Fundamental Concepts of Quality Improvement

Also Available from ASQ Quality Press:

Success through Quality: Support Guide for the Journey to Continuous Improvement
Timothy J. Clark

101 Good Ideas: How to Improve Just About Any Process
Karen Bemowski and Brad Stratton, editors

Root Cause Analysis: Simplified Tools and Techniques
Bjørn Andersen and Tom Fagerhaug

Quality Problem Solving
Gerald F. Smith

The Quality Toolbox
Nancy R. Tague

Business Process Improvement Toolbox
Bjørn Andersen

The Certified Quality Manager Handbook, Second Edition
Duke Okes and Russell T. Westcott, editors

Creativity, Innovation, and Quality
Paul E. Plsek

To request a complimentary catalog of ASQ Quality Press publications, call 800-248-1946, or visit our Web site at http://qualitypress.asq.org .

Fundamental Concepts of Quality Improvement

Melissa G. Hartman, Editor

ASQ Quality Press
Milwaukee, Wisconsin

Fundamental Concepts of Quality Improvement
Melissa G. Hartman, Editor

Library of Congress Cataloging-in-Publication Data

Fundamental concepts of quality improvement / Melissa G. Hartman, Editor.
   p. cm.
   Includes bibliographical references and index.
   ISBN 0-87389-525-8
   1. Quality control. 2. Quality assurance. I. Hartman, Melissa G.
   II. Title.

   TS156 .F86 2001
   658.5'62—dc21   2001005901

Note: As used in this document, the term "ISO 9000:2000" and all derivatives refer to the ANSI/ISO/ASQ Q9000-2000 series of documents. All quotations come from the American National Standard adoptions of these International Standards.

10 9 8 7 6 5 4 3 2 1

ISBN 0-87389-525-8

Acquisitions Editor: Annemieke Koudstaal
Project Editor: Craig S. Powell
Production Administrator: Gretchen Trautman
Special Marketing Representative: David Luth

ASQ Mission: The American Society for Quality advances individual, organizational, and community excellence worldwide through learning, quality improvement, and knowledge exchange.

Attention Bookstores, Wholesalers, Schools, and Corporations: ASQ Quality Press books, videotapes, audiotapes, and software are available at quantity discounts with bulk purchases for business, educational, or instructional use. For information, please contact ASQ Quality Press at 800-248-1946, or write to ASQ Quality Press, P.O. Box 3005, Milwaukee, WI 53201-3005.

To place orders or to request a free copy of the ASQ Quality Press Publications Catalog, including ASQ membership information, call 800-248-1946. Visit our Web site at www.asq.org or http://qualitypress.asq.org .

Printed in the United States of America

 Printed on acid-free paper

American Society for Quality

ASQ

Quality Press
600 N. Plankinton Avenue
Milwaukee, Wisconsin 53203
Call toll free 800-248-1946
Fax 414-272-1734
www.asq.org
http://qualitypress.asq.org
http://standardsgroup.asq.org
E-mail: authors@asq.org

Dedication

To LJR, as always;

and to Sara, Trudy, Aggie, and Rudy,
my devoted four-legged companions.

Table of Contents

vii

Preface

Much of the body of literature on quality improvement had its genesis in the manufacturing sector. It is only within the past 10 years or so that the benefits of quality improvement have begun to be realized in the healthcare, education, and service industries. This book approaches quality improvement from an "industry-neutral" perspective that highlights the similarities in approaches and techniques across a broad range of industries. In doing so, this book provides a very inclusive look at the fundamentals of quality and should appeal to a wide range of readers.

The chapters in this book were selected from articles that have appeared in Quality Progress magazine and papers that have been presented at ASQ's Annual Quality Congress and Annual Quality Audit Conferences. The material in this book was not selected for its contemporary nature; in fact, some of the writings contained in these pages date back to the late 1980s and early 1990s. This collection is intended to be timeless; an ensemble of expositions, professional musings, and case studies based on the basic, enduring principles of the quality movement.

Experienced quality professionals will benefit from reading this book because it serves as a refresher on principles, techniques, and tools. New or less-experienced quality professionals will learn from this book because of the number of different concepts and ideas that are addressed. People who are participating in continuous improvement or quality initiatives for the first time will find a considerable amount of helpful information in this book as well. Additional beneficiaries include middle- and upper-level managers who are trying to manage improvement initiatives, and small business owners who are striving to enhance organizational performance.

The layout and the amount of material in the book makes it well-suited for use by university professors and corporate trainers who are preparing courses on quality improvement. Instead of taking a single approach to quality principles, as is the case in many books, this book covers a very wide spectrum of ideas and philosophies. Students will have the opportunity to read about specific quality improvement techniques and subsequently design projects to implement those techniques in their own industry.

This book will be tremendously beneficial to individuals preparing for the American Society for Quality's (ASQ) Certified Quality Improvement Associate (CQIA) certification examination. The major sections of this book parallel the CQIA Body of Knowledge, which is included as an appendix so exam candidates can monitor their learning as they move through the book.

The quality improvement journey is fortified with many different approaches to enhancing organizational performance, and many of them are covered in this book. These pages provide ample opportunity for learning, for reflection, and for moving forward down the path to quality improvement. The quality improvement journey is a rich and rewarding one, indeed. *Bon voyage!*

Acknowledgments

I am grateful to many, many people for the role they have played in putting this volume together. First and foremost, I am indebted to the authors whose original works appear herein. They are the ones who did the real work and have made the real contributions to the field of quality. These contributors, in alphabetical order, are:

Linda M. Bayuk
John D. W. Beck
Stephen M. Beckstead
Robert W. Boggs
Dean L. Bottorff
John T. Burr
Joseph F. Castellano
Andrew Clark
Timothy Clark
Steven Crom
Martha L. Dasch
Art Davis
D. Keith Denton
Robert A. Drensek
Illona Dubaldo
Herbert France
Marie A. Gaudard

James Gelina
Howard S. Gitlow
Shelly J. Gitlow
Fred B. Grubb
Charles S. Gulas
Steven H. Hanks
Reuben Z. Hauser
Susan M. Heathfield
Ron L. Huber
Roy H. Johnson
Brian L. Joiner
Lynn Kaemmerer
Patricia Keehley
Theodore A. Lowe
Sue A. MacBride
Joseph M. Mazzeo
David A. McCamey

Marianne Murdock
John L. Niles
Jeffrey P. Nogas
Alan Oppenheim
Rosa Oppenheim
Alan J. Peterson
Michael W. Piczak
Richard L. Ratliff
R. Dan Reid
Harper A. Roehm
Norbert J. Salz
J. Stephen Sarazen
Gregory M. Scheessele
Marty Schildroth
Cliff L. Seastrunk
Zhiming Xue
Neil M. Yeager

My friends and colleagues in the ASQ Certification Department have done a tremendous amount of legwork to make this book happen. Sheila Connolly, ASQ Psychometrician, and Carmen O'Neill and Tanya Burton, ASQ Test Developers, worked diligently with the blessings of Sally Harthun, ASQ Certification Manager (and one of the finest leaders I have ever known), to help me locate and get my hands on articles to consider. Sharon Manassa and the staff in the ASQ Quality Information Center (QIC) were able to get hundreds of abstracts to me and dozens of articles that I thought (hoped!) might work well in communicating the fundamentals of quality improvement. I have the highest respect for the wonderful job that you all do time and time again. Thank you.

Dozens of volunteers in the ASQ CQIA exam development process also made a contribution to this book while I was chair of the CQIA examination. What they did is critical to any problem-solving process: they identified the stuff that wasn't there. Key among these vocal volunteers were Lynda Winterberg, the new CQIA examination chair, and Marty Mitchell, CQIA subcommittee member and volunteer recruiter extraordinaire. Specifically, they pointed out—and made a big deal about—the things that were missing from the current body of literature on the fundamentals of quality. They were right, of course, and I hope this book addresses at least some of their concerns.

Finally, Annemieke Koudstaal, ASQ Quality Press acquisitions editor, and Craig Powell, ASQ Quality Press project editor, have been absolutely delightful to work with. They have been patient, kind, diligent, and forgiving . . . all of which are traits of outstanding editors. Paul and Leayn Tabili, New Paradigm Prepress & Graphics, have combed through this manuscript with an eye for detail that exceeds any I have ever known. I do thank you all from the bottom of my heart.

Section I

Quality Basics

A ny discipline has a fundamental point from which all else follows. The discipline of quality improvement has evolved primarily from the work of a handful of prominent individuals who had the foresight to realize that there could be a systematic approach to doing things the right way. The articles in this section provide insight into the philosophies of those who many consider to be the founding fathers of quality: W. Edwards Deming, Joseph M. Juran, and Philip B. Crosby. Much has changed since they originally articulated their methodologies, but their impact has had an enduring influence on quality improvement.

In "Lessons Learned from the Masters: Experiences in Applying the Principles of Deming, Juran, and Crosby," Theodore Lowe and Joseph Mazzeo address the philosophies of the masters. They describe how one company integrated the three viewpoints to improve their quality processes. This article provides a clear example of how these classical approaches complement each other.

Harper Roehm and Joseph Castellano provide a detailed description of Deming's 14 points in "The Deming View of a Business." Unlike the typical presentation of these points, however, Roehm and Castellano have sequenced the points to provide guidelines for implementing cultural change. This article also provides a very useful description of Deming's PDSA cycle.

In "Variation, Management, and W. Edwards Deming," Brian Joiner and Marie Gaudard provide an in-depth explanation of Deming's theory of variation. Four types of variation—common, special, tampering, and structural—are defined, and appropriate managerial interventions for each are discussed. The impact of variation on each of Deming's 14 points is also addressed in this article.

"Ensuring Team Success in Continuous Improvement," by Susan Heathfield and Gregory Scheessele, focuses on three requirements for successful continuous improvement activities: demonstrated management commitment, support systems that encourage cultural change, and new managerial roles as essential aspects of success in a team-based environment. This enlightening article provides a thought-provoking conclusion to this section of articles on quality basics.

1

Lessons Learned from the Masters: Experiences in Applying the Principles of Deming, Juran, and Crosby

Theodore A. Lowe and Joseph M. Mazzeo

ABSTRACT

For the past several years, American companies have placed greater emphasis on improving the quality of the products and services they produce. In doing so, most of the individuals responsible to make this quality revolution happen have begun to implement the philosophies of Dr. W. Edwards Deming, Dr. Joseph M. Juran, or Philip B. Crosby. Unfortunately, some confusion has also developed as to the need and the approach to integrate the concepts of all three men together. This article addresses how companies can effectively utilize the quality management principles of Deming, Juran, and Crosby rather then being forced to choose among the three approaches.

This paper compares the different approaches and concludes that there is a consistent direction from Dr. Deming, Dr. Juran, and Mr. Crosby. The concepts, methods, and direction from the three experts that proved to be most valuable to us are documented. The paper reviews how the different strengths were integrated to help formulate the Truck & Bus Quality Improvement Process, and concludes with the "lessons learned from the masters."

INTRODUCTION

Most companies today have started on a journey that they hope will lead to world-class quality. Along the way, the companies have encountered many management philosophies and directions, including those from the three most reknowned quality experts in this country: Dr. W. Edwards Deming, Dr. Joseph M. Juran, and Philip B. Crosby. The directions have often caused disagreement within companies as to which one is the right direction to follow. But is it necessary, or even beneficial, to choose between the different approaches? Or can a company make faster progress by incorporating the best directions from all of the masters into its own road map to world-class quality?

While others have debated what is lacking with the direction from either Dr. Deming, Dr. Juran, or Philip Crosby, Truck & Bus looked for the right things from each. It was our position that the quality philosophies were 90 percent common and that they complemented each other. Therefore, we tried to understand and integrate the three approaches. By using the strengths from Deming, Juran, Crosby, and others, our organization has been able to accelerate our quality improvement journey. In order to help others who are beginning their journeys, we will review the lessons learned from the masters as we have developed and implemented the quality improvement process for the Truck & Bus Group.

In 1982, the Truck & Bus Group was formed by combining the truck operations of Chevrolet, General Motors Assembly Division, and the Truck and Coach Division. The Truck & Bus Group became responsible for the planning, engineering, manufacturing, and assembly of General Motors Trucks worldwide. Although there were different approaches in place at the various locations that formed the new Truck & Bus Group, we knew we needed to develop a common direction for our quality process.

LESSONS LEARNED FROM
DR. W. EDWARDS DEMING

At the start of the 1980s, Dr. Deming triggered the quality renaissance in the United States. It was at this time that Truck & Bus management started to look at how the quality of our products could be further improved and turned to Dr. Deming's principles.

Dr. Deming's philosophy helped challenge many of our past business practices and provided our organization with the encouragement to question traditional practices in the open. In addition to sparking the renaissance in thought, Dr. Deming gave our people a way to get at the "truth"—through statistical thinking. In studying the Deming process we learned about variation and the difference between common and special causes and how to use control charts to separate the special causes of variation from systemic problems.

Through Dr. Deming, as well as Dr. Juran's teachings, our organization came to understand that 85 percent of a company's problems are management controllable. It is management's job to initiate action on the system to eliminate the common causes of variation and improve the process capability of an operation. To understand whether processes were stable, capable, and on target, statistical tools were used, starting with the seven soft tools of Ishikawa and progressing to the Taguchi and other design of experiments techniques.

Dr. Deming helped us understand the need for ongoing improvement. His fifth point of his 14 Obligations of Management states to constantly and forever improve the system of production and service. This concept is illustrated by the Deming Circle, which symbolizes the problem analysis process. The elements of the Circle, which are plan, do, check, and act, also serve as a model for the quality improvement cycle of a company planning and designing a new product, making and selling it, checking customer satisfaction, and acting to further improve customer satisfaction.

At Truck & Bus, Dr. Deming's principles helped to establish a learning environment, which in turn gave a boost to the effectiveness of the training from the other experts. Dr. Deming, however, warned not to jump into statistical process control (SPC) training for the masses until all the roadblocks to quality had been removed. We did not heed this warning and learned the hard way that plants that trained selectively with a purpose were more successful than those that trained everybody top to bottom and were done with it.

The organization also found that the use of SPC was more difficult to apply in assembly plants and staffs. The journey in these areas was certainly tougher than in traditional manufacturing plants as there were no documented experiences or directions to follow. Often the common response from people in functions that used little variable data was: "How can I use it; we're different."

The implementation of the Deming process and SPC in general was more successful at the lower levels. The workers and quality engineers could make use of the SPC tools. Even though Dr. Deming directs his 14 points at management, the Deming process at Truck & Bus became a grassroots movement, centered around SPC training and application. However, the grassroots movement was successful for our organization, as it has led to the development of a quality process that over time has addressed his 14 obligations of management. Dr. Deming's principles triggered the start of Truck & Bus's quality process by helping to establish a participative and learning environment and by providing a means for getting at the truth through the use of statistics.

LESSONS LEARNED FROM DR. JOSEPH M. JURAN

Whereas Dr. Deming's 14 points were more of a final destination than an actual road map, Dr. Joseph Juran provided us with a more specific, system approach to quality control, improvement, and planning for all parts of the organization. Dr. Juran gave us an assortment of quality improvement approaches in addition to SPC, such as the project-by-project orientation and the application of the "breakthrough sequence." With his quality spiral and his "fitness for use" definition of quality, Dr. Juran left with us an orientation to meeting the customers' expectations.

Dr. Juran addressed Truck & Bus's top eighty executives for the first time in November 1983 and recommended four major thrusts in our quality improvement process: (1) establish annual quality improvement goals; (2) establish hands-on leadership toward quality improvement; (3) establish an executive steering committee to lead the quality improvement process; and (4) establish a vigorous education and training process. Our executive staff acted aggressively on his recommendations, starting with the creation of an Executive Quality Council and the implementation of Juran training.

Dr. Juran's education process gave the organization an understanding of the Juran trilogy of quality planning, quality improvement, and quality control. Quality planning focuses on creating a process that will from the start have a very low cost of poor quality. Quality improvement strives to lower the cost of poor quality in existing processes, and quality control's attention is to hold the gains and keep the process in control.

Many of our plants and staffs used the "Juran on Quality Improvement" videotapes. This training process is based on a project-by-project approach, with project being defined as a problem scheduled for solution. It can be used effectively to address the vital few problems in an organization. The Truck & Bus Group was also one of five companies chosen to pilot "Juran on Quality Planning." This training process facilitates projects that can be defined as processes scheduled for improvement. Because systems are responsible for 80 percent of an organization's problems, "Juran on Quality Planning" helps address what Dr. Juran calls the useful many and what General Motors calls the significant many.

In his quality management seminars at Truck & Bus, Dr. Juran stressed the need for establishing the problem-solving machinery required to achieve improvement. The third step in his breakthrough sequence is to organize for a managerial breakthrough in knowledge by creating problem-solving steering arms and diagnostic arms. The steering arm guides the overall problem-solving effort by establishing the direction, priorities, and resources to accomplish the task. The diagnostic arm is the work group with the investigative skills and mobility to follow the trail wherever it leads until the root cause is identified. Dr. Juran divides the problem-solving effort into two journeys—a journey from symptom to cause and a journey from cause to remedy. He states that the most difficult journey is from symptom to cause, because it is not clear where the responsibility lies.

To steer quality improvement efforts at Truck & Bus, customer satisfaction improvement teams were established in 1985 for each one of our product lines. The teams, which include representatives from all key disciplines, focus on increasing customer satisfaction. These teams have assessed the current quality position of their product, established objectives, and developed plans and projects to accelerate the rate of improvement. The customer satisfaction improvement teams operate on a project-by-project approach and have effectively addressed and solved many of the vital few product-related problems.

Dr. Juran urged Truck & Bus management to establish an annual quality improvement program, setting objectives and seeing that specific projects were chosen, year after year, with clear responsibility for action. His approach conformed readily with our five-year business planning process. Dr. Juran advised that the quality objectives must be set according to the marketplace. They should not be limited by elements outside an organization's immediate control or by what is thought can be realistically achieved with current resources. He stated that after upper managers set the broad improvement goals, it is up to the middle managers to establish the teams, resource requirements, measurements, and projects to meet the goals.

Dr. Juran's direction helped accelerate our knowledge and also got more members of our organization involved in the quality process. His training proved to be most valuable to the managers and quality professionals responsible for implementing and managing the quality improvement process.

LESSONS LEARNED FROM
PHILIP B. CROSBY

To further accelerate a company's quality journey, there is a need to achieve an awareness and involvement of the entire workforce, from top to bottom. The principal strength found in Philip Crosby's program is the attention it gives to transforming the quality culture of an organization. By stressing individual conformance to requirements, Crosby helps involve everyone in the organization in the quality process. His 14 steps, a "how-to" for management, provides an organization with an easy-to-understand, structured approach to launching the quality improvement process and starting the journey to world-class quality.

In line with Step 2 of Crosby's 14-step process, Truck & Bus implemented both a group quality improvement team and plant and staff quality improvement teams to run the quality improvement process. The quality improvement teams initially manage the "soft" or non-product areas covered in Crosby's 14 steps, such as awareness and communication, quality education, cost of quality, and recognition. The role of our quality improvement teams has gradually shifted from "implementing our quality improvement process" to "being the driving force in improving the quality of all of our business processes." However, the 14-step process provided the organization with the most defined, simple-to-follow road map for the initial legs of our quality journey.

Like Deming and Juran, Crosby starts his process with management commitment. But we were more successful achieving management commitment with the Crosby process. Perhaps, it is because the four absolutes of quality required by Crosby to achieve management commitment provided us with the new philosophy and a breakthrough in attitude that Deming and Juran require in their approaches.

An example of the commitment from our management was the establishment of an Executive Quality Council visit process to our plants and staffs. These visits that occur twice each month are solely for quality and for discussing progress and any obstacles to the quality improvement process. The theme for these visits is "how can I help?"

Crosby also asks for a management commitment to quality training and awareness for all levels and functions. Although Crosby's training does not go into the depth of Juran's training, it provided broader coverage for our organization.

Another distinction between the Crosby and Juran processes that we used to our advantage is their problem focus. Whereas Dr. Juran's project-by-project approach attacks the vital few problems, Crosby's error cause removal step and emphasis on conformance to requirements help to address the category of problems that Dr. Juran calls the useful many.

At Truck & Bus, we used Crosby training to help everyone focus on the quality of their business process and to understand their internal customer/supplier relationship. Every individual produces a product and has customers. Everyone must determine the requirements and satisfaction of their personal customers.

Individuals also have internal suppliers who provide products and services that are used to complete tasks. Requirements must be identified for the internal suppliers. Feedback mechanisms must be established to provide the internal suppliers information on the quality of the work they provide. This understanding of the customer/supplier relationship helped to further crystallize the concept of quality in our staff functions.

INTEGRATION OF DEMING, JURAN, AND CROSBY PROCESSES

At GM Truck & Bus we took "great pains" to make the Crosby training additive and integrated with the previous training. In adding the Crosby process to the existing focus on Juran and Deming, it was important for us to overcome the perception by some parts of our organization that the Crosby process was only a means of cheerleading workers to achieve zero defects. In that regard we were fortunate to have the depth of knowledge gained from Deming and Juran. The understanding of their philosophies allowed us to show how Crosby's concepts would fit into overall company strategy. This approach helped to minimize any potential confusion. The incorporation of Crosby also helped to reach those individuals who had not yet begun to understand their individual role and responsibility in the quality process.

The quality management practices and problem-solving techniques that were learned from Juran and the statistical techniques and management principles that were learned from Deming increased the effectiveness of Crosby's training in developing a new quality culture and implementing the quality improvement process. However, in conducting quality education programs on the three approaches, we had to overcome differences in terminology used by the experts. Often there was a need to serve as interpreters, translating Juran's language into Deming's or Crosby's terminology or vice versa.

An example of translating differences in terminology was in the definition of quality used by Crosby, Juran, and Deming. To Crosby, quality is conformance to requirements; whereas, Juran defines quality as fitness for use. Although Deming does not give an explicit definition of quality, he describes quality as a predictable degree of uniformity and dependability, at low cost and suited to the market. Dr. Juran relates his definition to Crosby's by stating that the quality mission of a company is fitness for use whereas the quality mission of departments or individuals is conformance to specifications. In their quality definitions, Crosby's emphasis is on doing things right while Juran is stressing the need to do the right things. Furthermore, General Motors has developed a definition of quality that encompasses all three ideas: "Quality is conformance to specifications and requirements that meet customer expectations."

Based on our experiences, we have concluded that understanding and following the directions from each of the leading quality experts is necessary, but not sufficient by itself for companies to reach their destination and meet their objectives. Crosby, Deming, and Juran are interdependent. Companies using one of their processes need to borrow concepts and techniques from the others to make their own processes more successful.

A Deming process, for instance, needs a Crosby 14-step process to assist management in transforming the organization. It also needs Juran's breakthrough process as a framework for applying statistics. Juran states that the breakthrough sequence must start with a breakthrough in attitude. Crosby helps achieve this breakthrough with his four absolutes.

The effectiveness of Juran's problem-solving approach is also enhanced by the application of the statistical tools that Deming promotes. A company using the Crosby process needs these tools and Juran's techniques. It also needs the teamwork that Deming and Juran emphasize to address the system problems that keep the individual worker from reaching zero defects.

In establishing a quality improvement process, organizations need to fit Crosby, Deming, and Juran into their process and not try to fit their process into one of the programs by Deming, Juran, or Crosby. In incorporating the best features of all three into a quality process, the organization must also avoid the perception that they are jumping from one "prophet" to the next.

To avoid the conflict that comes when an organization tries to choose the proper "champion," the benefits of integrating the concepts of Deming, Juran, Crosby, and others into the quality improvement process can be illustrated using the metaphor of three preachers, one religion.[1] Dr. Deming has been called the "fire and brimstone" preacher. He lays down the 14 commandments for management. He tells management that they are responsible for 85 percent of the sins and that they must repent or their businesses will go to hell. Dr. Deming also provides the congregation with an SPC "prayer book."

Dr. Juran is the theologist who has extensively researched the scriptures of quality management. He provides the quality "bible," the *Quality Control Handbook*.

Philip Crosby might be viewed as the evangelist of the three. He is exciting, positive, and generates enthusiasm. His message is simple: The Four Absolutes of Quality. He preaches that no level of sinning is permissible but he provides management with a way to get to heaven.

Management and the workforce make up the congregation, and they must learn to sit together and be more than Sunday Christians.

As organizations practice this quality religion, the process will become more homogeneous. Our experience has been that the different concepts and techniques that we have learned from Deming, Juran, and Crosby have lost their identity with the preacher and become part of the Truck & Bus quality process.

LESSONS LEARNED FROM THE MASTERS

The lessons that Truck & Bus has learned from the masters are best summarized by reviewing the tenets that our organization has established as the guiding principles of our quality improvement process. The definition of a tenet as we are using it is: "A principle, belief, or doctrine generally held to be true; one held in common by members of an organization."

1. *Quality improvement requires management and union commitment and leadership at all levels.* Leadership means comprehending the quality improvement process, developing a shared vision, communicating clear direction, gaining the commitment of the people, establishing a quality environment, developing a sense of trust among the people, and establishing a "can do" attitude.

2. *Quality improvement is necessary for providing a systematic approach to continuous quality improvement.* The structure requires the networking, teamwork, and cooperation of all groups within Truck & Bus, as well as throughout General Motors, our suppliers, and dealers. The strategy must be well defined, encompass all the elements in the quality improvement process, and provide a systematic and uniform approach that is clearly understood and followed throughout Truck & Bus.

3. *Awareness and open and free communications are necessary to create a climate of continuous improvement.* All employees must have a shared understanding of our quality issues, challenges, goals, commitment, and accomplishments if we are to establish a new quality culture. This group-wide awareness can only happen in an environment of open, free, and honest communications in all directions.

4. *Our quality culture is contingent upon an environment where all employees are learning to apply the quality concepts and techniques.* A climate of continuous learning and not just providing training is essential to a continuous quality improvement process.

5. *We (everyone) will continuously improve the quality of all of our products, services, and business processes.* Commitment and leadership, structure and strategy, awareness and communication, and education are all necessary prerequisites for the attainment of our fifth tenet.

Continuous improvement requires the following actions: (1) measurement, analysis, and continuous improvement of our business processes; (2) the use of cost of quality as a management tool to help gauge the effectiveness of our quality improvement process; (3) the use of statistical methods to identify, understand, and continually improve process capability; (4) a corrective action process that includes an error cause removal system; (5) a focus on preventive actions and on planning and providing capable processes.

6. *Employees will be recognized and rewarded on the basis of their contributions to a team approach as well as their contributions as individuals for their continuous quality improvement.* As an organization, we value a team approach as the way we get our business accomplished. Toward that end, our employees, as teams, will be given the appropriate authority to make decisions and will be, accordingly, rewarded for those efforts. This will not, however, take away from the need for all individuals to be creative, involved, and contributing, both on an individual basis and as a team player.

7. *A group quality culture will be achieved when each and every employee at Truck & Bus is constantly trying to improve the quality of his/her processes.* A work environment must be established where each and every employee understands and can contribute to the quality improvement process.

8. *Satisfying customers must be our foremost priority in every action and decision.* This tenet is the result of the previous seven and the glue that binds the first seven tenets together. From its inception, the focus of Truck & Bus Group has been on providing and improving customer satisfaction.

As a result of our quality improvement process, we are approaching and achieving world-class quality in many of our current product lines, as confirmed by our customers.

CONCLUSION

In conclusion, we have worked hard to develop a group-wide quality culture, involving all employees, in a process of continuous improvement. The true measure of our quality efforts is only seen in the marketplace, and employee involvement is critical in achieving customer satisfaction. The commitment and leadership of Truck & Bus management and the same commitment of the union are necessary ingredients in assuring employee involvement and customer satisfaction, and in the success of our entire quality improvement process.

The tenets of our quality process provide the basis for our future improvement and are, in essence, the lessons learned from the masters.

ENDNOTES

1. T. A. Lowe and J. M. Mazzeo, "Crosby, Deming, and Juran—Three Preachers, One Religion," *Quality* (September 1986): 25.

BIBLIOGRAPHY

Crosby, P. B., *Quality Is Free.* New York: McGraw-Hill, 1979.

Crosby, P. B., *Quality without Tears.* New York: McGraw-Hill, 1984.

Deming, W. E., *Quality, Productivity, and Competitive Position.* Boston: M.I.T. Press, 1982.

Lowe, T. A., and J. M. Mazzeo. "Crosby, Deming, and Juran—Three Preachers, One Religion." *Quality* (September 1986): 23–26.

Juran, J. M. *The Management of Quality.* 4th ed. New York: McGraw-Hill, 1981.

Juran, J. M. *Planning for Quality.* Wilton, CT: Juran Institute, 1986.

Juran, J. M. *Upper Management and Quality.* New York: McGraw-Hill, 1981.

2

The Deming View of a Business

Harper A. Roehm and Joseph F. Castellano

It is continually surprising: the number of executives, business faculty, and students who know little or nothing of the contributions of W. Edwards Deming. Those who have heard of Deming's work usually have some understanding of his 14 points for management and, to a lesser degree, his system of profound knowledge. What is often lacking, however, is an understanding of the connection between these two core elements of his teachings. This necessary and important integration between the 14 points and the system of profound knowledge would be better understood if those studying Deming's theory of management understood the relationship between these core elements and Deming's view of a business.

Deming viewed a business as a system that should be focused on delighting the customer. He was not the first to recognize that businesses are systems or that focusing on the customer is important. He was, however, the first to articulate a management theory based on these two issues. Deming's view of business as a system helps in understanding his system of profound knowledge and 14 points for management.

Deming did not specifically acknowledge that his now-famous 14 points follow a specific view of business, nor did he initially state that they followed from a system of profound knowledge. In fact, the phrase "system of profound knowledge," which was the subject of his last book, *The New Economics for Industry, Government, and Education*, does not even appear in *Out of the Crisis*. In *Out of the Crisis*, however, he did write that a business is a system that includes both the supplier and the customer. He also wrote that quality "should be aimed at the needs of the consumer, present and future."[1] Furthermore, he strongly believed that his 14 points flowed from an understanding of business as a system, the theory of variation, an understanding of psychology, and the theory of knowledge. These four elements were articulated in *The New Economics*, as was his system of profound knowledge.

Deming's view of a business saw the organization structured as a system whose purpose is to delight the customer. The system of profound knowledge flows from this view of a business, while the 14 points become a methodology for operationalizing the four elements of profound knowledge.

DEMING'S VIEW OF A BUSINESS

The first component in Deming's view of a business is the customer. In order to provide quality and delight the customer, it is necessary to know who the customer is and how the customer receives value from the product or service. Management must define the market and the customer being served, and it is responsible for understanding how the organization's product creates value for the customer. Quality can only be defined and understood in the context of the market and a defined customer.

Delighting the customer, in Deming's view, means more than just responding to customer needs, wishes, and expectations on a timely basis. While a competitive price, reliability, and functionality are required, they are not adequate for a business to remain globally competitive. It must exceed customer expectations.

To exceed customer expectations, the business must continually improve both its processes and its product. This continual improvement must add value for the customer. Equally important, the business must also continually innovate both its processes and product in a way that adds value for the customer. Improvement and innovation that do not add value for the customer are a waste of valuable resources. Furthermore, management must provide leadership in a way that fosters value-added continual improvement and innovation in both processes and product.

The second component of Deming's view is that a business is a system. Deming viewed the business, customer, and supplier as one system. A system is a group of interrelated processes (process and system are used interchangeably). The greater the degree of interdependency between the components of the system, the greater the need to manage the system. A central theme in Deming's view of business as a system is the belief that the aim of the system is to optimize the entire system, not its components.

Deming also believed that systems have a given capability and that this capability will exhibit variation. For example, assume you are building a bicycle. One of your processes is to cut tubing for the frame, and one of the cut tubings must be 600 millimeters long (or approximately two feet). After sampling 50 cut tubings from your process, the average cut is found to be 600.2 millimeters. From this sample you can prepare an X-bar chart of the cuttings. This particular process's capability is represented by the average of 600.2 millimeters; the variation around this average is shown on the chart in Figure 2.1.

Based on the earlier work of Walter A. Shewhart, Deming concluded that processes whose variation fell within three standard deviations of their mean were in control. For the example in Figure 2.1, three standard deviations from the mean has been computed as 604.1 millimeters (upper control limit) and 596.4 millimeters (lower control limit). The term "control limit" means that if an observation falls outside this range, the system is not in control. Since all of the variances in the chart fall within three standard deviations of the mean of 600.2 millimeters, this process is considered under control.

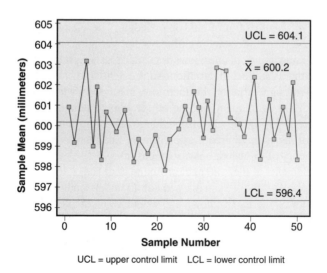

Figure 2.1 X-Bar chart of cutting operation.

Deming went on to conclude that variation within the control limits is considered common-cause variation and is the result of the normal random variation present in all processes. (He often stated in his four-day seminars that 94 percent of all variation comes from common causes.) Therefore, improvements aimed at reducing common-cause variation can only be achieved by changing the system (for example, buying different raw material or equipment). In contrast, observations falling outside the control limits are considered to be the result of special causes, and immediate corrective action should be implemented (for example, repairing a machine that is out of calibration). Finally, only those systems considered to be under control have a measured capability from which process improvement and innovation can occur. Systems must first be under statistical control before innovation and improvement can be initiated.

The components of a system that are responsible for its capability, and hence its results, are people, materials, methods, equipment, and environment. Deming believed that management is solely responsible for each of these components, and because these components determine product quality, management is also responsible for quality.

SYSTEM OF PROFOUND KNOWLEDGE

Deming's management theory is derived from a natural application of what he called a system of profound knowledge. The elements of profound knowledge are an understanding of a system, variation, psychology, and a theory of knowledge. If one views a business as a system—with a given capability that is subject to variation—it is essential to have an understanding of systems and variation. Furthermore, in a system where people are the most important component and the objective is to delight the customer, a knowledge of psychology is also required. Deming believed that almost every act of management requires prediction, and therefore, an understanding of a theory of knowledge is also necessary.

The elements of the system of profound knowledge are interdependent. For example, a study of systems without an understanding of psychology, variation, and a theory of knowledge would be incomplete. The 14 points for management become the methodology for operationalizing Deming's theory and for creating the environment necessary for a commitment to continual improvement, innovation, and delighting the customer. While Deming never prescribed a process for implementing the 14 points, the order presented here represents an approach that stresses commitment to employees and provides a foundation for changing a company's culture.[2]

THE 14 POINTS

Point 1: Creating Constancy of Purpose. Create constancy of purpose for continual improvement of products and services, allocating resources to provide for long-range needs rather than only short-term profitability, with a plan to become competitive, to stay in business, and to provide jobs.

Deming believed that for any system to reach its potential and be optimized, it should have a focused purpose. He stated in point 1 that for businesses to become competitive, stay in business, and provide jobs, they must have a long-term commitment to providing value to their customers. This can only be achieved through continual improvement to processes and products. Constancy of purpose is a recognition that one cannot manage for the short term at the expense of the long term. For example, foregoing preventive maintenance on machines to increase year-end profits will, in the long run, hinder product quality, foster customer dissatisfaction, and be counterproductive to the long-term survival of the business.

For all employees to be willing to serve the best interest of the organization—to innovate and improve products and processes and work together for the good of the customer—they must sense a long-term commitment from the organization and know that it is committed to providing a quality product for its customers. Improvement and innovation come primarily from people within the organization. Therefore, employees must know and believe in the aim and purpose of the organization. Likewise, for customers to remain loyal, they also must sense a long-term commitment to their needs. Without constancy of purpose, employees are not sure why the firm is in business or what its aim is. This creates instability, increases variation and fear, and reduces quality.

Point 2: Adopting the New Philosophy. Adopt the new philosophy. We are in a new economic age, created by Japan. We can no longer live with commonly accepted levels of delays, mistakes, defective materials, and defective workmanship. Transformation of Western management style is necessary to halt the continued decline of industry.

Point 2 says a transformation is required to adopt the Deming theory of management, and a change in style begins with personal transformation. Deming addressed the need for personal transformation in *The New Economics*, indicating that the first step is transformation of the individual, and this transformation comes from understanding the system of profound knowledge.[3]

Deming believed that once an individual understands the system of profound knowledge, he or she will be able to apply its principles in relationships with others and to personal decisions. Such an individual transformation serves as the basis for transforming the organization's culture. A new style of management will emerge, one that recognizes the creative talents of all employees and is committed to the aim of everyone winning over the long term. This new style of management is committed to continually improving the process and focuses all its efforts on delighting the customer. Therefore, adopting the new philosophy operationalizes the commitment to constancy of purpose. After management has committed to points 1 and 2, it is ready to lead the transformation. It is management's responsibility to lead the transformation, for a company cannot be transformed without strong leadership.

Point 7: Instituting Leadership. Adopt and institute leadership aimed at helping people to do a better job. The responsibility of managers and supervisors must be changed from sheer numbers to quality. Improvement of quality will automatically improve productivity. Management must ensure that immediate action is taken on reports of inherited defects, maintenance requirements, poor tools, fuzzy operational definitions, and all conditions detrimental to quality.

Because management is responsible for the system and all of its components, it is also responsible for quality. The most important component of a system is people. In order for the system to be optimized, management must recognize that people are not commodities or expenses but the organization's most important asset. Since the components are responsible for the system's output, it is a leader's responsibility to help employees do a better job. A leader must address some basic questions: Are employees properly trained, and do they have the necessary equipment and materials? Has the product and production process been well designed, and is the environment suited for optimum production? A leader's job is not to judge but to provide assistance on a timely basis. A leader must be able to blend the various strengths of individuals to optimize the performance of the system in a way that will exceed customer expectations. Managers who use this approach are often characterized as teachers or coaches, as described by Barry Hass, president of Jamestown Plastics, Jamestown, Ohio: "For years the foremen were probably 70 percent hands-on, and now that is going to shift to 30 percent. We are going to have to become educators. This is something that will be fairly new to us. We are going to have to become teachers and take what we learn and pass it to the people on the floor."[4]

Management must also understand and monitor processes so that, when problems arise, effective action can be taken. To avoid tampering with processes, management must understand variation and be able to distinguish between common-cause and special-cause variation. When effective corrective action is taken, quality is improved and productivity and cost are automatically improved. Leading the transformation requires management to provide employee training and education. While a change in leadership style is an essential step after implementing points 1 and 2, employees are often skeptical of changes in leadership style. Employee skepticism can be changed, however, by instituting training in which employees learn to better understand their jobs, systems and variation, and how to institute improvements.

Point 6: Instituting Training. Institute modern methods of training for everybody's job, including management, to make better use of every employee. New skills are required to keep up with changes in materials, methods, product design, machinery, techniques, and service.

Management must provide training so that employees are able to perform the specific tasks of their job, so that they understand processes and variation, and so that they are able to be more creative and solve problems. Diamond-Star Motors, a joint venture between Mazda and Chrysler Corp. in Normal, Illinois, spent three weeks sharpening employees' creative thinking skills and five weeks on job-specific skills, at a total cost of $13,000 per employee.[5]

If management expects employees to assist in managing the system and to offer solutions to problems and recommend improvements, it must provide training. Deming realized that innovation, improvements to systems, and the reduction of variation requires knowledge of problem-solving techniques, including the plan–do–study–act (PDSA) cycle (for more on this valuable tool, see the sidebar "The PDSA Cycle Explained"). Grand Rapids Spring & Stamping (formerly Grand Rapids Spring & Wire) in Grand Rapids, Michigan, recognizes the importance of understanding systems and variation and trains its employees in statistical process control. It also spends a great deal of time teaching employees problem-solving techniques, including the PDSA cycle, which they use daily to improve systems and solve problems. As an outgrowth of this training, employees better understand the relationship between their individual jobs and delighting the customer.[6]

While such training can be extremely effective in yielding process and system improvements, perhaps the greatest benefit is the increase in trust between management and employees. If management trusts employees to make improvements and solve problems without interference, employees in turn believe that management can be trusted.

Point 13: Encouraging Education. Institute a vigorous program of education, and encourage self-improvement for everyone. What an organization needs is not just good people; it needs people who are improving with education. Advances in competitive position will have their roots in knowledge.

While training is directed specifically at acquiring job skills and process improvement, Deming believed that it is also beneficial for both

THE PDSA CYCLE EXPLAINED

W. Edwards Deming realized that innovation, improvements to systems, and reducing variation require problem-solving techniques. A key element in this effort is the use of the plan–do–study–act (PDSA) cycle. The PDSA cycle is a vehicle for constant, continual improvement and innovation, enabling employees to solve problems and be more creative. PDSA involves the following four steps:

1. **Plan.** A change or improvement is planned.

2. **Do.** The change or improvement is performed on a small scale.

3. **Study.** The results of the tested change are studied, and from this study further action is determined.

4. **Act.** Either continued study is required, the change is implemented, or another change or improvement is initiated.

employees and the organization if employees are continually learning. James Brogden, president and chief executive officer of Master Industries, Ansonia, Ohio, a longtime believer in Deming's approach, believes that by encouraging education and self-improvement in all areas of interest, people feel better about themselves and thus become better employees.[7] Master Industries has an open education policy that reimburses employees for books and tuition for any course they wish to take, whether or not it is work related.

Providing the three levels of training—to perform one's job, to understand processes and variation, and to be more creative and able to solve problems—along with an open education policy, should begin to transform the culture and reduce skepticism. After extensive training, management and employees will better understand systems; variation; and the need to break down barriers, eliminate exhortations, and abolish arbitrary numerical targets.

Point 9: Breaking Down Barriers. Break down barriers between departments and staff areas. People in different areas, such as research, design, sales, administration, and production, must work in teams to tackle problems that may be encountered with product and service.

While constancy of purpose, leadership, training, and education can help a company become more responsive and competitive, these initiatives alone are insufficient. Deming observed that many business practices are counterproductive. For example, most organization charts stress departments and specific functional areas and do not seem to recognize that businesses are systems of integrated processes. He found that people often engage in activities that seem in the short run to be beneficial to themselves or their departments—at the expense of the overall business. He believed that this suboptimization can be avoided if people understand that they are a part of an overall system whose survival depends on delighting the customer. Furthermore, the system will function better if functional areas work together—not independent of each other. Deming believed that systems function better when people cooperate rather than compete with each other. He often cited the example of an orchestra: if individual musicians attempt to play their instruments without regard for the entire group, the orchestra will fail.

Rusch O. Dees, vice president of administration at Arkay Plastics, Dayton, Ohio, described his organization's attempt to break down barriers: "We knocked down the walls, took the offices away from people, took the carpeting away from them, took the couches and lamps away from them, and we put their desks in a T shape with their people. Why? So that if your people talk, you hear them. If you talk, your people hear you."[8]

Point 10: Eliminating Exhortations. Eliminate the use of slogans, posters, and exhortations of the workforce, demanding zero defects and new levels of productivity, without providing methods. Such exhortations only create adversarial relationships; the bulk of causes of low quality and low productivity belong to the system, and thus lie beyond the power of the workforce.

Deming felt strongly that the system and its components (people, materials, methods, equipment, and environment) are responsible for providing quality and delighting the customer. When systems are in a state of statistical control, they have a given capability. This capability can only be improved by changing or improving one or more of the components of the system. Because Deming believed that only management could change the system, he found the use of slogans, arbitrary numerical goals, and quotas to be offensive, ineffective, and harmful.

Management's role is not to create slogans, exhortations, and targets, but to work toward an understanding of the system and reducing variation through changes in the system. Slogans, exhortations, and goals for the workforce are never a substitute for the training, knowledge, or tools needed to continually improve the process.

Point 11: Eliminating Arbitrary Numerical Targets. Eliminate work standards that prescribe quotas for the workforce and numerical goals for people in management. Substitute aids and helpful leadership in order to achieve continual improvement of quality and productivity.

Point 11 challenges the basic assumptions of traditional management thought. The new philosophy recognizes that goals and numerical quotas are meaningless without a methodology for achieving them. It also recognizes the futility of setting standards or goals without an understanding of the system and the effects of variation. An understanding of variation must lead one to conclude that if the system is stable (that is, only common-cause variation exists) it is useless to specify numerical quotas or goals, since you will get whatever the system delivers. In short, you can't reach a goal beyond the capability of the system. On the other hand, if the system is not stable (that is, special-cause variation exists) there is no point in setting a goal since you cannot predict what the system will produce.

Real leadership requires an understanding of a system, variation, and how to improve a process. Managing by numbers and objectives will not provide this understanding. Once the system is stable, only management can improve it (that is, reduce variation). If employees are given quotas and goals with no method or process for achieving results, then fear, poor morale, low self-esteem, and loss of respect and trust will inevitably result.

The new paradigm requires focusing on the long run and understanding systems and variation. It requires management to take responsibility for the system rather than blaming employees. It requires leadership, knowledge, and a constancy of purpose directed at never-ending improvement of the system.

When employees better understand systems, variation, and the need for cooperation, and when barriers, exhortations, and arbitrary numerical goals have been eliminated, employees are prepared for the elimination of merit systems.

Point 12: Permitting Pride of Workmanship. Remove the barriers that rob hourly workers, and people in management, of their right to pride of workmanship. This implies, among other things, abolition of the annual merit rating (appraisal of performance) and management by objectives. Again, the responsibility of managers, supervisors, and foremen must be changed from sheer numbers to quality.

Establishing a constancy of purpose; instituting leadership, training, and education; breaking down barriers; and eliminating exhortations and arbitrary numerical goals do a great deal to build employee trust and empower the work force, but more is required. Deming believed that companies must provide joy in work, and that merit pay systems are the major obstacle to achieving this objective.

He gave several reasons for his belief. First, 94 percent of all variation is the result of common causes. Since this variation occurs randomly it makes no sense to reward or punish workers for what they are not responsible for. Second, it is difficult to measure someone's contribution in the short run. In fact, it is difficult to even identify an individual's true contribution without many years of observation. Third, when merit systems are used, employees concentrate on satisfying the short-term criteria of the merit system, not on the long-term goals of the company. Employees should instead be attempting to innovate and improve the system for greater customer satisfaction. Finally, people who operate systems must cooperate to optimize the system and delight the customer. Merit systems encourage competition between workers and are counterproductive to cooperation. They promote self-interest at the expense of the overall system.

PQ Systems of Miamisburg, Ohio, is a good example of a company that eliminated its merit system. It now uses a salary process based on market studies of various job categories and overall company profitability. Employees are involved in the process and in the annual market study updates. Salary increments are not tied to any specific performance measurements, only to market data. The emphasis is on assisting employees so that they can perform their jobs in a way that will delight the customer. Kurt Stueve, general manager, believes that employees receive far more feedback on performance now than when the merit system was used.[9]

Point 8: Driving out Fear. Encourage effective two-way communication and other means to drive out fear throughout the organization so that everybody may work effectively and more productively for the company.

After a company has a stated constancy of purpose, instituted leadership, encouraged training and education, attempted to break down barriers, eliminated exhortations and arbitrary numerical goals, and have fostered pride in workmanship by eliminating the merit system, it will have come a long way toward eliminating fear. In addition, Deming believed that management must encourage two-way communications with employees. It would be extremely difficult, however, to eliminate fear without first implementing all of the points already discussed. Without these points in place, the type of management-employee dialogue required would likely be impossible. Management can respond effectively to employees' needs only when employees feel free to express themselves and give their opinions.

Each of the previous points is directed at changing a company's culture. A company must first direct its efforts toward developing its own culture before it can be in a position to know what to expect from its suppliers and understand how to assist them.

Point 4: Ending Lowest-Tender Contracts. End the practice of awarding business solely on the basis of price tag. Instead, require meaningful measures of quality along with price. Reduce the number of suppliers for the same item by eliminating those that do not qualify with statistical or other evidence of quality. The aim is to minimize total cost, not merely initial cost, by minimizing variation. This may be achievable by moving toward a single supplier for any one item, in a long-term relationship of loyalty and trust. Purchasing managers have a new job, and must learn it.

Deming believed that the price paid by the customer at the time of initial purchase does not represent the total cost to the customer. The relevant cost is the total cost of use; therefore, he rejected the idea of selecting suppliers and awarding business solely on the basis of purchase price. Furthermore, he believed that to reduce variation and improve quality, companies need to work toward a single supplier relationship for component parts. Multiple suppliers will always create more variation than a single supplier. Deming spoke of a customer-supplier relationship in which the supplier is a part of the system. He concluded that companies must be cautious in their selection of suppliers and only choose those with whom trust has been established and total cost of use is lower.

After the company has begun to change its culture, understand systems and variation, and develop stronger and more meaningful relationships with suppliers, it is in a position to cease dependence on mass inspection.

Point 3: Ceasing Dependence on Mass Inspection. Eliminate the need for mass inspection as the way of life to achieve quality by building quality into the product in the first place. Require statistical evidence of built-in quality in both manufacturing and purchasing functions.

Deming believed that management's efforts should be directed toward improving the system in ways that will delight the customer. If management understands variation and its relationship to systems, there is no need for mass inspection of output. The system needs to be monitored and management must determine when the system is in control. When it is not, management must be capable of distinguishing special-cause variation from common-cause variation. Likewise, companies must assist suppliers in the management of their systems. If the emphasis is on management of systems, companies will not need mass inspection of either their output or their suppliers' output. This does not, however, imply elimination of all inspection—only the need for mass inspection of all output.

After the company has started to change its culture, strengthen its relationships with suppliers, and help employees better understand the system and its purpose, it is more capable of improving every process.

Point 5: Improving Every Process. Improve constantly and forever the system of planning, production, and service, in order to improve every process and activity in the company, to improve quality and productivity, and thus to constantly decrease costs. Institute innovation of product, service, and process. It is management's job to work continually on the system (design, incoming supplies, maintenance, improvement of equipment, supervision, training, retraining, and so on).

To remain competitive with products and services that will always delight the customer, companies must continually improve their processes and systems. A commitment to continuous improvement begins with knowing what the customer wants and how the product or service will be used. It also requires the recognition that quality begins at the design stage and continues downstream. Continual reduction of waste and improvement of quality in every activity (for example, purchasing, engineering, production, marketing) must be the focus.

A commitment to never-ending improvement also involves a recognition that simply allocating more resources will not bring quality. Improved quality must be viewed in the context of process improvement. Such improvements require knowledge about the process and the effects of statistical variation.

Point 14: Ensuring Top Management Commitment and Action. Clearly define top management's permanent commitment to ever-improving quality and productivity, and its obligation to implement these principles. Indeed, it is not enough that top management commit itself for life to quality and productivity. It must know what it is committed to—that is, what it must do. Create a structure in top management that will push every day on the preceding 13 points, and take action in order to accomplish the transformation. Support is not enough; action is required.

Deming was adamant in his belief that top management and the board of directors are responsible for seeing that the system continues to produce a product that delights the customer. In short, leaders must lead. Top management's role is to take responsibility for problems and mistakes and lead the organization in changing the system.

In the final analysis, what the transformation really involves is management's willingness to give up the old paradigms of management control (for example, management by objectives, management by the numbers, and merit systems). It must be willing to replace competition with cooperation. It must be willing to admit that an organization can be built on the empowerment of people and not on the basis of rewards and punishment. It must be ready to encourage innovation and risk taking, even though failures will occur. Only then can the organization begin its transformation.

LEVELS OF COMMITMENT TO EMPLOYEES

Much of what Deming wrote pertained to management's commitment to employees. He was appalled that many managers treated employees as expendable costs rather than their most valuable resource. While he did not include a 15th point called "levels of commitment," his 14 points define levels of management commitment to employees that must be present to support a culture of continuous improvement. And while Deming never suggested an order of implementation for his 14 points, the order specified here may help in creating that culture. It represents a strong commitment to employees and provides a solid foundation for change.

ENDNOTES

1. W. E. Deming, *Out of the Crisis* (Cambridge, MA: M.I.T., Center for Advanced Engineering Study, 1986): 4–5.
2. The wording for each of the 14 points has been taken from H. R. Neave, *The Deming Dimension* (Knoxville, TN: SPC Press, 1990): 287–405.
3. W. E. Deming, *The New Economics for Industry, Government, and Education* (Cambridge, MA: M.I.T., Center for Advanced Engineering Study, 1993): 94–95.
4. H. A. Roehm, T. Hayes, and J. F. Castellano, "Quality Addiction: True Confessions," *Organization Development Journal* (Fall 1993): 80.
5. W. J. Hampton, "How Does Japan Inc. Pick Its American Workers?" *Business Week* (Oct. 3, 1988): 84.
6. H. A. Roehm, D. Klein, and J. F. Castellano, "Springing to World Class Manufacturing," *Management Accounting* (March 1991): 40–44.
7. Roehm, Hayes, and Castellano, 73.
8. Ibid, 77.
9. K. Stueve, lecture given at University of Dayton, Dayton, OH, Spring 1995.

3

Variation, Management, and W. Edwards Deming

Brian L. Joiner and Marie A. Gaudard

Jack and Sarah were preparing for their monthly meeting. Jack, the vice president of sales, wasn't looking forward to it. Sales were down again this month, and he was going to have to confront Sarah, a regional sales manager. He really thought Sarah was doing a good job overall, and the fact that he needed to chastise here periodically frustrated him. But reprimanding Sarah usually improved sales—at least for a month or so.

Sarah wasn't looking forward to the meeting either. Even though she could easily come up with a thousand reasons why sales were down, they were the same reasons she had used many times before and would use many times again: absenteeism, sales force turnover, poor training, lack of product promotions, and a host of other factors that were mostly beyond her control. Even in those months when she was credited with unusually good sales, Sarah was nervous about the monthly meeting because she was never sure of exactly how she had improved sales.

At the meeting, Jack asked Sarah to explain the most recent drop in sales. Sarah gave her reasons. Jack pretended to believe her. He felt obliged to emphasize that her job was to keep sales up. Both felt this meeting was necessary, but both felt they hadn't really solved anything and that the same thing would happen again in subsequent months.

What were these managers doing wrong? Or, rather, what could they have done better? Both were acting in the best interests of the company.

Both were competent managers who had risen to high levels in the company. Yet Jack didn't enjoy reprimanding people, and Sarah felt uneasy each time she had to explain drops or rises in the sales figures.

What these managers and millions like them lack is a key piece of the management puzzle, a piece that W. Edwards Deming calls the theory of variation. In Deming's view, the first step is to recognize that variation is a part of everything: supplier goods, temperature, measurement systems, and even people's performance. But the real benefit comes from knowing something about the theory of variation so you can act on it. Understanding the theory of variation enables managers to recognize, interpret, and react appropriately to variation in the data, figures, performance, and outputs they deal with daily. Knowledge of the variation theory is one of the most powerful tools a company can develop in its quest for quality. It can improve a manager's effectiveness and create opportunities for continuous improvement. It is part of the foundation of Deming's management philosophy; each of his 14 points is based, in part, on the desire to reduce variation.

SOME BASICS ABOUT VARIATION

Variation is not a new concept. Statisticians and scientists have studied it for decades. What's new is that their awareness of variation and how it affects everyday activities is infiltrating the workplace. There are seven concepts about variation that everyone should know:

1. *All variation is caused.* There are specific reasons why your weight fluctuates every day, why sales go up, and why Maria performs better than Robert.

2. *There are four main types of causes.* "Common causes" are the myriad of ever-present factors (for example, process inputs or conditions) that contribute in varying degrees to relatively small, apparently random shifts in outcomes day after day, week after week, month after month. The collective effect of all common causes is often referred to as system variation because it defines the amount of variation inherent in the system.

"System causes" are factors that sporadically induce variation over and above that inherent in the system. Frequently, special cause variation appears as an extreme point or some specific, identifiable pattern in the data. Special causes are often referred to as assignable causes because the variation they produce can be tracked down and assigned to an identifiable source. (In contrast, it is usually difficult, if not impossible, to link common cause variation to any particular source.)

"Tampering" is additional variation caused by unnecessary adjustments made in an attempt to compensate for common cause variation.

"Structural variation" is regular, systematic changes in output. Typical examples include seasonal patterns and long-term trends.

3. *Distinguishing between the four types of causes is critical because the appropriate managerial actions are quite different for each.* Without this distinction, management will never be able to tell real improvement from mere adjustment of the process or tampering. In practice, the most important difference to grasp first is the difference between special cause variation and common cause variation.

4. *The strategy for special causes is simple: get timely data.* Investigate immediately when the data signal a special cause was present. Find out what was different or special about that point. Seek to prevent bad causes from recurring. Seek to keep good causes happening.

5. *The strategy for improving a common cause system is more subtle.* In a common cause situation, all the data are relevant, not just the most recent or offending figure. If you have data each month for the past two years, you will need to look at all 24 of these points.

In-depth knowledge of the process or system being improved is absolutely essential when only common causes are present. This knowledge can come from basic statistical tools, such as flowcharts, cause-and-effect diagrams, stratification analysis (used for measurement data such as process cycle time), and Pareto analysis (used for count data such as number of accidents). These and other tools can help identify fundamental changes to the system, but they should be tried on a small scale first to see whether results improve. Statistically designed experiments might also be helpful in identifying system innovations.[1,2]

6. *When all variation in a system is due to common causes, the result is a stable system said to be in statistical control.* The practical value of having a stable system is that the process output is predictable within a range or band. For example, if a stable order entry system handles 30 to 60 orders a day, it will rarely slip to fewer than 30 or rise to more than 60.

If some variation is due to special causes, the system is said to be unstable since you cannot predict when the next special cause will strike and, therefore, cannot predict the range of variation. If the order entry system just described were unstable and subject to special cause variation, it capability might sporadically (and unpredictably) drop sharply below or rise sharply above the 30 to 60 range.

7. *How much system variation is present can be determined by performing statistical calculations on process data.* Thus control limits can be set. Control limits describe the range of variation that is to be expected in the process due to the aggregate effect of the common causes. Calculating these limits lets managers predict the future performance of a process with some confidence.[3,4,5]

These seven fundamental concepts provide the framework for improving managerial effectiveness. The following example shows how.

THE PERNICIOUS PERIODIC REPORT

Managers often base decisions on data prepared daily, weekly, or monthly by their subordinates. These data are usually displayed in a table. Figure 3.1 is a typical example.

When asked what they look for in such tables, most managers respond "big negative variances." Like Jack in the opening story, they will focus on the undesirable figures and ask, "What happened? What is being done about it?" They'll say things like: "Manufacturing losses are up this month. Why? What are doing about it?" "Why have sales gone down two months in a row? What are you doing about it?" "Your project came in more than 10% over budget. Why?"

Look back at the description of what to do in response to special cause variation and common cause variation. Which one most closely describes these reactions? The answer is the strategy for special causes: seek out explanations for that data point and investigate how that point differs from the rest of the data.

Is this the appropriate strategy to follow? Although it is hard to tell without more data, the answer is probably no. Tables such as Figure 3.1 give no clue as to whether the undesired figure arose from a special cause or common cause. However, experience shows that the overwhelming majority of undesirable figures are, in fact, due to common causes. Not only do such tables hinder a manager's ability to determine appropriate action, they also reinforce the human tendency to overreact: if you receive a report, you feel the need to use it.

Yet the responses are characteristic of Western management: treat everything as a special cause. This invariably leads to tampering, which increases variation and makes matters worse, not better. The consequences of tampering can be fully appreciated only when a manager knows the alternatives.

Period 12—1986

Variances

	Actual	Plan	Fav. (Unfav.)	Volume	Usage	Spending	Price
Pulpwood	$131.63	$132.29	$7.66	$	$(1.98)	$	$9.64
Waste	27.18	33.61	6.43		2.36		4.07
Other Raw Materials	28.93	30.74	1.81		1.46		0.35
Labor	30.10	26.14	(3.96)	(1.30)		(2.66)	
Repairs	22.52	24.34	1.82	(1.22)		3.04	
Steam	32.01	35.37	3.36	(0.25)	0.82		2.79
Power	73.79	70.90	(2.89)	(1.76)	(2.20)		1.07
Wrapper	2.99	2.90	(0.09)				(0.09)
Clothing	11.11	10.18	(0.93)	(0.50)	(0.41)		(0.02)
Supplies	7.95	8.37	0.42	(0.42)		0.84	
Other Expenses	3.91	4.33	0.42	(0.22)		0.64	
Mill Burden	66.57	67.67	1.10	(3.38)		4.48	
Mill Depreciation	50.42	48.55	(1.87)	(2.42)		0.55	
Total	**$489.11**	**$502.39**	**$13.28**	**$(11.47)**	**$0.05**	**$6.89**	**$17.81**

Figure 3.1 Traditional presentation of management figures.

(continued)

Year-to-Date

	Actual	Plan	Fav. (Unfav.)	Volume	Usage	Spending	Price
Pulpwood	$133.96	$139.24	$5.28	$	$1.91	$	$3.37
Waste	29.84	33.71	3.87		1.41		2.46
Other Raw Materials	27.67	30.40	2.73		0.68		2.05
Labor	28.54	26.39	(2.15)	(0.61)		(1.54)	
Repairs	23.92	24.48	0.56	(0.58)		1.14	
Steam	36.67	41.52	4.85	(0.14)	1.96		3.03
Power	67.97	68.73	0.76	(0.77)	2.45		(0.92)
Wrapper	3.20	2.89	(0.31)				(0.31)
Clothing	11.21	10.41	(0.80)	(0.24)	(1.53)		0.97
Supplies	9.23	8.64	(0.59)	(0.20)		(0.39)	
Other Expenses	3.62	4.33	0.71	(0.10)		0.81	
Mill Burden	63.14	66.06	2.92	(1.50)		4.42	
Mill Depreciation	48.12	48.84	0.72	(1.15)		1.87	
Total	**$487.09**	**$1505.64**	**$ 18.55**	**$(5.29)**	**$6.88**	**$ 6.31**	**$10.65**

This chart was adapted from one used by Harold Haller of Statistical Studies Inc.

Figure 3.1   Traditional presentation of management figures *(continued)*.

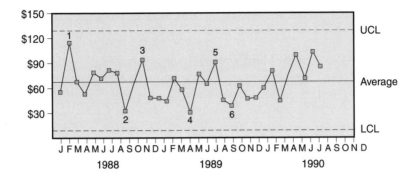

Figure 3.2 Monthly sales data (in $1,000s).

A BETTER WAY

Managers will do better if they use the theory of variation to react to figures. To use this knowledge, they must first look at the data in a different way. Figure 3.2 shows the monthly sales data for a product line. This presentation is different from Figure 3.1 in two important ways: the data are plotted in time order and the overall average and control limits are indicated on the plot. The resulting chart is a statistical control chart. (A product line with no growth in sales was chosen to simplify the presentation. If there had been a trend in sales—say, a 5 percent growth per year—the trend would be used as a center line and the control limits would be plotted parallel to that trend line.)

How does such a display help managers? It is immediately evident that all the points fall within the control limits. With a little training, a manager would also recognize that there is no evidence of special causes, patterns, or trends in the data. Thus the graph shows that the variation in this system is most likely due to common causes—it arises from the myriad of ever-present factors, each contributing a small amount to the variation seen each month.

In a system where only common cause variation is present, asking why the sales for a given month are lower or higher than the preceding month is a low-yield strategy, which means you won't get much payback for the time and resources you expend trying to answer the question. Worse, investigating one point will not give you the answers you need, and the problem will most likely resurface.

There are additional, less obvious costs incurred when variation is ignored or misinterpreted, including:

- Attention being diverted from more pressing problems that could be effectively addressed
- More variation in the system
- Loss of productivity
- Low morale
- Subordinates losing confidence in their manager
- Jobs/careers being put in jeopardy

TAMPERING REVISITED

Despite these costs of inappropriate reactions, treating everything as a special cause is exactly what most American managers are asked to do, and they learn to do it well. An example is shown in Figure 3.3.

Here the manager compared the pounds of product he predicted would be sold in a certain month with what was actually sold. As you can see, he came up with explanations for practically every pound of difference between the two numbers. His reaction to these figures was probably to chastise his salespeople for losing business to competitors. The implicit

February 1986 report for those accounts that are ±£ 5,000 from the budget.

Sales Region 1	**Actual**	**Budgeted**	**Total Variance**
	1,151,679	1,466,907	−315,228

Negative Variances		**Positive Variances**	
−115,000	lost to IJK	+6,000	Karl's, business up
53,200	Some branch closed	6,400	Biscuit Boy, business up
5,000	Upstate, Utica plant closed	6,550	Bayer's, business up
7,700	ABC, lost to XYZ yeast		
13,750	John's		
25,000	Modern Pastry		
9,300	R Rolls		
15,100	City Bakers		
19,000	Jane's		

Figure 3.3 Traditional explanations of variances.

Sales Region 2	Actual 2,308,382	Budgeted 2,969,161	Total Variance –660,079

Negative Variances		Positive Variances
–130,000	Stone Creek, PA. cycled out	(none)
113,000	Upstate, NY plant closed	
50,000	Upstate, OH lost to overseas	
47,000	Erie, PA, lost to IJK	
25,000	Ax's, Ft. Alban, no Feb. order	
10,700	Sadie, business down	
10,500	Biedermann, production shift	
25,200	THN, business down	
15,000	New Day, every other month	
72,000	Andrew, new plant delayed	
23,750	CBC, Dayton, lost to overseas	
24,000	Royal, OH, business down	
13,000	Savin, lost to IJK distributor	
15,500	Lee Foods, business down	
10,500	Benji Bakery, business down	
6,750	M.N. Engliz, MD, business down	

Sales Region 3	Actual 3,917,826	Budgeted 3,730,686	Total Variance +187,140

Negative Variances		Positive Variances	
–17.000	Upstate, Cicero, business down	+6.000	Upstate, business up
8,750	Edna's, lost to IJK	5,000	Diamond, business up
8,500	Gianni, Chicago, lost to IJK	9,000	Friendly's, gained from IJK
8,000	West, business down	121,000	Stone Creek, gained from IJK
9,240	AmBaCo, business down	113,150	Astor, moved production and closed Rockford
90,000	Q Baking, proof box in repair	33,750	ABCO, gained from IJK
8,400	RESA, Detroit, lost to IJK	150,000	CBC, gained from IJK
17,600	My-T-Fine Detroit, lost to IJK	10,000	Royal, business up
7,000	MNO's, Detroit, business down	10,000	GoodCo, new business, new account
6,000	Oldtime, lost to IJK	7,200	CBI, gained from IJK
5,000	H Supply, business down	84,200	CBC, Elkhardt, gained from IJK
6,850	Lake's, MN, business down	10,500	Hunter's, closed Green Bay, moved to Milwaukee
12,500	Weiss, Roseville, lost to IJK	17,500	Tommy's, business up
7,500	RDF, not buying from us in Canada	8,490	MoBaCo, bread special in Feb.
23,500	Jones' bakery, business down	24,000	Royal, business taken from SHAR
19,100	SHAR, 1/2 business to IJK		

Figure 3.3   Traditional explanations of variances *(continued)*.

assumption in this reaction is that there are special causes his salespeople could track and eliminate. As displayed, it is impossible to tell which of these figures could, in fact, be credited to special causes. His facts were correct, but his use of them (chastising salespeople) had only marginal benefit.

Another example of typical management practices is when managers concentrate on only the most recent data, although sometimes they might compare them with the previous year's. Figure 3.4 (which uses the same data as Figure 3.2) show the most recent monthly sales figure (indicated by an "o") and the figure resulting from the same calculation a year previously (indicated by an "x").

Compare this plot with the complete chart in Figure 3.2. Which is more useful? Which puts the manager in a better position to plan, predict, and improve?

Again the question of whether these approaches are adequate arises. The answer, again, is no. Figure 3.3 represents a failure to appreciate common cause variation. Like the causes that produced the data in Figure 3.2, the causes that produced the data in Figure 3.3 are most likely the same for all months. Trying to explain the reason for the exact increase or decrease in the latest point will most likely identify false causes and result in false solutions. Time, energy, and money will be wasted treating the wrong disease, exacerbating the situation instead of improving it—a perfect definition of tampering.

Figure 3.4 shows that managers are seriously handicapped if they cannot see all the data displayed on a control chart. Managers can make much sounder decisions that will lead to continuous improvement if they plot all the data on control charts and apply statistical theory to interpret what they see.

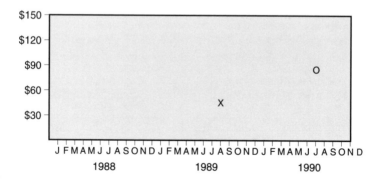

Figure 3.4 Annual comparisons.

Deming has often said that the use of statistical control charts should start at the top, not on the shop floor, to foster an understanding of variation among the leaders of the organization, to aid them in improvement efforts, and particularly in the early years of a quality improvement effort, to help them reduce their tendency to tamper. Improvements cannot really be made until tampering stops.

APPROPRIATE MANAGERIAL ACTION

Charts such as the one in Figure 3.2 provide the quickest, surest way to determine the appropriate reaction to variation. They enable managers to quickly distinguish common cause variation from special cause variation. Such plots also help managers predict system capability. For example, using the data in Figure 3.2, it's clear that unless something changes in the system, sales for this product will almost always fall between $10,000 and $130,000 per month.

What recourse does a manager have against common cause variation? If the manager is not happy with the range of variation, he or she would have to improve the system as a whole using basic statistical tools and methods.

Here's where data like those in Figure 3.3 are helpful. With such data, you can get a lot of mileage out of a common cause strategy. For instance, you might lump together the gains and losses over a series of months, not just single out the latest month or a month you don't like. You could look for patterns. You could stratify the data by categories: How much business is being lost to each competitor? How much to plant closings? How much to other factors? How much by region? You could also plot the data for each competitor on separate charts to see whether, over time, there were special causes within any one competitor that might be masked if just the aggregate data for all competitors were plotted. (This tactic could, for instance, signal that a competitor was using new promotions or introducing new products that were drawing away business.) And you could look for other ways to stratify and disaggregate the data.

If the data do signal the appearance of a special cause, you should find out what is unique about the particular month and then take action to prevent future problems. Failure to react in such a special cause situation would be inappropriate and costly.

Many managers say they are already using the common cause and special cause strategies. That's great, but it will only lead to rapid, continuous improvement if it is done systematically, if the focus is always on the appropriate strategy, if the manager reacts to the latest figure only when there is evidence of a special cause, and if employees are not wasting their time trying to explain why each month's figures are up or down. An article by Thomas Nolan and Lloyd Provost provides further background relative to common and special causes of variation.[6] Through numerous examples, the authors demonstrate the value of appropriate reactions to common and special cause variation.

The need for reacting appropriately to variation seems to be relatively easy for managers to accept when the data plotted are for widgets or processes. But what happens when knowledge of variation is applied to something much closer to home: the evaluation of employee performance?

VARIATION AND PEOPLE: "HALF BELOW AVERAGE"

Current managerial strategies used in this country show a lamentable lack of appreciation for simple math and variation. Managers are taught to reward employees who rank highest in groups, work with those employees who perform "below average," and punish those who rank lowest.

An average is simply a number calculated from data. By virtue of how it is calculated, roughly half the people in any group will perform below average, no matter how smart or talented they are. Even if you could improve the performance of those people "below average," as soon as you gathered new data, you'd find that the average had simply been raised and there are still people below the new average. When people are ranked according to performance, someone will always be highest and someone will always be lowest. These are incontrovertible facts. The issue for management is not whether this will happen—it will—but how to deal with this inevitability.

The red bead experiment, popularized by Deming, illustrates this.[7] Five workers draw beads from a box with a paddle that has fifty holes. The box contains both red and white beads: white represents good products, and red represents defective products. All workers use the same procedure for drawing the beads, with the five workers alternating draws until each worker has drawn five paddlefuls. At the end of the demonstration, the two workers who have the largest total numbers of red beads are fired. Since these workers did nothing different from the workers who were not fired, they are obviously victims of a game of chance. They were the ones who were "below average," yet they did nothing to merit being fired. They were merely working within a system of common cause variation. This scenario does occur in real life and has a demoralizing influence on the entire work force.

BUT PEOPLE REALLY ARE DIFFERENT

You might be saying, "But people really are different." Of course they are. The point is what to do about it.

The concepts of variation can help people understand what they should do when it is their job to guide other employees. Deming says that the manager's job is to learn who, if anyone, performs at a level outside the system—that is, above or below the "control limits"—the manager needs to follow a special cause strategy: investigate how this person's case differs from those of others working in the same process or system.

If this employee consistently performs better than anyone else, perhaps he or she uses different equipment or has invented more effective procedures. In that case, it is in the best interests of the company that this person's knowledge and insight be shared among all employees performing this task and that every effort be made to improve methods, equipment, and so forth.

If the person consistently performs worse than others, perhaps he or she was never properly trained or has a physical limitation (height, vision, hearing, dexterity) that impairs his or her ability to perform this particular job. In such a case, the manager owes it to the employee to identify the cause of the difficulty and work to eliminate the source of the difference, if possible.

If no one's performance falls outside the system of common cause variation, then the manager needs to work on the system to bring everyone to a higher level of performance with reduced variation. The common cause strategy described earlier is the high-yield improvement strategy in such a situation. Focusing on those who are below average or on the person with the lowest performance rating is not effective and has serious negative psychological effects. (An example of how the theory of variation relates to the supervision of salespeople can be found in the previously mentioned article by Nolan and Provost.[9])

VARIATION AND KICKING TUSH

It is very hard to get managers to apply common cause and special cause strategies to people. Their experience tells them to use what works: punishment and negative feedback. Praise an employee for exceptional work this week, and that employee's performance almost invariably worsens next week. But chastise an employee for poor work, and that employee's performance will probably improve.

The key to the puzzle is the fact that employees are usually functioning in a common cause system. A portion of the data used in Figure 3.2 is reproduced in Figure 3.5. Let's treat the data as if they represent one employee's performance over a 12-week period.

When Luella performs very well one week, achieving high sales, she's unlikely to perform better the following week. In fact, it's likely her sales figure will go down. But if Luella performs badly one week, then she's likely to perform at a higher level the following week. Thus, as many managers have discovered, giving praise for a good week seems to lead to worse results and kicking tush after a bad week seems to lead to better performance. The lesson is "obvious" to those who do not understand variation: kicking tush works better than giving praise! The kick tush approach to managing is just another example of destructive behavior nurtured by ignorance of the theory of variation.[10]

Learning the basic concepts of variation can prevent a lot of tension between managers and the people they lead and can create opportunities for real improvement. Had Jack and Sarah, the people in the opening story, understood the theory of variation, they could have dispensed with their monthly praise-or-blame sessions. Instead, Jack could have been helping Sarah figure out how to study and improve the systems and processes that affected her work and that of her salespeople. He could have helped her identify special causes and shape her tactics for tracking them down and preventing their recurrence. They could have worked on the common cause system to reduce variation and to bring all Sarah's salespeople to improved levels of performance.

In short, Jack and Sarah's working relationship would have changed. Knowledge of the theory of variation alters people's view of the world

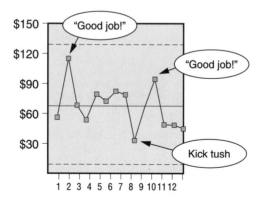

Figure 3.5 Luella's sales over a 12-week period.

forever. It influences practically every aspect of how companies are managed. That is why variation is a central theme of Deming's 14 points.

VARIATION AND DEMING'S 14 POINTS

Deming maintains that management's job is to optimize the enterprise as a whole, creating a win-win situation for customers, shareholders, employees, and suppliers. Think about what this would mean for your company. What would you have to do to make sure customers received high-quality goods and services all the time, shareholders were satisfied with their return, employees looked forward to coming to work, and suppliers worked closely with your employees to ensure the supplied goods were exactly what was needed? What would it take for you to do all this simultaneously?

That's the challenge that Deming presents. An in-depth understanding of variation is central to your ability to meet this challenge.

Point 1. Create Constancy of Purpose. Having a clear goal that everyone can work toward every day, month after month, allows employees to focus on tasks important to the organization and its customers. Changing the goal from time to time to meet managerial goals and quotas creates serious loss. Forcing a system to produce predetermined figures to delight executives or shareholders is extremely costly in terms of future profits, customer loyalty, and employee morale. Doing so represents a fundamental failure to understand that variation will inevitably be present in any system. Constancy of purpose toward delighting the customer each and every day is far better. It reduces variation because the employees will not have to constantly shift their priorities.

Point 2. Adopt the New Philosophy. We are in a new economic age, says Deming. Higher levels of quality at lower costs are possible if you learn to manage differently. Learning to manage differently involves learning how to improve systems in the presence of variation. As previously described, managing differently includes reducing variation in materials, people, processes, and products. Tampering and overreacting to variation, which only increase variation, must end.

Point 3. Cease Dependence on Inspection. Depending on inspection is like treating a symptom while the disease is killing you. The need for inspection results from excessive variability in the process. The disease is the variability. Ceasing dependence on inspection means you must understand your processes so well that you can predict the quality of their output from upstream activities and measurements. To accomplish this you must have a thorough understanding of the sources of variation in your processes and then work toward reducing the variation. Ceasing dependence on inspection forces you to reduce variability.

Point 4. End Purchasing on Price Tag. Reducing variation requires that you rethink your purchasing practices. Working with a selected supplier on a long-term basis of loyalty and trust reduces variation in incoming material and hence in the finished product. Involving the supplier in the collaborative design of new products further improves quality and reduces variation.

Point 5. Improve Constantly. You must constantly improve your production and service systems by understanding the causes of problems and seeking to reduce variation. Everyone in the company must participate in a disciplined way using the plan–do–check–act cycle.

Point 6. Institute Training. Some of the most insidious sources of variation are the lack of documentation on the best-known methods for performing tasks and the lack of standardized training for all employees working on the same function. The best-known methods quickly dissipate without training and retraining. Variation creeps in. Having the last worker training the next is a pervasive source of variation.[11]

Organizations must take action to train employees effectively and consistently. There is variation in how people learn, and training programs must accommodate it. How much training is needed should be addressed using common and special cause thinking.[12] In the words of Eddie "The King" Feigner, the famous fast-pitch softball pitcher who struck out more than 100,000 batters in his career, "Practice makes permanent, not perfect." Once the practice has reduced the variation to the point where only common causes are present, the effect of the training has become "permanent," and further training of the same kind is not likely to be effective. If the results are not good enough, moving to a new job with a fresh start at effective training is usually the best course.

Point 7. Institute Leadership. Managers who ask, "Why is that point up? Why is this one down?" are not leaders. Managers who merely find fault with their employees or who punish the lowest-ranking employee without knowledge of the system increase variability. According to Deming, a leader is someone who, enlightened with an understanding of variation, helps employees do their jobs better with less effort. Such a person works toward diminishing the differences among people by learning which employees are within the system and which are not and then acting appropriately. A leader also supports the goal of the company, focuses on internal and external customers, functions as a coach, and nurtures pride of workmanship. In doing these things, a leader provides constancy of purpose and helps reduce variation.

Point 8. Drive out Fear. Companies who have struggled with implementing Deming's 14 points know that fear is a powerful force that maintains the status quo and impedes many changes that accompany the transformation to a quality- and customer-driven organization.

Theodore Lowe and Gerald McBean identify six "monsters of fear" and discuss their consequences.[13] Fear of reprisal and fear of failure are closely related monsters that result in a please-the-boss mentality and an aversion to accepting risk or generating new ideas. Fear of providing information, which derives from fear of reprisal and fear of failure, leads to concealing information that could help identify and solve problems. This monster also encourages the fabrication of figures to please management and the accompanying increase in process variation due to tampering.

Another of Lowe and McBean's monsters is fear of not knowing. This monster emerges in organizations where managers are expected to control everything in their fiefdoms. The waste to the organization is incalculable. A manager in this environment gets involved in even the most obscure details of work and ends up losing track of the role his department plays in the organization—"he has his hands in all the ashtrays but doesn't know what the floor plan is."

Fear of giving up control lurks in organizations where management's job is viewed as controlling people rather than processes. This fear results in suboptimization, attaining one department's or group's goals at the expense of others, and squelches the workforce's intrinsic motivation. The final monster, fear of change, is an obvious impediment to process improvement.

Such fears create an environment where accurate data are nonexistent and where people are too protective of their jobs to accurately report on problems, failures, or defects. Without accurate data, it is impossible to describe or measure variation and thus impossible to reduce or eliminate it. Fear paralyzes a workforce that could otherwise be actively engaged in reducing variation.

Point 9. Break Down Barriers Between Departments. Separate goals and objectives for different departments result in variation and obstruction rather than cooperation. Reducing variation for the organization as a whole requires cooperation across departmental boundaries. An understanding of variation and cross-functional cooperation is required to optimize the organization as a system.

Point 10. Eliminate Slogans, Exhortations, and Targets for the Workforce. Someone once said, "Insanity is hoping for different results while continuing to do the same thing." Improvement comes only from changed processes and methods. Since most of the complexities and problems in work are due to common causes, only management can make the required changes. As shown in the cases discussed earlier, the results of slogans and exhortations aimed at the workforce only lead to demoralization, tampering, and increased variability rather than to effective change.

Point 11(a). Eliminate Work Standards (Production Quotas). Work standards are an assertion that there is little or no variation in a task. They presume, for instance, that the time to complete a job or the amount of work that can be done in an hour is the same for all people under all circumstances. This presumption obviously ignores variation in working conditions, materials, and methods. Another flagrant lack of understanding of variation is portrayed in the statement: "You've done it once, that proves you can do it every time." There will always be variation. Some days will be better than others. Work standards lead to a failure to measure and plan for variation, which in turn leads to missed deadlines, short shipments, sandbagging, and poor morale.

Production schedules are, of course, necessary and desirable. Knowledge of the variation in a common cause system enables managers to forecast what can be realistically produced. This can then be translated into workable production schedules. Knowledge of process variation helps managers plan for variation, thus minimizing missed deadlines, short shipments, sandbagging, and poor morale.

Point 11(b). Eliminate Management by Objectives. Management by objectives rewards people and departments for reaching short-term measurable goals. Management by objectives leads to suboptimization, one department's goals being reached at the expense of the company as a whole. For instance, it is common in many companies that sales sell products that production cannot produce. The sales department therefore reaches its monthly or quarterly goal, but the rest of the company (production, customer service, and so on) pays the price in stressed systems, employees who rush to produce the products, and backlash from unsatisfied customers.

Some managers fake conformance to goals. For example, they might store products that exceed this month's quota to meet next month's quota or fill the production quota at the expense of product quality. The system also breeds fear and hostility, encourages finger-pointing, and limits the amount of possible improvement.[14]

All of these consequences support mechanisms that increase real variability while often giving the illusion of reducing variability. In effect, they destroy mechanisms that might reduce real variability.[15] Management-by-objective systems reward results without paying sufficient attention to the methods by which they are obtained. A system that rewards people's efforts toward improvement would have greater value.[16]

Instead of pleasing the manager by providing the right figures, the focus needs to be on pleasing the customer each and every day. It should not be acceptable to have end-of-the-month rushes to meet quotas or goals.

Point 12(a). Remove Barriers to Pride of Workmanship for Hourly Workers. Examples of barriers to pride of workmanship for the hourly worker include pressure to use defective materials in production to meet daily quotas, inspection procedures that lack operational definitions, instruments and machines that do not function properly or are not in control, and poor supervision. Workers often have no way of knowing whether the job is performed correctly. In addition to contributing to the demoralization of the workforce, these barriers contribute to variability in output.

Point 12(b). Remove Barriers to Pride of Workmanship for Management and Engineering. In this point, Deming calls for the abolishment of annual or merit ratings and management by objectives. A merit rating system "nourishes short-term performance, annihilates long-term planning, builds fear, demolishes teamwork, nourishes rivalry and politics."[17] People working in the same common cause system can be rated quite differently when, in fact, their apparent performance is beyond their control. Managers should not act as judges, inspecting results at the end of the process; instead, they should be leaders, working upstream with employees to reduce variability at the early stages of the process. In short, merit-rating systems support behaviors that increase variation and destroy behaviors that reduce variation.[18,19,20]

Point 13. Institute a Vigorous Program of Education and Self-Improvement. Knowledge is needed for the advancement of an organization as well as society. Providing information on variation and other elements of what Deming calls "profound knowledge" (systems theory, theory of knowledge, and psychology) is an obvious place to start.[21] But, to have benefits, education and self-improvement need not be directly related to an employee's job. Any education or self-improvement increases an employee's self-esteem and potential to contribute to improvements in existing processes and advances in technology.

Point 14. Put Everybody to Work to Accomplish the Transformation. Coordinating the activities of everyone connected with the organization contributes significantly to the reduction of variation and the optimization of the entire system.

THE UNKNOWN AND UNKNOWABLE

Deming writes, "It was Dr. Lloyd Nelson who years ago remarked that the most important figures for management are unknown and unknowable. We could add that the most important losses and gains are not even under suspicion."[22] The effects of the reward system, the efficacy of the training program, losses that result from tampering, losses that ensue from suboptimization, and loss of market share due to unsatisfied customers all seem to defy quantification. Yet these are prominently among the most important figures for management.

The best weapons against these losses are embodied in Deming's 14 points: providing constancy of purpose, understanding variation and removing it from our processes and systems, and reducing fear. Only by internalizing the 14 points and understanding the role of variation will management be able to deal effectively with challenges in coming years.

ACKNOWLEDGMENTS

Sue Reynard did her usual outstanding job of improving the content and exposition in this paper. Many people have contributed to the knowledge presented here, including W. Edwards Deming, Thomas W. Nolan, John Dowd, Peter R. Scholtes, Kevin Little, Rob Stiratelli, and Harold Haller.

ENDNOTES

1. L. Finn, T. Kramer, and S. Reynard, *Design of Experiments: Shifting Quality Improvement into High Gear* (Madison, WI: Joiner Associates Inc., 1987).
2. G. Box, W. Hunter, and J. S. Hunter, *Statistics for Experimenters* (New York: John Wiley and Sons, 1978).
3. H. Kurne, *Statistical Methods of Quality Improvement* (Tokyo: The Association for Overseas Technical Scholarship, 1985).
4. D. Wheeler and D. S. Chambers, *Understanding Statistical Process Control* (Knoxville, TN: Statistical Process Controls, Inc., 1986).
5. *Continuing Process Control and Process Capability Improvement* (Dearborn, MI: Ford Motor Company, Statistical Methods Office, 1983).
6. T. W. Nolan and L. P. Provost, "Understanding Variation," *Quality Progress* (May 1990): 75–77.
7. W. E. Deming, *Out of the Crisis* (Cambridge, MA: M.I.T. Press, 1986): 346–53.
8. Ibid, 248.

9. Nolan and Provost, 75–77.
10. D. Kahneman and A. Tversky, "On the Psychology of Prediction," *Psychological Review* 80 (1973): 237–251.
11. T. J. Boardman and E. C. Boardman, "Don't Touch That Funnel!" *Quality Progress* (December 1990).
12. Deming, Chapter 8.
13. T. A. Lowe and G. M. McBean, "Honesty without Fear," *Quality Progress* (November 1989).
14. B. L. Joiner and P. R. Scholtes, *Total Quality Leadership vs. Management by Results* (Madison, WI: Joiner Associates Inc., 1985).
15. Lowe and McBean.
16. S. M. Moss, "Appraise Your Performance Appraisal Process," *Quality Progress* (November 1989).
17. Deming, 102.
18. R. D. Moen, "The Performance Appraisal System: Deming's Deadly Disease," *Quality Progress* (November 1989).
19. P. R. Scholtes, *An Elaboration on Deming's Teachings on Performance Appraisal* (Madison, WI: Joiner Associates Inc., 1987).
20. Moss.
21. W. E. Deming, "Foundation for Management of Quality in the Western World," unpublished manuscript (1990).
22. Ibid.

4

Ensuring Team Success in Continuous Improvement

Susan M. Heathfield and Gregory M. Scheessele

SUMMARY

Setting up teams is easy. Making empowered teams effective contributors to bottom-line organizational success and to the continuous improvement of operations requires consistent, dedicated leadership; a redefined organizational culture; new roles and responsibilities for all company members; and redesigned support systems that emphasize teamwork and expanded levels of empowerment.

KEY WORDS

Cultural change, empowerment, leadership, management, work teams.

INTRODUCTION

Manufacturing companies who compete within the global manufacturing community know that their continued supplier relationships are dependent upon their ability to continuously improve. Continuous improvement requires: reductions in cost and delivery time, increases in quality, utilization of data and statistical methods, tracking and improvement of measurable performance indicators, systematic approaches to problem solving, reporting on process as well as product, and close relationships with customers.

Companies that adopt the philosophy and methodology of continuous improvement are most likely to succeed in this environment. Continuous improvement, as discussed in this paper, means intentional, ongoing, incremental progress and growth in every aspect of work. Changes in how workers clean and organize the manufacturing facility, in how they run their machines, and in how they relate to each other and the management of the operation, constitute the guts of continuous improvement.

The heart of continuous improvement is people. The competitive advantage of a manufacturing company is the ability and commitment of the people the company employs. The second competitive advantage is the stockpile of improvements implemented by these workers that differentiate, for example, one metal stamper with a 600-ton press from the stamper down the road with the same press. Because the competitive advantage of a company is its people, helping people develop their talents and skills, providing ways in which people can contribute ideas, and designing systems that encourage these contributions is critical. This paper describes three key requirements for the company that wants a successful continuous improvement through teams process:

- Provide consistent, visibly demonstrated management (and in a represented facility, union) commitment and involvement

- Recognize that adopting the philosophy and methodology of continuous improvement is a cultural change; company systems must be redesigned to support this change

- Redesign and mentor the new role of managers and supervisors

DEMONSTRATE MANAGEMENT (AND UNION) COMMITMENT AND INVOLVEMENT

"It is easy to adopt the tools and management mechanisms of a CIP (Continuous Improvement Program). It is much more difficult to live up to the underlying philosophy." (Schroeder and Robinson 1991) These authors "have recently observed or participated in the installation of a number of CIPs that were implemented at great expense, with extensive retraining, and accompanied by much fanfare, only to wither into perfunctory exercises as soon as it became obvious to the workers and lower management that an uncommitted upper management was merely introducing the program to be fashionable, or in response to corporate or customer pressures."

In companies that successfully implement continuous improvement processes, the attention and the commitment of executive management and the union leadership is constant. When this constancy of purpose is demonstrated, resistant company members become convinced over time that the continuous improvement process will not go away, or be replaced by the next program of the month. There are specific ways in which leaders can demonstrate this commitment.

First, to truly convince people that a change is underway, executive leaders must demonstrate their commitment to the change by changing. The organization will not change, and cannot be expected to change, if the leaders do not change. In traditional organizations, people do what they think their boss wants them to do. The actions of the leader send a much more powerful message than his or her words. If company leaders want to create a company that is focused on continuous improvement in a team environment, they must act as if they are leading a company that is focused on continuous improvement in a team environment. In this way they build and foster the trust that is essential if they wish to transform their workplace. In companies that successfully adopt this philosophy, the leaders may not always perfectly support the process but their commitment to the process is always visible to their people.

This trust begins with the communication of a clear vision that is formulated with input from other members of the company. This vision is a picture of the kind of work environment the leader wants to create. The vision is communicated regularly in company meetings, in personal conversation, and in daily actions. Working with as many members of the company as possible, the leader then develops the critical strategic goals necessary to accomplish the vision. These goals are communicated to every company member. One mid-sized manufacturer scheduled meetings for all employees at external facilities to communicate the vision, the strategic direction, and the goals.

Following this communication, each manager must then make certain that each individual employee clearly understands how he or she can contribute to the accomplishment of these goals. This gives all employees a clear sense of direction and helps people align their personal and team improvement activities with the overall direction of the company. When the most important goals are clear, company members select the most important projects and improvements to pursue in their teams.

No company member wants to exert time and energy on something that is not important. At a Florida manufacturer of microporous membrane, members of one department were focusing team efforts only on issues such as: purchase a storage cabinet, buy a mat for the floor, and get a pencil holder for this machine. When the department manager clearly communicated the department goals, and asked department members for help in specific areas, team members changed their emphasis to scrap reduction and increasing productivity.

When the vision has been communicated, the goals established, and the daily actions that will support the accomplishment of these goals agreed upon, leaders must model the behavior they want to see in other members of the company. Swooping into the workplace with daily changing demands and directions; telling workers what to do and how to do it; arguing with or denying a team decision that was delegated; giving an assignment and, when unhappy with the results, taking the work back; suggesting a new idea or approach to a manager, but then implementing it before he has the chance; are all seen by the workforce as examples of lack of trust and commitment. And they are examples of lack of trust. Moreover, actions of this type will destroy a continuous improvement process.

When nurturing the continuous improvement process, the leader must demonstrate commitment in actions, often before his or her inner comfort level catches up with the outward actions. As an example, when forming continuous improvement teams, providing each team with a self-directed budget can be worrisome for a leader. Relinquishing control of the money demonstrates trust, but many leaders have to experience the responsibility with which most teams handle resources before they become true believers. In fact, at companies in the authors' experience, many teams are tighter with the purse strings than the leaders. At one company, a several thousand dollar capital budget with recurring expenses was established by management for a team of machine operators to implement a clean room gown cleaning process. The team implemented a solution that met requirements with no capital outlay and saved $17,000 per year in expenses over the original method.

The leadership of a continuous-improvement-through-teams process cannot be delegated. The visible commitment and interest of the leader must be demonstrated daily. There is a tendency in the workplace for people to go about their business as usual unless the leaders are cheerleading and encouraging the change. Especially in the early days of a team process, momentum must be assisted. When workers have experienced some successes, less championing of the process is necessary. The need for leadership and demonstrated interest, however, never ceases completely.

When problems occur and forward movement is not as fast as the leaders desire, leaders must resist their natural tendency to revert to their old management style. Through this commitment, they gain the trust of the other members of the team. This is probably the single most important factor in building the momentum of any continuous improvement effort. Should the leader fail in this regard—and most will at one time or another—he or she must make note of their failure to the workforce.

Apologize and explain that they are learning how to work in the new system as well. Do not let the failure go undiscussed; it will be talked about by the workforce either with the leaders or without them.

When starting a continuous improvement process, leaders must reassure their workforce that responsible participation will not result in any penalties. Some penalties are not as obvious as others. One company scheduled all improvement activities on overtime thinking that the workers would appreciate the extra income. Wrong. The workers were already working more overtime than they wanted to work. Another company allowed teams to meet only when production was caught up. People indicated that they felt they had to work like dogs to get to meet with their team.

The leader must take the position that failure is expected when company members are contributing to improvement. At the same time, managers in a continuous improvement process cannot allow a team improvement to fail if their input or assistance would have prevented the failure. Leaders walk a fine line between providing experience and information and taking over the work of the team. Training team members to become more independent of the manager pushes out the boundaries within which team members can contribute. Teaching team members to obtain the information they need by monitoring their own processes and making their own vendor and internal resource contacts helps team members grow and contribute more.

Finally, leaders must create an atmosphere that is free of fear for real continuous improvement to flourish. When asked if their employees are afraid, many managers will answer with a resounding *no*. Yet other company members, when responding to the same question, mention fear of retaliation as one of their most serious concerns. These workers state that many operators are afraid to tell the truth about what happened at their workstation to cause damaged parts or a malfunctioning machine.

They fear that they will look bad, be "written up," or in some way receive punishment for their honesty. So the job of the repair person is multiplied because he must guess what really happened as he repairs the problem. This same fear interferes with problem solving and process improvement. At the problem analysis step, operators must be free to state exactly what happened. Otherwise, improvement will not occur.

One manufacturer recently pressured workers to abide by shop rules that had not been regularly enforced for several years. One of the most devoted employees in the company was working in shipping. A procedure that had never been enforced was not followed and bad parts ended up on their way to a customer. When the employee realized what had happened, he called his manager at home and woke him up to tell him of the problem. He also called every other possible person to keep this problem from reaching the customer.

Rather than reinforcing service to the customer via the need for the procedure, communicating that the procedure would in future be enforced, and following up to assure that the procedure was followed, the managers "wrote up" the employee for not following the procedure. In this union facility, the employee won in the grievance process. Unfortunately, the company lost more than the simple grievance. Management taught other employees a powerful lesson in truth and consequences. Weeks after the incident, other company members claimed that admitting error and/or telling management what really happened was personally risky.

The amount of time spent addressing the issue of leadership in this paper is directly related to the importance of this issue in a continuous improvement process. At the same time, the authors believe in the power of and necessity for buy-in and support from the entire organization. Even the most powerful leader cannot drag an entire work force in a particular direction indefinitely. Therefore, it is also important that companies focus on helping all company members understand the importance of the process through communication, training, demonstrated support and success, and recognition of accomplishments.

Without the commitment and support of both the company leaders, and in a represented workplace, the union leaders, the continuous improvement process will not produce the desired impact on the company bottom line. With appropriate leadership that provides goals, direction, support, training, trust, expectations of measurement, and feedback loops, the continuous improvement process will thrive.

DESIGN SUPPORT SYSTEMS THAT ENCOURAGE THE CULTURAL CHANGE

The second key requirement addressed by this paper is that organizations must recognize that the transition from a traditional manufacturing environment to a team-based, continuous improvement–focused operation requires changing the culture of the company. Companies must make the transition from the traditional hierarchical triangle in which a few people control information and decision making to a culture in which influence, responsibility, and accountability are shared. Importantly, studies indicate that only when a company addresses continuous improvement as a cultural change of this type and magnitude, and designs appropriate support systems, will the company reap maximum reward from its investment.

In a continuous improvement process, "right the first time" becomes a problematic rallying cry. Making data visible and working to improve processes is a switch from hiding numbers to look good. Having a clean, organized manufacturing facility on a daily basis is a change from spending hours on cleaning the day before a major customer visits. Asking people what they think they should do is different from telling people exactly what to do. This transition requires changing systems; habits; and traditional ways of interacting, providing information, evaluating performance, developing people, and making decisions. This type of cultural change can require two to eight years of effort. Most companies do, however, experience some bottom-line results within the first six months, when pitfalls are avoided.

The main purpose of a continuous improvement process or system is to provide a framework in which company members can effectively contribute. The goal of the system designed is to eliminate operating processes, procedures, and barriers that keep people from contributing. Companies are most successful when they concentrate efforts on changing how the organization does work (the setup of systems) rather than on changing the people. An example of this is illustrated in the following case. Traditionally, relationships between the automotive companies and their suppliers have been tedious and stressful. The automotive companies tend to dictate methods, objectives, and sometimes even staffing to their suppliers. This has had limited success. But this does not have to be the case. One relationship that concentrated on how the two organizations worked together has continuously yielded improved component quality, lower costs, and shared savings for four straight years. The key difference occurred when corporate management stepped aside after providing clear direction, and allowed their product focus teams (engineering, production, design) to work together.

Each company needs to examine their own systems to identify those that are preventing people from maximally contributing to major bottom-line impact. Generally, the company's methods for providing information; sharing decision making; involving employees in planning; and evaluating, motivating, and developing company members, undergo changes in a continuous improvement, employee empowering process. (Vogt and Murrell 1990) Additionally, how companies reward and recognize the contributions of company members usually changes when continuous improvement is emphasized.

Organizations experience the following issues. Every organization that begins this process finds that employees do not have enough information to make responsible, educated decisions. Most companies find they must schedule more frequent production meetings. They find they must provide more information about what is done with the parts the operators produce. They find they must help people develop and react to process feedback and measurement systems through such methods as training in statistical process control (SPC), trend analysis, flow diagrams, and so on. Organizations find they must provide systematic problem solving and process improvement methods and information about how to overcome interdepartmental barriers. Companies find they must make the plant schedule visible if they want people to move on to their next task without the direction of a supervisor.

They discover that customer is a nebulous word until employees have spent time directly interacting with the people in the next process who use the part they produce. They find that their sales organization, and often their engineering organization, have so effectively interacted with the customers that no one else knows they have one. For continuous improvement, every company employee must identify and know the requirements of both their internal and external customers. The single most effective way to do this is for company members to visit their customers and spend time discussing customer requirements and needs. (This assumes the teams have been trained in how to satisfy internal and external customers without the risk of losing either.)

Additionally, companies discover that company members need regular feedback about performance. Indeed, companies that implement self-directed teams discover that two areas of great importance for exceptional performance are the most difficult to cover. Teams report that they do not receive performance feedback regularly. They also report that without supervisors, they do not receive company information. For continuous improvement, both of these systems are essential and must be addressed for success. Organizations must redesign performance feedback systems so the peer role in feedback gradually increases. Company members must learn to develop and understand information that is present in and communicated by the process.

Systems examination and change begins with company leadership. Then, involving the workforce in planning and designing their own system is important. This is an effective strategy as people take real ownership of the system they are creating. This eliminates most, although not all, of the need for selling people on participating in a management-designed system and then having to police the system later. Something as simple as assisting a team of employees to figure out their own way to inventory, organize, and distribute gloves in a welding department helps people walk the path of continuous improvement.

Involving workers in systems design and improvement takes time, energy, and training. First, the leaders of the organization have to understand the current and needed systems. Then, the leaders need to acknowledge the value of involving and training workers in systems design. Leaders need to recognize that how they involve workers in system design is also critical. Involving people on the front end, when decisions are made, generally eliminates much of the selling and policing managers must traditionally do on the back end. Additionally, the involvement of people builds their trust and helps the cultural change progress more rapidly.

DESIGN AND MENTOR THE NEW ROLE OF MANAGERS AND SUPERVISORS

In the third key requirement for successful continuous improvement through teams, studies indicate that only one-third of all supervisors initially see the process as benefiting them. Additionally, other studies indicate that supervisors express the greatest degree of dissatisfaction and frustration with any continuous improvement process. Supervisors often cite a distrust for ongoing management support of their efforts when these programs are implemented. Their general experience has been that after the training classes and all the hoopla that accompanies the kick-off of a new program ends, they are left alone in the field to make it work.

Additionally, many supervisors and managers regard these processes with great suspicion and concern for job security. These concerns are warranted. In one recent study by Development Dimensions International, of 20 companies studied, 13 had fewer managers after the institution of a team process. Fifty percent had fewer layers of management. One company had replaced 80 managers with eight facilitators. (Wilcox 1994)

Supervisors also experience confusion about their new role. Many people have difficulty handling any type of change. Supervisors and managers not only have to cope with the change but they experience assorted human feelings about the loss of power and control. Supervisors who experience these feelings can display passive nonsupport of the continuous improvement efforts, or even subtly sabotage the planned process.

Working with managers and supervisors to help them identify new roles and contributions is one of the most crucial steps in implementing continuous improvement. This work must begin first, before any continuous improvement process is rolled out to the general workforce.

The supervisor or manager must begin to see him- or herself as a team leader or coach and must learn new skills. The supervisor must do the following:

- Become a teacher and a coach rather than a director

- Provide the teams, or teach the teams how to obtain and use, information about business needs such as cost, quality, and production schedules, and help the teams use this information effectively to set goals, solve problems, and make decisions

- Help teams of employees know where to go when they have a problem

- Help teams of employees set specific, measurable goals and review the team's performance in team meetings

- Help teams confront and resolve personality problems, leadership problems, conflict, and performance issues in the team

- Provide information about and access to customers and suppliers

- Build a team, develop the people in the team, work with team members on performance management issues, and link the team to the wider organization

The following management actions will assist supervisors and managers to support the continuous improvement through teams process:

- Provide a regular opportunity for supervisors to get together to express their real fears and concerns as the transition is taking place.

- Involve supervisors in the goal-setting and planning processes. Encourage them to participate in planning teams and steering committees.

- Encourage supervisors and managers to serve on teams that interest them as a participant, not as the leader.

- Schedule regular meetings between the supervisors, the managers, and the leaders of the change process.

- Provide training and role clarification classes for a period of time for supervisors and managers.

- Provide some control over team rewards and recognition, and input to these matters through the normal leadership channels.

- Hold supervisors accountable for assisting the continuous improvement process. Provide assessment and rewards based on their willingness to utilize the talents and resources of the people they supervise. The focus of these efforts is growth and development, not punishment.

When companies pay attention to the roles of the mid-level managers and the supervisors, they magnify their opportunity for success with continuous improvement. Committed supervisors are the lifeblood of the process.

CONCLUSION

It is difficult to cover all aspects of creating continuous improvement through teams in this brief paper. We have concentrated on three of the more important aspects: leadership of the change; changing company culture and support systems to support the change; and the changing role of the manager or supervisor in a continuous improvement process. Other important aspects of an effective system include creating an organized, managed, team process; measuring the results of and success of the process; using systematic problem solving and process improvement methods, providing frequent rewards for, recognition of, and review of team progress, and providing clear direction to teams.

Part of the process is that companies need to experiment and continuously improve the process they embark upon. Making an agreement with the people in the company from the beginning that all the pieces of the program are not in place is important. Emphasize that the goal is to continually improve the system in which people are contributing to improvement to maximize their ability to do so.

REFERENCES

Berry, T. H. *Managing the Total Quality Transformation.* New York: McGraw-Hill, 1991.

Imai, M. *Kaizen, the Key to Japan's Competitive Success.* New York: Random House, 1986.

Jablonski, J. R. *Implementing Total Quality Management.* Albuquerque, N.M.: Technical Management Consortium, 1990.

Joiner, B. L. *Fourth Generation Management: The New Business Consciousness.* New York: McGraw-Hill, 1994.

Juran, J. M. *Quality Control Handbook.* New York: McGraw-Hill, 1988.

Scholtes, P. R. *The Team Handbook.* Madison, WI: Joiner Associates, 1990.

Schroeder, D. M., and A. G. Robinson. "America's Most Successful Export to Japan: Continuous Improvement Programs." In *Sloan Management Review* (Spring 1991): 67–81.

Suzaki, K. *The New Shop Floor Management: Empowering People for Continuous Improvement.* New York: The Free Press, Macmillan, 1993.

Vogt, J. F., and K. L. Murrell. *Empowerment in Organizations: How to Spark Exceptional Performance.* San Diego, C.A.: University Associates (Pfeiffer and Company), 1990.

Wilcox, J. "Teamwork Brings Changes for Managers." ASTD Management Development Report (Fall 1994).

Section II

Teams

The notion of people working together to achieve a common goal is certainly not one that originated with quality professionals. This concept probably dates back to the first days of cave men and women who struggled together and allocated duties with the common goal of survival. Quality professionals caught on to this idea of shared goals pretty quickly; teamwork has been at the very heart of quality improvement for decades. The articles in this section address some of the opportunities and challenges of working together to achieve a common goal.

In "The Use and Management of Teams: A How-To Guide," Richard Ratliff, Stephen Beckstead, and Steven Hanks discuss various aspects of teams. First, they identify four organizational situations that indicate the need for teams. Then they summarize four different types of work teams and provide simple guidelines for determining optimal team size. Finally, they tie it all together with easy-to-use models for team management.

Cliff Seastrunk, Roy Johnson, and Ron Huber discuss team types and organization in "Effective Use of Teams in Continuous Improvement." They provide a model describing team membership, direction, duration, and participation for four types of teams. Their article clearly defines team roles for leaders, facilitators, and recorders.

R. Keith Denton, in "Building a Team," addresses factors that are essential to team success. Denton identifies characteristics of effective team leaders and summarizes problem-solving and team-building roles for the team leader, facilitator, recorder, and resources. His article concludes with a wonderful summary of effective team communication techniques.

In "Self-Directed Work Teams: A Guide to Implementation," Michael Piczak and Reuben Hauser define self-directed work teams (SDWTs) and describe their many benefits. They distinguish SDWTs from other types of teams and provide useful guidelines for team implementation.

The remaining two articles in this section address team failure. "Why Teams Poop Out," by John Niles and Norbert Salz, addresses that tricky question of why well-trained teams lose momentum and have less-than-desirable outcomes. Niles and Salz present a four-part model for diagnosing team performance and finding remedies for low-performing teams. In "How to Prevent Teams from Failing," John Beck and Neil Yeager address many aspects of teamwork. Their primary focus is on leadership, team dynamics, and empowerment as important attributes for team success. They conclude with a discussion of four important steps that team leaders should take to prevent teams from failing. Together, these two articles provide some very useful guidelines for heading off team problems.

5

The Use and Management of Teams: A How-To Guide

Choosing the Right Type for Your Projects

Richard L. Ratliff, Stephen M. Beckstead,
and Steven H. Hanks

The use of teams has become a key fixture in today's organizations. Managers of many organizations have realized the significant benefits of teams. Others, however, have only become frustrated.

The authors' observations of hundreds of teams in numerous organizations on four continents, including many world-class companies, have suggested some simple guidelines for the effective use and management of teams in any kind of organization.

This article presents a basic team framework designed to answer the following questions that managers must consider:

1. What conditions call for the use of teams? Are there conditions when teams are not beneficial? If so, what are they?

2. What types of teams should be formed? Are there conditions that guide this decision?

3. How should teams be managed? What factors influence team size and team duration? Should different types of teams be managed differently? If so, how?

WHEN TO USE TEAMS: FOUR ENABLING CONDITIONS

The authors' observations suggest that four enabling conditions give rise to the need for teams.

> *Condition 1:* When there is more work to do, usually of one kind, than one person can do in the allotted time

> *Condition 2:* When a single job is best performed as a sequence of tasks and is required to be completed faster than a single person can do it

> *Condition 3:* When a single job requires the coordination and integration of different roles or expertise

> *Condition 4:* When the solution to a problem requires the combination of more knowledge than one person possesses

In situations where one or more of these conditions exist, managers should give careful consideration to forming a team to accomplish the work at hand. When none of the enabling conditions is present, jobs and tasks should be assigned to individuals.

Teams used in the absence of these conditions usually end in disappointment for all concerned, with team members getting in each other's way and productive members being resentful of those who do not contribute. Morale, efficiency, and productivity all tend to suffer. There is little, if any, benefit in employing teams when none of the enabling conditions is present.

FOUR BASIC KINDS OF TEAMS

The authors' research has identified four basic types of teams:

1. Simple work teams

2. Relay teams

3. Integrated work teams

4. Problem-solving teams

Each team type is associated with a particular enabling condition. Thus, the appropriate choice of which type of team to employ is related to the enabling conditions present. Table 5.1 illustrates the relationship between team type and the four enabling conditions.

Table 5.1   Enabling conditions and team types.

Primary Enabling Condition	Corresponding Team Type	Application
More work of one kind than one person can do in the allotted time	Simple work team	Surlyn cover injection teams, Wilson Sporting Goods Golf Ball Division
Sequential work process with handoffs	Relay team	Sandwich assembly teams, McDonald's
When a single job requires the coordination and integration of different roles	Integrative work team	Surgical teams, Logan Regional Hospital
When the solution to a problem requires the combination of more knowledge and expertise than one person possesses	Problem-solving team	Kaizen teams, Gates Rubber Siloam Springs Plant

In defining these four types of teams and their associated enabling conditions, illustrative applications are drawn from four organizations: McDonald's; Wilson Sporting Goods Golf Ball Division, Humbolt, Tennessee; Gates Rubber Company, Siloam Springs, Arkansas; and Logan Regional Hospital, Logan, Utah.

McDonald's is a world leader in the fast-food industry. The other three are award-winning organizations that use teams to drive production, quality improvement, and customer satisfaction.[1]

Simple Work Teams. Teams responding to the first enabling condition—when there is more work to do than one person can complete in the required time—may be called simple work teams. The focal role of simple work teams is to complete a large task within a limited period of time. Each employee performs basically the same task.

Wilson Sporting Goods' surlyn cover injection teams, with 12 to 15 members each, are examples of simple work teams. Here, injection mold operators place golf ball cores in a mold with the appropriate dimple pattern. The surlyn cover material is injected around each core. As thousands of golf balls are produced each day, this requires a team of operators, all doing essentially the same task, to complete the daily volume requirements.

Other generic examples of simple work teams include assembly teams, on which each person does total assembly of a unit, such as at Wilson; painting teams; and short-distance delivery teams, where one person is responsible for one or more complete deliveries.

Relay Teams. Teams responding to the second enabling condition—when a sequence of tasks must be performed on an object (good or service) in a specified order, one following the other—are called relay teams. Here the object is passed from one team member to the next in sequence, although all team members may be working on other objects in various stages of completion.

The assembly of sandwiches at a McDonald's restaurant is an example of a relay team. Although the matching of tasks to specific workstations varies slightly from one McDonald's to another, the basic assembly process requires that each sandwich go through the following series: bun preparation, dressing (sauce, lettuce, onions, and so on), meat placement, wrapping, and queuing.

Other examples of relay teams include traditional in-line manufacturing; long-distance mail delivery teams, where intermediate exchanges are required; and newspaper writing–editing–production teams.

Integrated Work Teams. Teams responding to the third enabling condition—when different roles must be coordinated—may be called integrated work teams. These teams combine a variety of related tasks to produce a product (good or service). In integrated work teams, several tasks are performed at the same time.

Logan Regional Hospital's surgery teams are an example of integrated work teams. Surgery is a service requiring several different kinds of tasks that must be carefully coordinated, focusing on some specific aspect of the patient's body.

The lead surgeon has primary responsibility for the team and performs the surgical procedures. A consulting or assisting surgeon often is present to provide additional expertise and a second pair of hands to perform surgical procedures required to support the lead surgeon.

A lead, or circulating, nurse supervises the setup of the operating room and patient preparation, at the lead surgeon's instructions. A surgical technician helps set up the sterile components of the operating room and prepare the patient in the operating room. The surgical technician also hands the surgeon the instruments, and both the circulating nurse and the surgical technician count instruments, sponges, and needles, and provide ad hoc surgical support as needed.

An anesthesiologist, or nurse anesthesiologist, is responsible for administering anesthesia and working with the lead surgeon to ensure the proper level of brain activity and to monitor the patient's vital signs during the surgical process.

All of these tasks are required for a typical surgery, and all are integrated and focused on the successful completion of the surgical procedures on an individual patient.

Other examples of integrated work teams include book production teams, road production teams, and advertising production teams. The main purpose of these teams is to produce an identifiable product as efficiently as possible, using a diversity of skills and careful integration of those skills.

Problem-Solving Teams. Teams responding to the fourth enabling condition—when the task is unstructured and/or the solution to a problem requires more knowledge or expertise than one person has—may be called problem-solving teams.

Gates Rubber's quick changeover *kaizen* team is an example of a problem-solving team. Kaizen teams map processes, find waste, use cause-and-effect analysis to determine causes of waste, design and implement countermeasures, and check to be sure improvement has been made.

Kaizen teams are typically formed for a few days and disbanded when the problem is solved. Gates Rubber also uses problem-solving teams to achieve cycle-time reductions, increase throughput in production cells, and reach proper staffing levels for manufacturing processes.

Other generic examples of problem-solving teams include quality improvement teams, crime prevention task forces, and design teams. The work of these teams is primarily cerebral. The main purpose of these teams is to combine and focus brain power in addressing workplace problems. Solutions are generally reached by consensus.

WHAT TO DO WHEN MULTIPLE CONDITIONS ARE PRESENT

When more than one of the enabling conditions occur simultaneously, there is likely a need for more than one of the four basic team types and their corresponding activities. When this occurs, rather than devising some new form of team, successful teams become multiconditional. First, tasks are segregated into different categories corresponding to the existing conditions, and then the subtasks are performed according to the basic team activities required.

One example of a multiconditional team is a typical site evaluation team for a quality award, such as the Shingo Prize or Malcolm Baldrige National Quality Award. When conducting a site visit, the team of examiners often encounters all four of the enabling conditions simultaneously, as well as conditions calling for individual tasks.

Time constraints often require team members to examine different parts of a company's operations separately, all looking for approximately the same sorts of things (simple work team). Team members also coordinate different roles during site visits: data collection, analysis and evaluation, and report preparation (relay team, integrated work team). Finally, members must combine their knowledge and expertise to reach a consensus opinion on the team evaluation (problem-solving team).

TEAM SIZE

Important to the organization of any team is determining its size. Each of the four kinds of teams and their associated activities suggest a different strategy for determining the number of members required. While a variety of factors may affect team size, only a few factors in each case are most likely to drive team size. The primary factor for all types of teams is the size and scope of a required project. Beyond this basic consideration, however, certain factors appear to come into play when determining the appropriate size for each type of team.

Simple Work Teams. The principal factors driving the size of simple work teams are:

- The amount of work to be done

- The amount of time available to do the work

- The amount of work one person can do in the available time

With this information, it is a simple matter to divide the total estimated work to be done by the amount of work one person can do in the available time period, giving the number of people required to do the work in the required time.

For example, suppose 50,000 square feet of surface must be cleaned in five hours, and one person can, on average, clean 5,000 square feet in the five-hour period. Ten people, then, would be required to complete the job in the allotted time.

Relay Teams. The main factors influencing relay team size are:

- The differentiation of tasks to be performed in sequence

- The balancing of task assignments to ensure a smooth flow of work without bottlenecks or unnecessarily idle resources

- The cycle time required

A single work process may be divided into, say, three, five, or eight separate tasks, depending on how the tasks are defined. For example, in some McDonald's restaurants the task of dressing a sandwich bun may include placing the meat on the bun, while at other restaurants, dressing may include everything other than the meat, and placement of the meat is a separate task.

To balance the work flow, it is necessary to assign the tasks to individual workstations so that units of work pass through the sequence smoothly. Tasks may be combined or redifferentiated to accomplish this balanced flow.

For example, one McDonald's restaurant divides the six-step sandwich assembly process into four workstations: bun preparation (step 1), dressing the bun (step 2), cooking and meat placement (steps 3 and 4), and wrapping and queuing (steps 5 and 6). A second restaurant, one with less customer demand, uses only two workstations. Bun preparation, dressing the sandwiches, and meat placement are combined, and cooking is taken off the assembly line entirely. Cooking is an off-line support, just-in-time process.

Integrated Work Teams. The principal factor driving the size of integrated work teams is the differentiation of the required tasks. To determine team size, the integrated production process must first be planned, standardized, and balanced to ensure an integration of tasks without creating bottlenecks or slack points. Once the integration and balancing of the tasks have been accomplished, team size is determined by the number of integrated human tasks required to run the production process.

For example, Gates Rubber, as well as other companies that use cellular manufacturing techniques, uses this approach to determine the number of team members for each production cell. First, daily production numbers are determined. These are usually tied to customer requirements.

Next, "takt time" is calculated. Takt time is calculated by dividing the productive time available in a given period by the number of units required by the customer during that period. Takt time is sometimes referred to as the "heartbeat" of the customer. Working to a takt time is one step in getting production to flow more smoothly.

Third, cycle time (the time to complete each operation in the cell) is calculated. Cycle time is the actual run time of the operation. Each worker in the cell is then assigned operations that as much as possible equal takt time, thereby minimizing the number of operators in each cell.

Problem-Solving Teams. The principal factor driving the size of problem-solving teams is the number of dimensions of the problem significantly affecting the solution. Generally, the more dimensions, the larger the team. Of course, in some circumstances, one person may cover more than one dimension, which would reduce the number of team members required. In other cases, one dimension may be so complex that more than one person may be required to cover it.

As an example of determining the size of a problem-solving team, the design of a new golf ball by Wilson might include consideration of quality, cost, customer requirements, production capability, and customer service. Consequently, this product design team would likely include a quality expert, an accountant, a research and development specialist, supplier representatives, at least one production specialist, and a marketing specialist. This team might include as many as 10 people.

OTHER FACTORS AFFECTING TEAM SIZE

Beyond issues related to team type, additional factors must be considered in determining the appropriate size of a given team. These include the periodic need for reserve team members, consideration of technological capabilities and sociological needs, and the need to vary team size during a project.

Need for Reserve Team Members. The more critical the need to meet specific project criteria, the greater the need to assure the performance of each team member. This need sometimes requires alternate or substitute team members held in reserve. The number of reserve members will depend on the importance of the task and the probability that substitute members will be needed to fill certain positions. A surgical operating team, for example, is likely to have reserve support readily available for each key team function (that is, lead surgeon, assisting surgeon, lead nurse, surgical nurse, and anesthesiologist).

Technological Capabilities and Sociological Needs. One question that arises in determining the size of teams is whether teams can become too large. The answer seems to hinge on two factors: technology and sociology. First, technology seems to determine the limits of effective communication, integration of roles, and effective handoffs, for example, on integrated work teams.

A typical surgical team, because of the restricted confines of the operating room, restricted view of the patient, and close work space, is limited to spontaneous, in-person voice communication between team members to coordinate the various tasks. Electronic media (audio and video) can be used to allow the participation of a few off-site team members whose knowledge may be required, but such participation is awkward at best.

Technology should facilitate team efforts, not hamper them. When a team reaches a size where the available technology cannot support the team effort, or the technology required for the team to function begins to interfere, the team is too large. In either case, technology should not reduce the team's effectiveness and efficiency.

Second, the sociology of teams includes a psychological and emotional identification with the team. As the team becomes too large, such identification can be difficult to establish and sustain. In general, it seems that as teams grow to the point where team members are less familiar with each other, both by person and by role, they are less likely to hold a strong psychological and emotional identity with the team as a whole.

Of the specific companies surveyed for this article, the upper limit was about 15 team members, as seen on Wilson's simple work teams. Integrated teams ranged between five and eight members, and problem-solving teams ranged up to 10 members. Relay teams observed at McDonald's ranged up to eight members, with two people at each of four workstations.

Technically speaking, however, relay teams conceivably could involve an endless sequence of handoffs. The primary limitations on the size of relay teams seem to be the size of the project and team members' sociological needs. For example, the production, assembly, and delivery of automobiles requires hundreds of individual tasks to be performed in sequence at different locations, resulting in hundreds of handoffs. In a large sense, perhaps everyone involved might refer to the team effort required, but individuals are likely to feel more of a team relationship with others working on the same shift or in the immediate area. In this case, the team would range from two or three members to perhaps two dozen.

Changing Team Size. Some teams may vary in size during a project. Generally, there is a core group of team members present for the entire project, while other team members may join the team temporarily to complete specific tasks.

For example, audit teams frequently employ specialists who join the team only long enough to perform a specific procedure. But while they are present, these specialists are very much a part of the team: their work is focused on the team project; they communicate directly with other team members in the performance of their work, which must be coordinated with other team tasks; they become part of the team social network; and they and other team members understand their role in completing the overall project.

TEAM DURATION

Teams can be permanent or temporary. If the conditions leading to the establishment of the team are stable over long periods of time, it is appropriate to assign team members on a permanent basis. When conditions, or the nature of the work, change often or are of limited duration, it is generally best to form teams on a temporary basis. Under such circumstances, teams can be established on an ad hoc basis and dissolved when the work of the team is completed.

MANAGING TEAMS

Whether teams are self-managed or have a designated team leader or supervisor, effective teams require effective management. Mismanagement can cause—and has caused, in too many situations—dysfunctional teams. Like the issues of team type and size, team management should be tailored to the type of activity required.

In analyzing effective team management, the authors have identified certain management tasks that must be performed in all teams regardless of team type. These are designated as foundation tasks. These tasks form the foundation of team management activity and represent the tasks required for effective management of simple work teams. Beyond these, the authors have identified unique additive team management tasks that must be applied when other enabling conditions are present and the management task becomes more complex.

For each type of team activity, a unique strategy is called for, forming a hierarchy of team management tasks. This hierarchy is illustrated in Table 5.2.

Managing Simple Work Teams. Simple work teams are the simplest team form; they usually perform less complicated work requiring less coordination and, often, less direct supervision. Effective management of simple work teams involves the six foundation tasks identified in Table 5.2:

1. *Identification of work to be done.* The work to be accomplished by the team must be clearly identified. Associated with this task is the need to ensure that a team is really called for—that at least one of the four enabling conditions calling for the use of teams is present.

2. *Team selection.* The appropriate team members must be selected, including possible reserve members.

3. *Allocation of work.* This involves ensuring that the work is allocated in such a manner that all required work can be completed in the allowed time, and with as little overlap as possible.

4. *Coaching and facilitation.* These are required to ensure that all team members understand and perform their assigned tasks, that they have the tools and resources required to do the job effectively, and that problems are resolved.

Table 5.2 Hierarchy of team management tasks.

	Simple Work Team	Relay Team	Integrated Work Team	Problem-Solving Team
Enabling Condition	More work of one kind than one person can do in the allotted time	Sequential work process with handoffs	Single job requires coordination and integration of different roles and expertise	Solution to a problem requires the combination of more knowledge and expertise than one person possesses
Foundation Tasks: Identification of work to be done; Team selection; Allocation of work; Coaching and facilitation; Coordination with suppliers and customers; Cheerleading				
Additional Task No. 1: Managing handoffs/transfers between individuals or teams				
Additional Task No. 2: Coordinating and scripting complex, integrated routines				
Additional Task No. 3: Providing structure and facilitating the problem-solving process				

5. *Coordination with suppliers and customers.* This must occur on an ongoing basis, with both internal and external suppliers and customers, to ensure effective quality is achieved in the team's work.

6. *Cheerleading.* This is essential to the recognition and celebration of quality work and team accomplishments.

Managing Relay Teams. Relay teams are a relatively simple form, but somewhat more complex than simple work teams. The reason for their greater complexity is the use of handoffs, or transfers of work units between workstations. Careful coordination of the effectiveness and efficiency of transfers from one task to another is the primary distinguishing feature of relay teams.

Beyond the six foundation tasks, effective management of relay teams requires the management of these handoffs. A good handoff is one in which the object is properly secured to avoid dropping or breakage, is transferred in good form and ready for the next task, and is transferred quickly with as little expense and movement as possible.

To manage the handoff of sandwiches between workstations at McDonald's, sandwiches are placed six at a time on a single tray, which is then moved down a stainless steel counter to each subsequent workstation. The workstations are balanced to avoid bottlenecks and smooth the flow from station to station.

All employees are carefully trained and coached to operate each machine and handle the work flow, and to perform their individual tasks and the handoffs to preserve the appearance, taste, and nutritional quality of the food. Each manager also is trained to carefully facilitate the work process by making proper workstation assignments and providing well-maintained and properly designed equipment, well-designed work processes, immaculate facilities, and a friendly, productive work climate.

Managing Integrated Work Teams. Integrated work teams are distinguished from relay teams by the complexity and direction of handoffs. Handoffs in integrated work teams tend to be multidimensional and more complex. Thus, the additional task associated with integrated work teams is coordinating and scripting complex integrated routines.

Surgical teams, for example, typically consist of several specialists. Each team member is responsible for filling certain roles at various phases of the surgical procedure. Most surgical procedures have an established protocol wherein team members play their varying roles. These are scripted in advance, and are refined over time as team members gain experience working together.

Beyond formal scripting, team members actively observe the overall process, stepping in and assisting as necessary, in response to formal and informal cues provided by the team leader or other team members. Thus, the management task involves formal scripting of team protocols and routines, training team members to understand their role in the entire integrated process, clarification of cues, and mechanisms for informal adaptation and team learning.

Managing Problem-Solving Teams. The defining need of problem-solving teams is to provide structure that helps the group process take advantage of every team member's potential contribution, combining them to achieve a single solution. Usually, the people recruited to these teams already possess the requisite individual knowledge or expertise.

The management problem is to generate a single solution from the individual parts. Successful management of these teams usually includes additional coaching in the team problem-solving process and leading and facilitating that process.

Team problem-solving processes usually include several features: team orientation to the problem, individual consideration of the problem, individual input, synergizing, and consensus building. Each part of the process is crucial. Team orientation focuses all efforts on the required solution.

Individual consideration and input ensures everyone's contribution. Synergizing allows team members to brainstorm together, considering the problem collectively. Consensus building develops a single solution. Techniques using all of these features include brainstorming, focused group, and Delphi techniques. The best kaizen teams also include these features, although there is no well-established, standardized kaizen team process.

At Gates Rubber, kaizen teams are organized to effect significant change in a five-day period:

Day 1: Team members are trained and familiarized with the area to be improved.

Day 2: The current situation is analyzed. Time analysis, machine capability, cycle time, and takt time are examples of some measurements taken early on the second day. Later during the second day, data are analyzed and cause-and-effect analysis begins.

Day 3: Countermeasures are designed and implemented.

Day 4: The effect of the changes is checked, and additional changes are made to increase the gains in time, productivity, or quality. Near the end of the fourth day, new work standards are written based on the improvements, and reports documenting the kaizen team's work are prepared. Follow-up items are then listed, with individual responsibilities and deadlines, to ensure that the gains made during the week are not lost due to poor communication or lax implementation.

Day 5: The morning is spent reporting to supervisors and managers.

In managing the team problem-solving process at Gates Rubber, the team leader or facilitator plays a vital role in training team members in the kaizen methodology, ensuring that the structured process is followed, and managing the process to ensure that key milestones are met.

OUTSTANDING TEAMS, OUTSTANDING ORGANIZATIONS

The guidelines included in this article (summarized in Table 5.3) represent a synthesis of hundreds of informal observations in many different organizations—public and private, small and large. Specific examples come from four organizations recognized for their excellence, and that strongly emphasize the use of teams. Violations of the guidelines, except in exceptional situations, seem to occur consistently among mediocre or dysfunctional teams in struggling organizations. While these guidelines are general and there may be exceptions, they are used consistently among outstanding teams in outstanding organizations.

ENDNOTE

1. Wilson Sporting Goods Golf Ball Division and the Gates Rubber Siloam Springs Plant were 1993 recipients of the Shingo Prize for Excellence in Manufacturing. Logan Regional Hospital, affiliated with Intermountain Health Care, is a recipient of the 1991 Healthcare Forum/Witt Award and the 1996 National Quality Healthcare Award presented by the National Committee for Quality Healthcare.

Table 5.3   The use and management of teams.

	Primary Enabling Condition	Primary Factors Affecting Team Size	Primary Team Management Approach
Simple Work Team	More work of one kind than one person can do in the allotted time	Amount of work to be done, available time, and amount of work one person can do in available time	**Foundation Tasks:** Identification of work to be done Team selection Allocation of work Coaching and facilitation Coordination with suppliers and customers Cheerleading
Relay Team	Sequential work process with handoffs	Work process tasks, work balancing requirements, and cycle time required	Foundation tasks, plus managing handoffs
Integrated Work Team	When a single job requires the coordination and integration of different roles	Degree of differentiation and integration needed to balance the production process	Foundation tasks, managing handoffs, plus coordinating and scripting complex, integrated routines
Problem-Solving Team	When the solution to a problem requires the combination of more knowledge and expertise than one person possesses	Number of dimensions of the problem that affect the solution	Foundation tasks; managing handoffs; coordinating and scripting complex, integrated routines; plus providing structure and facilitating the problem-solving process

6

Effective Use of Teams in Continuous Improvement

Cliff L. Seastrunk, Roy H. Johnson,
and Ron L. Huber

SUMMARY

There are several key criteria needed to successfully implement the use of continuous improvement teams. These include organizational structure, an understanding of the different types of teams, and the roles within a team. In this paper, the effective application of teams is demonstrated through industry examples and case studies.

KEY WORDS

Facilitator, implementation, leadership, problem solving, project management.

Teams have existed for centuries in one form or another throughout many cultures, countries, and political climates. Most executives within U.S. companies recognize the value of teams and are quick to suggest that they be used. Although some of these companies have experienced great success in their application, many others find teams to be a waste of time and most do not utilize teams to their fullest potential.

Why is this? We have found in practice that although most companies are quick to "buy off" on the team concept they do not have the patience nor do they make the full effort to ensure their success. Teams are often confused with teamwork, project teams are not differentiated from work teams, control teams are not distinguished from improvement teams, and so on. The purpose of this paper is to clarify the different types of teams that can be utilized. Further, a case study will be given to demonstrate the effective use of teams in a U.S. carpet yarn company.

ORGANIZATION OF TEAMS

Based on our experiences with various companies, we have found that there are certain common factors found in organizations that successfully apply the team process. Some of these key items include: (1) Supportive culture, (2) leadership from upper management, (3) education and training, (4) development of strong facilitators and SPC coordinators, (5) clearly set goals and objectives, (6) well thought out selection of team members and assignment of team roles, (7) team leader development, (8) efficient project time management, (9) presentations to management, (10) rewards for successes, and (11) strategic follow-up on implementing project recommendations.

The culture needed for the team process is one that not only demonstrates an early excitement for the value of teams but also must be one whose support lasts over the long haul. Success does not occur overnight nor are all projects going to be successful. With patience the early incremental successes of a few teams can lead to exponential improvements as the number of teams and the experience factor is magnified.

As is the case with all areas of continuous improvement, the long-term success of implementation will depend greatly on the active commitment to the process demonstrated by upper management. Early on, a steering committee of key organizational players must carefully guide the team process. The steering committee must take an active role in all of the areas discussed in this paper. Further, we have found it extremely motivational to the associates when upper management is directly involved in the improvement teams. Particularly helpful to the "buying-in" process is to assign high level improvement projects to steering committee members. With maturation of the team process, the organizational steering committee must delegate management of the project teams to plant or departmental steering committees since the responsibilities greatly increase over time.

Education and training must come early in the process and work best when following a top-down approach. A working knowledge is often needed initially in the following key areas: (1) team building, (2) communication skills, (3) tools for quality improvement, and (4) problem solving. As the team process matures, further skills will be needed in such disciplines as SPC and design of experiments. Specialty skills can be administered later where needed. The key here is to ensure some training before attempting to utilize teams.

For ongoing management of the continuous improvement process it is necessary to develop and train resident facilitators and SPC coordinators. These are key players in the implementation of the continuous improvement process. A general rule of thumb is that a facilitator, on a full-time process can manage up to 10 teams that meet on a weekly basis. The coordinator(s) is your resident expert in the application of statistical tools and should be readily available for the project teams. Facilitators and coordinators also fill an important role in training others within the organization.

For successful projects it is imperative that the improvement opportunity be clearly defined. Early on it is necessary that the steering committee establish this criteria to ensure that the projects are consistent with the organization's vision and quality goals. In addition, this will improve the chances for upper management "buy-in" if they are involved in the selection process. As the process matures and the associates become further trained and more fully empowered, then the teams will play a more active role in choosing their own projects.

In the early stages of an organization's attempt to set up a team approach to problem solving it is also necessary for the steering committee to become actively involved in the selection of team members. Such criteria as technical expertise in the project area, the need for interdepartmental versus departmental teams, the amount of training needed, among others, must be carefully considered. As the team implementation process matures, then more of these responsibilities can be passed on to plant/departmental steering committees.

Next to management commitment one of the most important keys for successful project teams is the team leader. The skills needed for this must carefully match those chosen for this team role. If the abilities are there but not the skills then training must precede the assignment. Other roles such as recorder and assistant leader must also be carefully assigned to the appropriate individuals. Early in the development of a team, the facilitator will likely have to actively support each of these role players, particularly the team leader.

A problem that teams often face midstream in their project and also one that frequently disrupts team meetings is a lack of focus which causes inefficiencies in time management. Teams often get caught up in activities rather than accomplishing predetermined objectives. We have found that utilizing problem solving steps such as those shown in Figure 6.1 leads to

1. Clearly define the problem/opportunity

2. Develop a clear understanding of the process being studied

3. Plan collection of data to study problem, develop a hypothesis for anticipated results

4. Collect and analyze data

5. Study results—test theory—make conclusions

6. Determine causal factors—prioritize major causes

7. Develop alternative solutions to problem—evaluate and prioritize for "best" solutions

8 Develop action plan for next steps to implement solutions—continue continuous improvement cycle until goals/objectives are achieved

9. Develop a plan to maintain the gains that have been achieved

Figure 6.1 Steps to follow for problem solving.

more successful projects. An additional tool that can be utilized is shown in Figure 6.2. This time chart features projected completion dates for project objectives and actual times for comparison purposes. In this figure another effective tool is demonstrated that can help ensure efficient time management—progress reports and final presentations to management. In our experiences we have found that nothing seems to press the urgency for completion as much as a presentation to management.

Rewards for successful projects take on many forms. Successful utilization of them depends almost entirely on the cultural environment within the particular organization. Some examples of rewards we have seen utilized in various companies for participation in and/or for successful projects include jackets, caps, or other apparel, selected "best" projects for presentations within and outside the company, percentage of savings cash rewards, time off, personal recognition, and so on. It is best to learn what really motivates your associates over the long term before deciding which reward you choose.

Project: SPC@By-Pass   Matrix for Sliver Stability Using SPC at By-Pass Plant
Team Start Date—3/16/94

	Number of Weeks Projected	Actual	1	2	3	4	5	6	7	8
Flowchart process	1 week	1	3/26							
Brainstorm causes of instability	2 weeks	2		4/15						
Data collection and charting	2 weeks									
Cause and effect corrective action	6 weeks									
Group sampling	3 weeks									
Cause and effect corrective action	4 weeks									
Analyze drawing frame sliver	2 weeks									
Determine spec limits	1 week									
Design of experiments	6 weeks									
Goal achieved	Total 27									

Team members: William Johnson
Jeff Walters
Scott Butler
Johnny McVay
Gary West
James Bradford
Paul Sands

Figure 6.2 Time chart with project objectives.

Many successful projects are not implemented properly because of a lack of follow-up. There seems to be a finality concurrent with the final presentation that ends the project. This can be alleviated by submission of a plan for implementation of improvement recommendations by the project team. This plan must be adopted (if accepted) by management, and responsibility assigned for follow-up to ensure long-term success.

Although much has been said and written about the value and success of utilizing teams and promoting participation by all levels of associates, it must be pointed out that there are just as many, if not more, examples of where teams have failed in the workplace. We have just covered some of the key items needed for successful team implementation. We now want to look at two of the major reasons why teams often fail: (1) A lack of understanding the different types of teams and (2) not defining the roles within the team.

TYPES OF TEAMS

We have listed in Table 6.1 four types of teams commonly used in organizations that have been successful in implementing continuous improvement: (1) continuous, (2) quality improvement, (3) customer/supplier, and (4) work teams.

Most organizations have some type of continuous teams (or committees) that are in place even if no formal organization or structure for teams are implemented. An example of this type of team is the safety team (or committee). They are normally made up of people from different areas of the organization. The team is usually in place permanently even though team members are normally rotated on some regular schedule. Care must be taken that this type of team not fall into the trap of "just going through the motions" instead of being an active, productive team.

Quality improvement teams may have members from the same general work area or from different areas. Most organizations first utilize these teams to solve problems or emergencies. More mature organizations actually allow these teams to work on improvement opportunities even if "something ain't broke yet." A common problem for improvement teams is

Table 6.1 Typical types of teams.

Type of Team	Membership	Direction	Duration	Participation
Continuous (committees)	From different departments	Self-directed	Permanent	Voluntary
Quality improvement	From different departments	Guided	Temporary	Voluntary
Customer/ supplier	From different departments	Guided or self-directed	Temporary	Voluntary
Work teams	From same department	Self-directed	Permanent	Mandatory

to solve a problem or improve a process and not put any measurement system in place to prevent slippage back to the previous state.

Customer/supplier teams have been recognized for being beneficial in improving (or in some cases, opening) lines of communication, resolving differences or conflicts and bringing about overall improvement in the partnership. The focus of these teams must be on meeting customer needs and continuous improvement, not just solving routine or procedural problems.

Many organizations are utilizing work teams with varying degrees of success. In order to be successful, three areas must be addressed: (1) adequate training, (2) well-defined objectives, and (3) complete understanding of the responsibilities and authority for the team. Many companies have implemented group incentive or recognition systems. We have found that some measurement of quality must be a component of that system.

ROLES WITHIN A TEAM

Understanding and filling the various roles within the team is essential for a successful team. These roles include the team leader, facilitator, recorder, and team member. We will look briefly at the leader, facilitator, and recorder roles.

Team leaders must possess both good leadership and communication skills. In most cases, these skills need to be improved by specific training prior to assuming this role. The leader must assist the facilitator and provides the link between the team and the rest of the organization. The leader must also carry out the decisions and recommendations of the team. A strong team leader is critical to a successful team.

The facilitator works very closely with the team leader prior to each meeting in preparing agendas, collecting background information, and assisting in administrative tasks. During the meeting, the facilitator assists the team in choosing the proper tools to use, keeps the team focused and on-track, and has to remain open-minded for feedback from all the team members. The facilitator's role is often assumed by the leader in smaller teams and organizations.

The recorder is an extremely vital member of successful teams. Taking minutes of the meetings, distributing the minutes to team members on a timely basis, and keeping historical records for the team are the main responsibilities of this role. Failing to carry out these responsibilities accurately and in a timely manner can have an extremely adverse effect on the success of the team.

SUPPORTING TEAM PRIORITIES

Most teams need outside help at some time to be successful: for specialized training, technical expertise, financial approvals, and so on. Therefore, it is important for all teams to work with a trained team facilitator who has the responsibility to provide for these needs.

Obviously, all teams need basic team training as previously discussed. However, it is essential that team leaders receive additional training for the role that they have accepted. The team facilitator must see that the team leaders function in a positive manner or correct the problem. It is the program coordinator that works with the facilitators and the steering committee to ensure the success of the total program.

All teams should initially prioritize the activities of the team by preparing a team flowchart with an estimated time schedule for each activity as approved by the facilitator.

There are many types of support that a team might need. Each team has a unique personality, an extension of the individuals on the team. Some need discipline, technical abilities, moral support, information, computer skills, and so forth. The list can go on and on. It is the facilitator's responsibility to find a way to fill the voids.

We will now look at two case studies that will illustrate the importance of supporting team priorities in order to achieve long-term continuous improvement through the effective use of teams.

One example is the "15 Card Pick-Up Crew," a process improvement team at Candlewick, whose mission is to control and reduce product weight variation at the carding process. This team first needed a better understanding of the machinery and how the machine settings contributed to process variation. The team facilitator and department manager arranged for the OEM to conduct on-site training to key team members. Also an inspector was brought in to inspect for differences in the 15 cards that represented two different models, each of which also had been modified. This pointed to several points of control in the machinery that have been added to PM schedules.

The "Even Heaters," another process improvement team working on the reduction of variability in the Suessen heatsetting process, needed to understand the thermodynamics of thermoplasticity. A seminar was set up on-site to provide this training.

CONCLUSION

Teams can be valuable assets in the continuous improvement process when utilized properly. Success does not happen, however, without a great deal of effort and patience. We must understand that an organizational framework must be initially set up to provide for direction in the implementation process. Training prior to "meetings" is necessary to provide understanding for the different types of teams, the roles of team members, and other technical skills that will be needed. Selection of appropriate facilitators/coordinators is necessary to maintain and provide continued success.

REFERENCES

Katzenbach, J. R., and Smith, D. K. *The Wisdom of Teams: Creating the High-Performance Organization.* New York: HarperCollins Publishers, 1994.
Scholtes, P. R. *The Team Handbook.* Madison, WI: Joiner Associates, 1988.
Technicomp. *Teams for Excellence.* Cleveland, OH: 1991.

7

Building a Team

D. Keith Denton

Teamwork is an essential part of effective teams. You do not need a team to have teamwork, but you do need teamwork to have a team.[1] For a team to be effective, its members must include the necessary experts or those most familiar with the problem. Its members must be able to compromise and to respect each other's views.

From a team standpoint, individual goals should not get in the way of team goals. While individual goals are important, they must be compatible with the team's goals. In turn, team goals must be compatible with the organization's goals. Finally, there is no substitute for unity of purpose. Every team must have a common purpose and goals.

The need for a clear purpose and team goals is illustrated by two organizations with extensive team management experience. Ford Motor Co. states that, to be effective, a team must have common goals.[2] Without these shared goals, time and energy are wasted and little will be accomplished. To build team purpose, Ford management emphasizes asking whether the group's goals are clear to all team members and whether everyone is trying to achieve the same goal. To ensure goals are understood and accepted, each member should help decide what they are.

Metropolitan Life Insurance Company (MetLife) defines a team as a group of people with specific roles and responsibilities, organized to work together toward common goals or objectives, in which each member depends on others to carry out responsibilities to reach those goals and objectives.[3]

MetLife identifies "depends" as the key word in this definition. A team must be able to depend on its members to carry out its tasks. Teams also depend on members to communicate and listen effectively. Team members must also put the team's needs above their own, and they must help each other. Good teams also depend on good team leadership, feedback, and common goals and objectives. In other words, a team is not a team unless it behaves like one.[4] There must be trust, cooperation, and mutual respect among members.

TEAM BONDING

To unify a team, members must know their goals and roles and work out relationships with other team members. There is no best way to do this. Sometimes it takes something special for a team to bond. Ford management tells of a chief engineer and his group who kept trying, with little success, to clarify their goals, roles, and relationships. At first, the team tried to do this through regular meetings in his office, but there were constant interruptions. The team then decided it would be best to go off-site for a one-day team development session. After the meeting, all unanimously agreed it was time well spent. There was more trust, better understanding of goals and roles, and more frequent and open communication.[5] It was then and only then that the members became a team.

TEAM-BUILDING ELEMENTS

Regardless of how a team forms its identity, there are several elements that must be worked out before teams can function with any degree of teamwork. MetLife says that problem solving and team building have three elements: establishing teams' roles, using certain communication techniques, and following specific problem-solving steps.

MetLife shows that team building can be compared to a house (Figure 7.1). This team-building house has, first, a foundation (the task that brings the group together). The posts of the house that support its walls and roof are the roles team members assume. The bricks that make up the walls are the sequence of steps that teams follow to solve problems. The mortar that holds the bricks together is the communication techniques used by the group. Finally, the roof of this house is the action plan used to implement team ideas and solutions.[6]

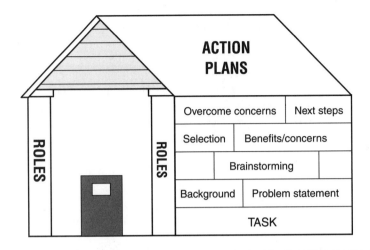

Figure 7.1 The team-building process.

Source: Courtesy of Metropolitan Life Insurance Co.

ROLES AND RESPONSIBILITIES

Every team needs to have certain roles assumed by or assigned to its members. Each member of the team should know exactly what role he or she is to play. Only when these roles are clear does the team achieve its goals. Make sure that each team member accepts and is able to handle the responsibility of his or her assigned role. It is also important to make sure the workload is equitable and no one member is overburdened. Assignments should not just be dumped on people. When too much is required of them, people feel threatened and might even reject participation or assignments. For this reason, team members should have the opportunity to participate in the assignment of work.

Ford emphasizes that, regardless of the purpose of team meetings (setting goals, establishing plans, or solving problems), the best team meetings are those that are well planned. Ample time should be taken in advance to ensure all necessary arrangements have been made. Poor planning produces poor performance.

If team members' roles are well planned, participants will have a clear idea of the purpose of the meetings. They will also tend to agree on the agenda and procedures and will understand the project better and commit to it more fully. Good planning ensures that meetings start and end on time.

TEAM LEADERSHIP

The success of team meetings also depends on the team leader's skills. Leaders should be able to supply essential information and clarify issues. They should encourage all members to participate and, at the same time, protect individual members from being attacked. If conflicts do occur, they should be resolved quickly. Leaders also help the group stay on track so all issues are covered. Other general criteria for effective team leadership are shown in Figure 7.2.

MetLife provides some concrete suggestions for improving leadership. It notes that a common weakness of team leadership is that one person has two different responsibilities: the problem the meeting is supposed to address and the way the meeting goes.[7] This is a heavy burden for one person, and it often leads to the team's failure. For instance, a leader with both responsibilities might focus so much on resolving a problem that the meeting itself is out of control. As a result, many good ideas can get lost in the shuffle. MetLife's experience shows that, when a team leader tries to manage both items, there is a tendency to lose control, or a leader will impose his or her will and others won't participate.[8]

Because of these problems, MetLife's managers recommend that team leadership be divided into two roles: client and facilitator.[9] The client is the team leader who asks for help to solve a problem. This person is responsible for what team meetings are supposed to address. Specifically, the client provides background information for the team, clearly describes the problem, and identifies what is to be achieved. The client also selects the most promising ideas provided by the group so they can be evaluated in greater detail and completes the team's action plan.

The facilitator is responsible for the way the meeting goes. Facilitators have four basic responsibilities: helping other team members keep time commitments, keeping group members on track, remaining neutral about the meeting's content, and clarifying group members' ideas and making sure other members' ideas are protected from attack.[10]

Both client and facilitator roles are essential leadership roles, but they are not the only ones. The recorder does not have leadership responsibilities but plays an essential role nonetheless. His or her role includes using flip charts to take notes so that every member of the group can see what has been agreed on before the meeting is over.

Recorders are also responsible for what MetLife calls headlining. This involves first noting and then recording key ideas and relevant phrases on a flip chart using words the team agrees on. Flip charts are used not only so everyone can see the key facts and ideas generated, but also to help members understand what future steps will be needed. These charts help

Effective leadership is essential to teamwork. Effective leaders can add enormous strength to the process and can have a positive effect on the teamwork climate. Effective team leaders:

- Understand and accept their obligation to the team.

- Deal fairly and consistently with everyone.

- Believe that people want to do a good job.

- Are open, forthright, and consistently do what they say they will do. When they can't, they explain why not.

- Care about people and respect them as individuals.

- Believe that when their work groups do well, they themselves do well; they take pride in the groups' achievements and share credit for work the groups have done.

- Act as they expect others to act.

- Solicit ideas and listen carefully when ideas are offered.

- Are dedicated to improving people's work lives, to their safety, and to the efficient production of quality products and services.

- Seek out education, training, and development opportunities for team members, including themselves.

- Are willing to coach and advise and not rely solely on the authority of their positions.

- Keep themselves and members of their teams aware of the needs of other teams and those of internal and external customers.

- Meet regularly with their counterparts to openly exchange information and ideas.

- Support team efforts and get help for the team when it is needed.

- Strive for continuous improvement in themselves and in their relationships with people.

- Seek information that pertains to their work groups and regularly share it.

- Demonstrate their support for the groups and the individual members when things are not going smoothly.

- Conduct themselves as professional representatives of their respective organizations—with pride.

Figure 7.2 Characteristics of effective team leaders.

Source: From "Team, We Are a Team," an information package from Ford Motor Co., 1988, p. 17.

problem solving because they ensure each person has a uniform record of team efforts. When the meeting is over, the flip charts should be typed and distributed to members.

The remaining role for all team members is that of being resources. In the resources role, members contribute ideas and provide support for the process. Figure 7.3 contains a summary of these roles, MetLife notes these roles support the team structure, and effective communication strengthens this structure.

Roles	Responsibilities
Client	Owner of the task • Provides background information • Formulates problem statements • Selects and prioritizes ideas for the group • Accepts ultimate responsibility for completion of the action plan
Facilitator	Caretaker of the process • Keeps group focused on process (roles and responsibilities) • Remains neutral about content of meeting • Helps group keep time commitments • Clarifies/paraphrases group members' contributions
Recorder	Keeper of the group memory • Remains neutral about content of meeting • Writes down key ideas, pertinent phrases, benefits, and concerns agreed to by group • Transfers flip charts to typed format and distributes them to the group
Resource	Contributor of ideas • Uses interpersonal skills to ensure positive outcome • Generates ideas fully, builds on ideas • Refrains from judging the value of client's problems • Works hard to overcome concerns

Figure 7.3   A summary of problem-solving/team-building roles.
Source: Courtesy of Metropolitan Life Insurance Co.

COMMUNICATION TECHNIQUES

Interpersonal communication is the key to teamwork. Communication is important because of human nature. Almost anyone who hears of a new idea or approach tends to be skeptical and to look for reasons why it will not work. Such negative reactions are natural. Likewise, MetLife points out that people tend to assume there is only one right answer and to try to discourage those ideas that do not agree with their own past experiences or beliefs. For all these reasons, it is important that ideas not be seen as either totally acceptable or totally unacceptable.

MetLife uses five interpersonal communication techniques to help its teams improve both communication and problem solving (see Figure 7.4).

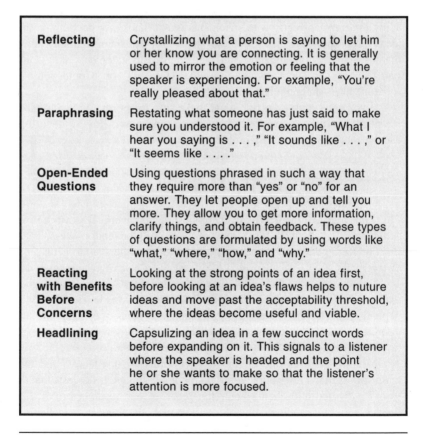

Reflecting	Crystallizing what a person is saying to let him or her know you are connecting. It is generally used to mirror the emotion or feeling that the speaker is experiencing. For example, "You're really pleased about that."
Paraphrasing	Restating what someone has just said to make sure you understood it. For example, "What I hear you saying is . . . ," "It sounds like . . . ," or "It seems like . . . ."
Open-Ended Questions	Using questions phrased in such a way that they require more than "yes" or "no" for an answer. They let people open up and tell you more. They allow you to get more information, clarify things, and obtain feedback. These types of questions are formulated by using words like "what," "where," "how," and "why."
Reacting with Benefits Before Concerns	Looking at the strong points of an idea first, before looking at an idea's flaws helps to nuture ideas and move past the acceptability threshold, where the ideas become useful and viable.
Headlining	Capsulizing an idea in a few succinct words before expanding on it. This signals to a listener where the speaker is headed and the point he or she wants to make so that the listener's attention is more focused.

Figure 7.4 Summary of communication techniques.

Source: Courtesy of Metropolitan Life Insurance Co.

PROBLEM-SOLVING STEPS

While it is important, communication alone will not ensure successful team problem solving. MetLife recommends a seven-step sequence to ensure problems are thoroughly resolved (see Figure 7.5).[11]

MetLife points out that the sequence is not learned merely by discussing it. To enhance problem solving, the sequence must be applied.

MetLife emphasizes that it is extremely important for a team member, in the role of client, to coach team members in problem solving as it progresses. These individuals should monitor communication skills used by team members and encourage them to stay on track by following the problem-solving steps.

Facilitators also have to encourage team members to use this problem-solving sequence. Facilitators can do this by praising members when they apply the steps correctly with statements like "Thanks for budding on that idea." Facilitators can also encourage use of the sequence by simply pointing out when team members should be using it with statements like "Could you express your concern in a how-to statement?" or "Could you—or someone else—help me headline that idea?"

When setting up an action plan, make sure to set up a time and place for necessary follow-up meetings to discuss progress. Having done this, choose another high-priority problem.

TEAMWORK

For teams to function effectively, there must be teamwork. Teamwork is not something you just wish for; it must be built in to the team process. There must be team goals and a clear purpose if team members are to get a sense of teamwork.

Teams are more than goals and objectives. As MetLife says, good teams consist of people with specific roles and responsibilities who depend on each other to achieve those goals. It takes good planning and good team leadership to ensure each member is happy with the group and his or her role.

MetLife believes one of the reasons teams are ineffective and lack teamwork is that a few people try to do too many things. It suggests that the team be divided into client, facilitator, recorder, and resources roles. It is then essential that a wide range of interpersonal communication techniques be used to ensure ideas are thoroughly explored. Finally, building a good team depends on following specific problem-solving steps.

Step 1:	Defining current situation with background	State relevant facts and activities that help identify that a problem exists. Include actions or thoughts that have already been considered and define the desired results by using this problem-solving process.
Step 2:	Formulating the problem statement	Develop a concise action statement beginning with "How to," include an action verb that denotes accomplishment, and state what has to be done and when.
Step 3:	Brainstorming	Begin the problem-solving process by developing thoughts, wishes, suggestions, and recommendations for accomplishing the identified objective.
Step 4:	Selecting ideas	Select a single idea or group of ideas for further development. Sometimes, if all ideas are promising, the facilitator asks the client to prioritize them.
Step 5:	Analyzing the benefits/concerns	Develop a list of at least three benefits before listing concerns. Phrase concerns as potential problems in how-to statements. For example, "How to get the resources we need to implement this idea."
Step 6:	Overcoming concerns	Generate ideas to overcome any concerns that must be addressed before the selected idea can be implemented. In other words, recycle concerns through the sequence of steps as new problems, if necessary.
Step 7:	Creating the action plan	Identify the next steps that will ensure that the chosen idea becomes a solution to the problem. During the process, the individual or group identifies next activities and sets up appropriate controls to monitor progress and communicate results.

Figure 7.5 Summary of steps.
Source: Courtesy of Metropolitan Life Insurance Co.

ENDNOTES

1. "Teamwork—More Critical Today Than Ever Before," *Quality Performance* (May 31, 1990).
2. "Continuous Improvement through Participation," a booklet by Ford Education and Personnel Research Development (September 1984).
3. The National Work Team Leaders Guide to the Quality Improvement Process, Metropolitan Life Insurance Co., 1986.
4. "Continuous Improvement through Participation."
5. Ibid.
6–11. The National Work Team Leaders Guide to the Quality Improvement Process.

8

Self-Directed Work Teams: A Guide to Implementation

Michael W. Piczak and Reuben Z. Hauser

It seems virtually impossible to pick up a current edition of a business publication without finding an article about self-directed work teams (SDWTs). SDWTs, also called semi-autonomous work groups or self-managing teams, have been implemented in an increasing number of companies with varying degrees of success. Such companies include Chevron Chemical, Coca-Cola, Federal Express, General Electric, General Motors' Saturn Division, Motorola, Procter & Gamble, and Xerox. The idea appears to be catching on outside the United States as well, with such Canadian companies as Babcock & Wilcox, Boart Longyear, Campbell Soups, Dofasco Steel, Honeywell, Northern Telecom, and Steelcase Equipment reporting various stages of implementation.[1]

The list of U.S. and Canadian companies adopting teams covers a broad spectrum of industries. Self-managing teams can be found in petrochemical, electronics, consumer products, heavy manufacturing, and pharmaceutical companies.

SDWTs are often viewed as an extension of or a vehicle for the continuous improvement process, which may have begun with statistical process control training. Teams are also seen as a logical structure for the implementation of total quality management, ISO 9000, or lean production techniques. Some firms see SDWTs as part of world-class manufacturing, which can include such techniques as total predictive maintenance, just-in-time manufacturing, and employee involvement. The business literature consistently refers to gains attributable to teams in the areas of quality, productivity, flexibility, commitment, and customer satisfaction.

This article provides a road map for the successful implementation of SDWTs. The points raised here are based on a review of the literature, field visits to a number of organizations experimenting with the team concept, an examination of and participation in SDWT Internet forums, and hands-on experience in implementing teams with several organizations.[2]

Also set out in this article are key success factors that must be managed in the course of SDWT implementation. Recommendations are provided on what should be done, how it should be done, and by whom. In addition, some caveats—or key failure factors—are issued so that these practices can be avoided or, at least, anticipated and managed.

SDWTs DEFINED

It is helpful to begin the discussion armed with a working definition of SDWTs. Briefly stated, an SDWT is a highly trained group of employees (generally 6 to 15 volunteer or assigned members) that is fully responsible for turning out a well-defined segment of finished work (in this case, finished in the sense of processing responsibility).[3]

SDWTs are distinguished from most other types of teams in that they often have more resources at their disposal, a broader range of cross-functional skills, much greater decision-making authority, and better access to information. Such teams plan, set priorities, organize, coordinate with others, assess the state of processes, and take corrective action. They take on responsibilities typically assigned to frontline supervisors; in this way, the job of supervisor can evolve into a coaching or mentoring role, or the supervisor can be redeployed into some other position. Organizations might wish to consider eliminating this level of management, but the timing of such a change should be planned carefully.

Unlike earlier employee structures, such as quality circles or people involvement programs, SDWTs are not organizational appendages that require employees to engage in activities after work or apart from their daily activities. Self-directed teams do for themselves what they think needs to be done and, in this way, engage in a new and expanded set of activities.

SDWTs represent a different way of working whereby individuals behave as though their sphere of activity were their own business. In this sense, SDWTs take a step backward in time to an era when there was a greater degree of individual ownership in work. At the same time, SDWTs represent a step forward for organizations that are trying to instill a sense of ownership or entrepreneurial spirit in the workforce. SDWTs require a change in the way work is organized and executed. Team members should have genuine input into substantive decisions that affect their work lives. If employees perceive their participation as being limited to marginal decisions, or worse, that management is simply engaging them in a program of the month, they will regard teams as a naked attempt to get them to work harder. In reality, SDWTs represent a new paradigm of organizational life for both team members and those who interact with them.

The transition to team-oriented work can be wrenching for all concerned. New expectations are created for members of the team as well as for members of management. Support staff must be prepared to deal with individuals for whom work has become a new and possibly intimidating experience.

SDWTs: A DEPARTURE FROM CONVENTIONAL WORK DESIGN

Conventional approaches to job design divide work into narrow segments, thereby capitalizing on the benefits of specialization and division of labor as espoused by economist Adam Smith and management theorist Frederick W. Taylor. When stretched to the limit, however, these philosophies deliver the unanticipated side effects of low morale, poor quality, attendance problems, decreased commitment, and feelings of alienation.

The human relations movement helps alleviate these problems with the concepts of job rotation, horizontal job enlargement, and vertical job enrichment. Job rotation and horizontal enlargement can be viewed as extensions of the traditional approach to work design; rotation involves exchanging jobs, while horizontal enlargement expands the scope of work by adding extra duties. Both approaches attempt to reverse the damage done by over-specialization, but they are anemic attempts to inject some life into sterile job descriptions. Arguably, they are a step in the right direction, but such approaches do little to bring breadth or depth to jobs in any meaningful, permanent way. Continued detachment from the job, no sense of contribution, and job narrowness do little to eliminate apathy and alienation.

Vertical enrichment, by contrast, aims to fundamentally dismantle jobs with the intention of building motivational factors into the job package. As the job becomes more complex and challenging, the motivation to perform increases, particularly when the worker desires personal growth.[4]

SDWTs represent a practical application of vertical enrichment. Each member of a self-directed team performs many activities, and opportunities for personal growth are maximized through cross-training. Managers leave team members alone, staying out of their way as long as the team's output meets or exceeds established standards. Decisions typically within the domain of the supervisor are delegated to the team. A range of reward and recognition systems provides additional motivation.

SDWTs are a genuine departure from the usual way of organizing work. Rather than performing apparently meaningless job fragments that create distance between workers and the organization, members of SDWTs are part of a process: an inclusionary structure whereby decisions are shaped through the input of the people directly affected by them.

THE SCOPE OF SDWTs

A frequently asked question about SDWTs is how much autonomy teams should be given. The answer to this question is far from simple because it varies by organization. At Honeywell Canada, for instance, the scope of SDWTs expanded over time as the teams matured and demonstrated a willingness to assume greater responsibility. (Honeywell's approach is instructive; see Table 8.1 for a summary.) The company anticipates that, in the future, team members' duties will expand yet again. But, after three years of experience, no team has progressed to the advanced stage.

By contrast, teams at Boart Longyear Canada, a mining bit manufacturer in Mississauga, Ontario, were already making decisions before being formally commissioned. Now, the Boart Longyear pilot team makes or participates in decisions about shift scheduling, training rotation, production

Table 8.1 Honeywell's approach to team responsibilities.

Scope of Work for Team Members		
Basic Responsibilities	**Intermediate Responsibilities**	**Advanced Responsibilities**
• Multiple work skills • Housekeeping • Movement to point of need* • Safety • Customer satisfaction • Material replenishment • Quality at the source • Rework on the line • On-the-job training	• Total productive maintenance • Conflict resolution • Team meeting administration • Model changeover • Vacation scheduling	• Team member selection • Cost control • Performance appraisal

*Refers to reassigning personnel as required to clear bottlenecks in the operation.

A CASE STUDY: BOART LONGYEAR

To gain a clearer sense of how an organization goes from traditional management to self-directed work teams (SDWTs), consider Boart Longyear Inc., a manufacturer of mining machinery that has been experimenting with teams for over three years at its Mississauga, Ontario, operation.

The interest in teamwork at Boart Longyear evolved as a result of the company's intention to embrace world-class manufacturing (WCM) techniques to improve competitive position. Management recognized that the employees were key to WCM, and continuous improvement teams were established throughout all areas of the business. No crisis precipitated the move to SDWTs; instead, a planned approach was adopted. SDWTs were viewed in a broad context and thus fit easily within the company's WCM program, which also included total predictive maintenance, quality management, just-in-time supply management, and employee involvement. The shift to teamwork was expected to deliver a number of benefits, including a greater sense of identification and ownership of the product for employees, improvements in productivity, and a higher standard of quality.

In preparation for the move to teamwork, Boart Longyear management anticipated that the union, while not vigorously resistant, would not publicly embrace SDWTs. In addition, because of the number of changes that had taken place at the company recently, management expected a certain amount of skepticism from employees—they might view SDWTs as just another fad and choose to ignore the movement. Management knew that communication and education would be necessary to deal with employee concerns. Fortunately, upper management and corporate support was evident.

A design team was formed composed of staff members from all levels and functions in the organization. This multifunctional group included representatives from engineering, operations, the shop floor, and the union. The group's task was to arrange site visits, gather information, analyze data, choose the pilot project, communicate with others in the company, and select consultants. Once the pilot project was under way, the design team disbanded.

Continued

To keep employees well informed, presentations were conducted both for senior managers and plant employees. Presentations to senior management were made by plant management, while consultants presented information to plant employees. These sessions were conducted not only to provide a general overview, but also to invite participants to buy into the teamwork concept.

Team preparation consisted of training by outside consultants, who provided 60 hours of instruction to members on topics such as interpersonal skills, leadership, group decision making, and running meetings. Training was achieved through a combination of lecture presentations, group discussions, field visits, videos, and self-assessments. Part of the training involved practice sessions in which fledgling teams made decisions about training schedules, work rotation, and team member selection.

One key stakeholder group that kept watch over employee interests was the union. Time was taken to assure the union of the company's intentions; discussions took place both informally and during contract negotiations. Management knew that it needed the union to understand that SDWTs were not in conflict with the collective bargaining agreement. Parameters were set for how far team members could pursue various activities. For example, it was decided that team members would not be allowed to become involved with disciplining individuals, making strategic decisions, or addressing issues that required interpreting the collective bargaining agreement. In many ways, these discussions set the groundwork for the future, when certain job functions might evolve into new roles.

In terms of start-up problems, one of the greatest sources of frustration proved to be employees who were only comfortable being told what to do. Although the new culture called for more employee control and freedom, the first reaction of many was to ask their supervisor what to do next. There still appears to be a reluctance to step forward and assume responsibility, and no one person has emerged as a leader. This lack of leadership has resulted in unnecessary delays in decision making. (To avoid this, groups should begin to identify leaders early in the training process.)

Continued

One key factor contributing to the success of teams at Boart Longyear is the role played by plant manager Rick Langdon. Langdon has championed the SDWT effort in this organization, ensuring that training takes place, identifying prospective teams, and working closely with those supervisors who have since become coaches and mentors.

According to Langdon, the benefits of SDWTs to date include:

- Productivity has increased by an estimated 10% to 15%

- Teams work harder because they do not want to appear to be underperforming

- Individuals carry their weight, believing that they might otherwise be reprimanded by team members

- Employees participate in regular meetings where quality- and production-related issues are discussed

- Former supervisors work for the teams by obtaining information and securing resources

- Employees like the concept of SDWTs because of the degree of control that they enjoy

Langdon points to a number of fundamental concepts related to introducing teams, including doing preparatory homework, introducing a cross-functional design task force, and starting with a pilot approach. It should be emphasized that much of the work should be done up front, before start-up. The right work done at this stage saves headaches later. Failure to plan can doom implementation, cause frustration, displease the union, and make SDWTs look like just another program of the month.

prioritizing, and increasing crew requirements. In addition to holding these types of responsibilities, teams at Dofasco Steel make promotion decisions, and Motorola teams determine members' pay increases based on peer performance appraisals. Moving teams to these levels of responsibility takes time, and management must be satisfied that the teams can handle such duties.

Given these and other examples, it can be concluded that considerable variation exists when it comes to defining team scope. Deciding how quickly to escalate team responsibilities hinges on management's inclination, organizational culture variables, team members' needs and wants, and overall team maturity.

IMPLEMENTING SELF-MANAGED TEAMS

Several key variables must be carefully managed when implementing SDWTs. Inadequate planning will doom the initiative to failure, setting back the introduction of team concepts for many years as frustrated employees and protective unions fortify their resistance. Key factors to be considered include:

- Management commitment
- Unions
- Training
- Communication
- Empowerment
- Rewards

MANAGEMENT COMMITMENT

SDWTs can represent a radical departure from business as usual for most organizations. Benefits and gains from SDWTs can take many months or years to be realized. Organizations seeking a quick fix should look elsewhere for a remedy. Tangible results at Dofasco Steel, for example, were not realized until two or three years after SDWT implementation. Boart Longyear's pilot team, however, realized a 10% to 15% increase in productivity only a few months after installation (see the sidebar for details on Boart Longyear's implementation).

Clearly, an SDWT initiative must be delivered from the top down, as resources—and the green light for changes in operating practices—come from upper management. Patience and a willingness to stay the course are critical ingredients for success.

Management should devise a policy or statement of intention with respect to SDWTs. Articulating such a policy puts management on record—in the minds of employees, customers, and unions. Management might wish to include in the statement that there will be no layoffs due to the introduction of SDWTs and, where displacements do occur (for example, frontline supervisors and middle managers), retraining will be provided for alternate positions and income will be maintained at current levels for a specified period. Management should also outline the drivers for the introduction of SDWTs (for example, competitive pressures or the need for flexibility) and show a tie-in with previous improvement initiatives to provide a sense of continuity and integration.

The policy statement should be as timely and widely disseminated as possible. All members of management should also be formally advised of the organization's new direction. Making the assumption that everyone knows what is going on is a grave error.

A member of senior management should be selected as the champion and supporter of SDWTs. This will ensure that the initiative stays its course when progress is perceived to be slow, when disputes arise, and when key decisions must be made. In addition, this individual can allocate or lobby for funds to sustain training initiatives, special projects, equipment purchases, or customer visits. Such a champion can counsel organization members to be patient while SDWT results unfold. The SDWT vision will reside in this individual; he or she will be viewed as its keeper.

Management must seize every opportunity to speak out positively in favor of SDWTs. Walking the talk has become cliche, but the importance of behaving consistently with the new approach cannot be emphasized strongly enough. Lip service is not sufficient; walking the talk means making public statements in support of SDWTs, enthusiastically promoting this approach to employees and unions, and actively supporting team initiatives when requests are made for resources. Holding small, informal meetings with fledgling teams can do much to sustain the initiative. Detractors will be ever vigilant for any cracks in management commitment, and SDWTs can come to a grinding halt if there is a reluctance to spend a few dollars. Management must be in for the long haul.

UNIONS

Seasoned management will anticipate that unions, in their effort to advance and defend employee interests, will be concerned about the implementation of SDWTs. Union resistance is to be expected and planned for accordingly. At best, management can hope for cooperation and enthusiasm; at worst, fierce opposition and sabotage. Most likely, a middle ground can be anticipated, in which the union does not speak out publicly against SDWTs. If the union does not denounce the initiative, moderate—albeit silent—support for SDWTs can be inferred. While it is preferable to have the active support of the union, passive acceptance greatly facilitates implementation.

The Canadian Auto Workers (CAW) is one union on public record as being philosophically opposed to programs involving risk sharing or participative management. The CAW has a standing committee that visits auto supplier operations where SDWTs and lean production techniques have been installed. Its major criticism of SDWTs is the lack of substantive decision making on the part of teams. Teams are viewed as a thinly disguised attempt on the part of management to exact greater output.[5]

One way to counter this type of skepticism is to include union representation on the SDWT design team. Organizations must seriously consider the attitudes of their unions before implementing SDWTs. Clearly, this responsibility rests with management. Securing union support should be an ongoing activity that begins prior to making the decision to proceed with SDWTs. The subject of a team-driven work environment can be broached during contract negotiations or at a regular problem-solving meeting.

TRAINING

Richard Teerlink, Harley-Davidson's chief executive officer, has stated that if employees are empowered without the proper training, the only thing that will be certain is "you get bad decisions faster."[6] The definition of SDWTs used in this article suggests that these teams are composed of highly trained individuals. But announcing that a dozen individuals have been made into a team and turning them loose on production problems is a recipe for disaster because, for most employees, management decision making is unknown territory.

Training must address a spectrum of skills that vary in importance across employee groups. For instance, before proceeding to quality training or advanced technical skills, it is necessary to ensure minimum literacy and numeracy levels.[7] Studies consistently report illiteracy levels of 20% to 25% across North America, depending on the definition used; across Canada, figures range from 16% to 38%.[8] While management may believe that such illiteracy problems are challenges faced only by other organizations, it can be quite revealing to find the same level of inability resident within one's own company. In fact, prior to implementing its quality program, one Malcolm Baldrige National Quality Award winner found that the average numeracy and literacy skills of its workforce were well below the high school level.

Training in technical, administrative, problem-solving, quality management, productivity improvement, and interpersonal skills is necessary to varying degrees across teams and organizational levels. Table 8.2 suggests the type of training to be considered for various constituencies within a company. The numbers in the table represent the order of priority for training across groups in the organization.

Table 8.2 Training skills across constituencies.

Skill Group	Technical	Interpersonal	Administrative	Problem Solving	Quality Management	Productivity Improvement	Literacy and Numeracy
Team Members	2	3	6	5	4	7	1
Support Groups			2	3	4	1	5
Coaches and Facilitators	5	1	2	3	4	6	

The numbers in the table represent the order of training priority; the smallest number indicates the highest priority. Support groups refer to technical support staff in middle management; coaches and facilitators are those who assist with team functioning.

Before pursuing the training identified in Table 8.2, it is recommended that all members of the organization receive awareness training. It should not be assumed that employees know what is happening simply because upper management has decided to proceed with SDWTs. Employees should be formally notified, and the implementation plan should be clearly explained to them.

Awareness training would cover such topics as the company's mission statement, structure and functions of SDWTs, the relationship between SDWTs and ongoing quality and productivity programs, reasons for the shift to teams, the transition to teams, new roles and responsibilities, team member selection, pilot projects, compensation and reward structures, team scope, and job security.

Consultants should be contracted to provide a substantial portion of the training. While lacking in company-specific experience, they bring a wealth of information and experience from their work in other organizations. Further, they are often more believable and competent teachers than insiders.

COMMUNICATION

One of the most awkward adjustments for management is sharing information and data. Company information traditionally has been the exclusive domain of management, not to be divulged to the employees and certainly not to the union. If the organization is to work together as a team, however, full disclosure of relevant information is necessary. Employees must have access to all the information they need to do their jobs. Of course, certain confidential information, such as others' personnel files, or information that is of no direct relevance to the situation or decision at hand, should remain off limits to employees.

The group that will likely find this new policy disturbing is middle management, which regularly generates and manipulates data to produce information for decision making. Research has shown that middle managers can be among the most significant contributors to the failure of employee participation programs.[9,10,11] Middle managers often feel threatened by such programs, which enable employees to propose—to upper management—solutions to problems deemed insoluble by middle managers.

Upper management must make it clear to managers and support staff that whatever information SDWTs need is to be provided without hesitation. Coaches and facilitators can be instrumental in securing data and information in the short term and, in the long term, educating team members in how to access this information for themselves.

EMPOWERMENT

The ability to make decisions and assume responsibility requires a suitable amount of authority to act autonomously. Richard S. Johnson, in his article "TQM: Leadership for the Quality Transformation," defined delegation as responsibility plus authority plus accountability.[12] The lesson here is that management must delegate increasing amounts of responsibility to teams as they show themselves capable of handling more. Where authority for spending is given, limits should be established in the same way that signing authorities and limits exist for various levels of management.

Traditionally, decision-making authority has rested firmly in the hands of the managers, who create systems and procedures, set performance standards, control and measure results, and take corrective action. With SDWTs, there will be a gradual transfer of operational decision making from managers to work teams. Such a transition can be traumatic for both parties—for managers it means giving something up; for workers it means dealing with something new. Moving too quickly can spell disaster. A division of a major Canadian steel company discovered this when it made an aggressive movement toward teams and simply turned them loose on the organization. Declaring that teams are up and running hardly makes for a sound, full implementation.

There are no easy, cookbook answers as to how much authority to give employees and when. One possible approach is to monitor the amount of authority necessary to achieve particular goals and be ready to hand over more authority as the situation dictates. Teams must let their coaches or facilitators know, through their deeds and words, when they are ready to take on new responsibilities. The frontline supervisor, as coach, should stand ready to assist the team should it stumble, or expand its responsibility when it is ready.[13]

A note of caution: too little authority hamstrings teams and is not much of a departure from the old way of doing things. But providing too much authority can confuse members who are unaccustomed to making decisions. Management must be ever vigilant for signs that it is time to extend or retract decision-making authority.

REWARDS

A problematic area associated with SDWTs relates to reward systems. The issue is thorny for several reasons:

- Most organizations already have established compensation systems

- Most employees want to know what's in it for them when they join an SDWT

- Unions are typically not interested in changing or renegotiating compensation systems

Unions will likely resist dismantling hard-won wage structures. Such structures represent certainty for employees in terms of take-home pay, and employees are not generally willing to expose their pay to potential loss. In the minds of many employees and unions, risk is management's problem.

For reward systems, management has a number of options, including:

- Adding no incentive to the present pay system

- Using a performance-based incentive system

- Switching to a profit-sharing system

- Introducing a one-time-pay incentive system for suggestions implemented, based on a percentage of savings to the organization

- Giving knowledge-based pay

Each of these options comes with a unique set of advantages and disadvantages. A detailed examination of each option, however, is beyond the scope of this article. Companies poised to proceed with SDWTs should carefully think through their policies, as the question surely will arise during awareness meetings.

SOME TECHNICAL DETAILS

A few final concerns should be addressed before embarking on the journey to SDWTs. Frontline supervisors are among the most concerned when it comes to SDWTs because their position might evaporate or evolve into a set of new responsibilities. While perhaps fewer supervisors will be required, it is clear that some amount of frontline supervision will always be needed, for the following reasons:

- Making decisions that the group is not allowed to make (such as disciplinary action, reviewing plant policies, and compensation)

- Resolving intragroup conflict

- Intervening when the interests of group members appear to conflict with those of the company

In an environment of self-managing teams, frontline supervisors can also anticipate facilitating the work of the team, assisting in problem solving, leading training programs, and negotiating for resources with upper management. Thus, while the traditional role of the supervisor might disappear, there will be enough meaningful work to keep the new coach and mentor more than busy.[14]

In unionized environments, job control and bumping rights are significant philosophical and operational concerns, and various questions will need to be addressed. For example, when positions open up in the team, must management respect seniority and job bidding arrangements, or can these be put aside for SDWTs? An associated issue is that of cross-training team members, where such training can result in individuals becoming eligible for higher-paying jobs. Union members outside the team may believe that they have been denied such training opportunities and decide to submit a grievance. When cutbacks are apparent, will the usual bumping into other departments prevail? The implication is that individuals who have not been trained in SDWT techniques will parachute into teams and disrupt team functioning. (Individuals who replace departing team members should attend training with other teams as they are assembled.) An analysis of the collective bargaining agreement and a review of the workplace culture can be useful to head off such difficulties.

Management must decide whether team membership is to be voluntary or mandatory. It is preferable, of course, for individuals to join teams of their own accord. But, because of the realities of job classifications, contractual language, and so on, it is not always possible to have volunteers only. If an individual is opposed to joining a team, he or she should be excused from membership and reassigned as needed. Forcing employees to partake in team activities will merely poison the initiative.

It is advisable to establish a design or steering team representing all levels of the organization to assist the SDWT champion in planning and organizing the introduction of teams.[15] If applicable, union representation on the design team is also recommended.

Finally, job postings for positions within the team should state clearly that weekend, three-shift work, and other commitments could be part of team membership. Full, written disclosure will head off problems and eliminate surprises.

SDWTs CAN WORK

The benefits of SDWTs are real and many. The business literature provides evidence that organizations willing to move in this direction will be handsomely rewarded for their efforts. Visits to such companies will encourage management to proceed with this new form of organization. But courage is needed to undertake this bold initiative. Prosperity and marketplace survival will be the reward for those with the vision to empower employees to do the job they are capable of doing.

ENDNOTES

1. "The Celling Out of America," *The Economist* (Dec. 17, 1994): 62.
2. J. Clauson, "Cyberquality: Quality Resources on the Internet," *Quality Progress* (January 1995): 45.
3. R. Field and R. House, *Human Behaviour in Organizations: A Canadian Perspective* (Toronto, ON: Prentice Hall Canada, 1995): 137.
4. R. Hackman, G. Oldham, R. Janson, and K. Purdy, "A New Strategy for Job Enrichment," *California Management Review* 17, no. 4 (1995): 62
5. D. Robertson, J. Rinehart, C. Huxley, J. Wareham, H. Rosenfeld, A. McGough, and S. Benedict, "The CAMI Report: Lean Production in a Unionized Auto Plant," Canadian Auto Workers Union Research Department (Willowdale, ON, 1993).
6. "Now Hear This," *Fortune* (Aug. 22, 1994): 20.
7. J. Ryan, "Employees Speak on Quality in ASQC/Gallup Survey," *Quality Progress* (December 1993): 51.
8. "Adult Illiteracy in Canada: Results of a National Study," Statistics Canada (Ottawa, ON, 1991); B. Perrin, "Literacy Counts," National Literacy Secretariat (Ottawa, ON, September 1990); and W. Fagan, "Adult Literacy Surveys: A Trans-Border Comparison," *Journal of Reading* (December–January 1995): 260–69.
9. R. Collard and B. Dale, "Quality Circles: Why They Break Down and Why They Hold Up," *Personnel Management* (February 1995): 82.
10. M. W. Piczak, "Quality Circles Come Home," *Quality Progress* (December 1988): 37.
11. C. N. Weaver, "How to Use Process Improvement Teams," *Quality Progress* (December 1993): 65.
12. R. S. Johnson, "TQM: Leadership for the Quality Transformation," *Quality Progress* (March 1993): 91.
13. V. Hoevemeyer, "How Effective Is Your Team?" *Training and Development* (September 1993): 67.
14. S. Calminiti, "What Team Leaders Need to Know," *Fortune* (Feb. 20, 1995): 93.
15. S. Phillips, "Teams Facilitate Change at Turbulent Plant," *Personnel Journal* (October 1994): 110.

9

Why Teams Poop Out

John L. Niles and Norbert J. Salz

SUMMARY

Cross-functional teams are responsible for making a wide variety of process improvements. Many produce mediocre results. The paper identifies the most common causes of team fatigue and recommends preventive action.

INTRODUCTION

Our business involves training teams to solve problems. A glance at our client list finds many of the largest banks, insurance companies, manufacturing businesses, and oil companies. Most of the hundreds of teams we have trained have been extraordinarily successful. Teams routinely report improvements of 75 percent to 90 percent in the task they were asked to improve. The reader may wonder why, with such a track record, we are writing about teams pooping out. The answer is simple. Many clients come to us after they have had unsuccessful experiences with teams, and some of the teams we have trained have pooped out. Our research shows that teams poop out for several reasons. A manager who understands this could intervene and cause the team to rethink some key issues that would allow it to continue and be successful.

A physician speaking on a talk show was asked why he had to order so many tests when trying to find out what was wrong with a patient. He answered that he ordered as few as he could and would need to continue because patients seldom arrive with a diagnosis written on their foreheads. The same is true for teams. A manager can usually determine that a team has not made progress against a goal just as the doctor can recognize that a person is not well. But it takes a structured and probing assessment to determine why a patient is not well or why a team is pooping out.

THE MODEL

The model we recommend is easy to remember because it takes the shape of a triangle under an umbrella. When teams seem to poop out, they have probably either neglected to be specific and thorough in developing their goals, roles, and procedures, or they may not be connected effectively with the system within which they operate. This relationship is depicted in Figure 9.1 and discussed following.

System

The system is made up of the formal and informal structures of the organization. It includes such elements as reporting relationships and organization

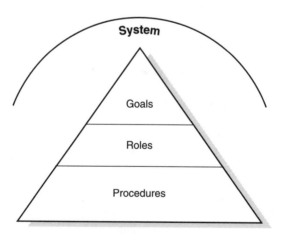

Figure 9.1 Model for successful teams.

structure, the power structure, formal and informal communication patterns, the compensation and reward system, how problems are solved and decisions are made, the overall climate and culture of the organization, and so on. People who know and understand "how to get things done around here" are skillful at making the system work for them.

One of the greatest challenges for any team comes from the paradox of working within the system while trying to make changes which are frequently at odds with some part of that system. Perhaps the most frequent example we encounter is that first-line and middle managers are often not adequately included in the change process, and so they may naturally resist or withhold necessary support and resources. Team members often experience this as not having adequate time to spend on the team's task, or not being acknowledged or rewarded for their contributions to a team. Another example is that some team members may be ostracized by their peers if the team selection process was seen as unfair. Or perhaps the team's efforts may be at cross purposes with another effort in another part of the organization. It is not unusual to hear about competition across shifts in the same department undermining cooperative team efforts.

Both the team and management should consider several questions as they plan on making the team's results an effective part of the system:

- How will the system be affected by the team's work?

- In what ways does the formal system support the team? What reward is there for team contributions?

- How might the system (either deliberately or unwittingly) thwart the team? In what ways does the team threaten the existing system?

- How will the team's efforts and results be communicated?

- What is being done to ensure that all stakeholders are included appropriately?

Goals

Let us start at the top of the pyramid. Some will say that it is obvious that a team must have a goal. We say maybe it is just as obvious that a car must have gas in the tank to reach a destination. Yet every day people are stranded by the side of the road because they forgot to check.

When a team is not making progress toward its goal, they (or management) should undertake an examination of the goal. This should be done in a team meeting with active participation of all team members. Some questions that should be asked are:

- When the goal is reached, how will it contribute to company profits? How is it a "worthy" goal?

- Is the goal supported by management?

- Do team members understand the goal?

- Can the goal be measured accurately?

- Is the goal specific and written? Is it dated?

- Does each team member see how they will benefit? How does it make their job easier? How does this affect their job security? How will it impact the job frustrations they encounter?

- Has each team member adopted the goal as his personal goal?

If the goal is not written or is not specific concerning what is to be achieved, have the team write it or write it again. If the goal is to prepare the company's federal tax return in 75 percent less manhours, say so and be specific concerning how the 75 percent will be measured.

Developing a sense of personal ownership in the team's goal is a powerful force and comes from the team members having the opportunity to "work" the goal—to understand it, to challenge pieces of it, to adapt it to their realities—and to come to a complete and thorough understanding of the goal.

Roles

In teams, members are asked to perform functions somewhat like an actor does when performing a part in a play. Some team members assume their roles naturally and others need some training. Specific roles each team needs include:

- Team leader

- Team recorder

- Team observer

- Team members

Team Leader. The team leader role is critical. It requires someone who is goal-oriented, sensitive to others, and skillful within the organization. Team leaders have a sense of how to get things done within the company. A team leader is doing his job if you can see the following behaviors:

- The leader uses tools such as a prepared agenda, team ground rules, and frequent team self-evaluations.

- The leader encourages all team members to participate actively. Differing views are encouraged and understood. Differences are confronted openly and straightforwardly.

- The leader holds herself to the same high standards of discipline as other team members.

- The leader encourages disciplined problem solving such as data collection and discussion of relevant facts before calling for decisions.

- Work to be done between meetings is divided on an equitable basis.

- The leader develops skills and resources within the team as well as encouraging the use of resources from outside of the group.

- There is a commitment to ongoing improvement and learning as demonstrated by honest self-evaluation and behavior changes within the team.

Team Recorder. Each team needs a record of its meetings, both during the meeting so misunderstandings are minimized, and following the meeting so that the thread of thought is not lost and everyone is clear about next steps. These break out as two separate tasks. The recorder acting as scribe records the flow of the meeting on a flip chart to help the team stay focused and to ensure a common understanding of the proceedings. The second task is one of reducing those flip charts to a few pertinent facts, such as:

- Date and time of the meeting

- Attendees

- Topics discussed

- Decisions made

- Action steps agreed to

Team Observer. The task of the team observer is to stand back, away from the team, and see how well the team follows its own rules. A good observer can help the team leader steer the course much like a navigator helps a pilot. The observer can identify events such as team members not contributing, meetings starting late, minutes not recorded, or when decisions are made without appropriate data.

Team Members. The role of a team member is as important as that of the leader and recorder. The members are responsible for:

- Using their talents and energy to reach the goal
- Picking up tasks from the team
- Meeting deadlines
- Working together collaboratively with other team members
- Participating in meetings
- Taking on team leadership as appropriate
- Advocating for their perspective while also listening and keeping the larger picture in mind

This all adds up to members taking responsibility for full partnership in the team's task. Frequent team meeting self-evaluation, occasional in-depth team self-evaluation, taking advantage of an outside observer or consultant perspective and input, and reporting progress on both the task and teamwork are important tools in monitoring and improving team member performance. Poor member performance must be confronted openly so that the root cause of that performance is identified and addressed. Frequently such problem solving is invaluable in improving the individual's skills and performance.

Procedures

The purpose of a team meeting is to make progress on the task at hand. Effective procedures provide tools, such as meeting management, problem solving, decision making, and conflict management that will help the team achieve its goal. Procedures should help teams focus on reaching their goal. Our experience is that almost everyone has good things to say about a meeting that starts on time, stays focused on the announced purpose of the meeting, encourages each member to speak, develops and uses meaningful data to make decisions, and ends on time. At a minimum, every team should develop and use procedures in the following areas. When appropriate, training must be provided to the team in these areas.

- Meeting management
- Decision making
- Problem solving
- Conflict management

Meeting Management. Like a stool, meetings will work effectively when they have three solid legs upon which to stand. They are objective, content, and process.

Each meeting needs an objective. The meeting content must be clear; an unambiguous agenda will identify specific topics covered and decisions to be made; the logistics of time, place, and materials such as flip charts and markers must also be handled. The team must have an effective meeting process which describes how the team works together in and outside of the meeting.

The team leader is the manager of the meeting. He should follow a written agenda and move through a series of events such as:

- Discuss the agenda

- Review meeting rules, such as, smoking, starting on time, only one person speaks at any one time

- Finish each agenda item before taking up the next

- Make sure the recorder is writing

- Use flip charts to focus attention

- Keep an asides list for items not on the agenda

Members should play their roles and encourage the leader to lead if he forgets. Once the leader, recorder, and the members understand their roles, a meeting should proceed in a fairly orderly fashion.

Part of the meeting process takes place outside of the team meeting. Before the next meeting the leader should:

- Remind members about the next meeting

- Discuss problems

- Make sure meeting records are filed in an orderly way, such as in a notebook

The team leader should follow up with team members between meetings. Most often a simple, "don't forget our meeting next week," is all that is required. It lets the meeting member know that the team leader is thinking about the goal and establishes a level of importance in the team member's mind.

A good leader will anticipate problems and discuss them with team members and other appropriate people before the team meeting. The purpose of "touching base" is to make sure that the team meeting will proceed according to the agenda. Touching base between meetings can also reduce the tension that accompanies strong differences of opinion and solves problems that are better handled one-on-one than in a group discussion.

Decision Making. Teams poop out when they make poor decisions, if they spend too much time making decisions, or when they are not able to gain acceptance for the decisions they have made.

There are three basically different ways to make decisions. Unilateral decisions are those made by an individual. A second way to make decisions is called consultative. That is, one person again makes the decision, but only after open and meaningful consultation with others who may be knowledgeable about or affected by the decision. A third way to make decisions is group decision making, which may be further divided onto "majority rule" and "consensus." Majority rule is simply using our democratic tradition of debate and voting to decide. Consensus requires a more complete discussion with explicit attention paid to understanding others' ideas and positions, as well as advocating one's own thinking.

We advocate what may be called "situational decision making." That is, different circumstances call for different approaches to making decisions. When the theater is on fire, we don't want to assemble a group and invest two hours in developing an evacuation plan! The amount of time available is a critical factor in choosing the most appropriate decision-making style.

Often a decision requires special knowledge in order to be high quality or "technically correct." When broad acceptance and support are necessary, it is more appropriate to include others in the decision-making process. We have two tools to help teams as they make decisions. The first is a chart summarizing the relationships between decision-making style and the three critical factors of time, quality, and acceptance.

The second is *decision charting*, which offers explicit choices about whether people should be directly involved in making the decision (D), be consulted prior to a decision (C), be informed of the decision (I), or manage the decision process to ensure that a decision is made (M). Using decision charting clarifies when consensus is a good investment, supports role clarity within a team, and gets people to consider who else may be affected by a decision.

Problem Solving. Few teams poop out because they lack problem-solving skills. If they understand the system they are operating in and do well with their roles, goals, and meeting procedures, they can usually find a resource who will teach them problem solving. A good problem-solving procedure is:

    a. Define the problem

    b. Identify possible solutions

    c. Gather data

    d. Analyze data

    e. Select the best solution

    f. Test the solution

    g. Go back to Step "a"

Successful teams will follow the above procedure until they have found the root cause of any problem. A solution to a root cause cannot be improved by further problem solving.

Conflict Management. One advantage of teams is their diversity of perspectives and resources. Teams poop out when conflict gets the best of them, and interpersonal strife overshadows the creative use of diversity in solving problems and achieving results.

Team members need to identify and discuss how they each bring similarities and differences in terms of their approach to conflict, their problem solving and learning styles, their perspectives on the team's task, and what they may individually expect from each other and from being on the team.

This awareness leads to understanding conflict as an energy source— a wellspring of ideas and possibilities that can fuel the team. Building upon this understanding, teams need tools and skill building that enable them to use conflict constructively to their great advantage rather than to be stymied by it. Most tools or structures are quite simple; usually, it is in the implementation that the difficulties arise. Thus, it is through application and evaluation that teams can analyze and improve their knowledge and skills in teamwork.

CONCLUSION

Teams poop out because they do not have a model to follow and management does not have a model to teach them. The model presented in this paper has been used with hundreds of teams and works because it is easy to apply and makes sense to the average person. The model can be remembered as a triangle under an umbrella. The area outside the triangle and under the umbrella is called the system. The system identifies the forces outside of the team that it must deal with if it is to be successful.

The system includes managers and employees who are not on the team, formal and informal company policies, and the organization culture. A team begins its interaction with the system when it receives its assignment or charge from the group who created the team. Team members' work experience also helps them understand how they must work within the system to be successful. At the top of the triangle are *goals*, then *roles*, and at the bottom *procedures*. Goals should be specific, measurable, supported by management, and understood by team members. There are four important roles on every team; they are leader, recorder, observer, and team members. Each has specific tasks to perform on a successful team. The team leader's role is critical. A good leader is goal-oriented, sensitive to others, and skillful within the organization. The leader makes sure that each meeting has a written agenda and follows a meeting plan. The recorder concisely records the events that occur at each meeting. The observer makes sure that the team follows its own rules and points out departures from the rules to the leader and team members. Team members use talents and energy to reach the goal.

Procedures help the team achieve its goal by providing structure or a framework that ensures results when followed. There are four areas of procedures: meeting management, decision making, problem solving, and conflict management. Teams poop out for several reasons. A manager or team member who understands this model could intervene when a team is pooping out, causing the team to rethink some key issues, which would allow it to continue and be successful.

10

How to Prevent Teams from Failing

John D.W. Beck and Neil M. Yeager

The quality director of a midsize manufacturing firm is struggling to keep the company's quality initiative alive. Senior management is on his back because the quality teams aren't focusing on significant problems that affect the bottom line. At the same time, team members are ready to quit because the projects they want to work on never get management's approval.

This quality leader is not alone. The senior vice president of human resources in a high-tech company is frustrated by the inability to turn analysis into shop-floor actions. Despite an all-out commitment to the total quality management process, the only real change has been the amount of time employees spend in unproductive meetings. One team leader describes this process as "consensus run amok." Another asks, "Can't anything be done by an individual anymore? Does it really take a team to change a light bulb?"

Meanwhile, the president of a major oil company wonders why the managers who were charged with making the quality program a success have failed to produce the results he wanted. "I told them they could do whatever it took to get the job done," he complains. One team leader's response to his complaint is, "That's a nice theory. In reality, we're on our own, having to beg, borrow, and steal every bit of time and money we can get. We've got no resources and have had trouble getting managers to take us seriously."

Finally, a regional bank vice president laughs when anyone asks her how the continuous improvement process has improved bank operations. "It's a joke," she says. "After those first meetings, people have been off doing their own thing. We almost never come together as a team to assess our progress or rethink our plans. And when we do, it's a waste of time. People just play politics and second-guess each other."

These are common complaints from the trenches, where disappointment has replaced much of the enthusiasm that used to accompany the quality movement. Quality teams often fail because:

- They don't focus on a mission that both the team and management are committed to solving

- They are trapped in a groupthink mind-set in which no actions are taken until everyone agrees with every decision

- Individual assignments aren't accomplished because there is no support for the time and resources needed to achieve the results

- The team stops holding meetings to coordinate efforts and check progress because departmental politics get in the way

Not every quality initiative is a bust. Most teams accomplish something, and many produce outstanding results. When a team succeeds, who gets the credit? The team does—people usually say that it was a team effort that got the job done. When a team fails, who gets blamed? It could be management, the union, the consultants who introduced the process, or a team member with a strong personality. But, typically, people don't point their fingers at the team as a whole.

One of the biggest causes of failed quality initiatives, however, is poor teamwork. If success is always attributed to effective teamwork, doesn't it stand to reason that ineffective teams might be a cause of failure?

Quality initiatives are typified by employees being sequestered in conference rooms with fishbone diagrams, Pareto charts, histograms, process maps, and affinity diagrams. There are timekeepers, gatekeepers, scribes, facilitators, and even people called leaders, but is anyone really leading? Tools are being used, but what are the outcomes? Employees are playing textbook roles, but to what end?

Tim "The Tool Man" Taylor, the main character in the popular television sitcom *Home Improvement*, offers a poignant metaphor for why quality initiatives often fail. In one episode, Tim retrofits a power screwdriver with a gasoline engine, complete with sputtering sounds and spewing smoke. When he attempts to drive a series of screws through a sheet-rock wall, his over-engineered tool proves to be a disaster. He drives the screws, the screwdriver, and his own arm through the wall!

When quality teams have the tools to analyze a problem but lack the tools for effective teamwork, the result is often over-engineering. The focus becomes the analytical tools; the people and the process end up serving the tools rather than the other way around. When that happens, teams create elaborate schemes that lead nowhere instead of finding the best way to attach screws to a wall.

The concepts of total quality and continuous improvement work, as do analytical tools. So where is the breakdown? Why do so many quality initiatives fail? Because they require people to work together in teams. Most team leaders receive inadequate training in the fundamentals of how to make a team effort produce results. They get trained in how to use analysis and problem-solving tools, but they don't get taught the most important lesson: the leadership skills needed to turn a group of people into a team.

LEADERSHIP IS THE KEY TO SUCCESS

If a quality initiative is going to succeed, the quality teams making the improvements will need solid leadership. The people leading the teams will need to know how to get individuals to work together effectively. A simple template that can help in this effort is called *the leader's window*.

To understand the leader's window, it helps to be familiar with the four leadership styles that most managers tend to use. Figure 10.1 contains a snapshot of the four styles. Each style, referred to as S1, S2, S3, or S4,[1] is defined in terms of decision-making methods, communication skills, and recognition strategies. These leadership styles are not new, but the way they are put together in the leader's window provides a new approach to successful teamwork.[2]

Each leadership style offers a potential blessing and a possible curse. It's a blessing when the leadership style matches the conditions; it's a curse when there is a mismatch between the leader's actions and what followers need in that situation. Figure 10.2 shows how the four leadership styles can be effective if they are used at the right times and equally ineffective if they are used at the wrong times. To be effective, team leaders can use the leader's window, which provides unconventional wisdom on how to use group dynamics and how to empower individual team members.

Figure 10.1 The four leadership styles.

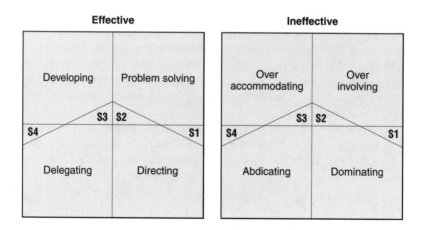

Figure 10.2 The four leadership styles can be equally effective and ineffective.

TEAM = INDIVIDUALS + THE GROUP

Team leaders have to realize that a team consists of individuals and the group dynamics that surface when these individuals come together as a team. Too often, managers think of individual assignments and group efforts as polar opposites—that an individual is the antithesis of being a team player. Many trainers even use the line, "There are no i's or u's in the word 'team.'" The implication is that teamwork means involving everyone in a "we" exercise.

This kind of thinking results in the mistaken notion that teamwork only happens when all of the team members are together in a conference room. The reality is that not every team requires a carefully orchestrated group effort, like that demanded by basketball, hockey, or football teams. Some teams—such as golf, tennis, or track teams—require individual excellence and very limited group interaction.

Most business teams require both types of interaction. So, to lead a successful team effort, team leaders have to know how to lead the group dynamics, but they also need to know how to translate the group effort into individual accountabilities.

LEADING EFFECTIVE GROUP DYNAMICS

To lead a group effort, the team leader must understand the predictable stages of development that groups go through. The conventional wisdom that most people have been taught is the forming–storming–norming–performing model of group development. This model, developed by Bruce Tuckman in 1965, was based on a review of literature that was predominated by research with therapy groups, sensitivity-training groups (often referred to as T-groups), and other leaderless groups.[3] Despite this, Tuckman's model has been attractive in the business world for several reasons:

- The terms are simple

- It is comforting to believe that storming is natural

- It is nice to believe that storms give way to productive norms

- It is reassuring to believe that the endpoint will be performing

Unfortunately, Tuckman's model distorts the realities of teamwork:

• *Distortion 1:* Forming simply means meeting teammates. In reality, forming requires much more than meeting the other members of the team. It requires clarifying the team's mission, defining goals and roles, and establishing procedures for getting the work done. At the outset, a team needs to form around a clear purpose and then get focused on the best ways to accomplish that purpose.

• *Distortion 2:* Storming is inevitable. In reality, many teams have become focused and productive without experiencing storms. While storming often occurs, it is not a required stage of group development. Of course, if someone believes it is supposed to happen, that belief can become a self-fulfilling prophecy.

• *Distortion 3:* When storming occurs, it eventually turns into norming by itself. Many team leaders and facilitators are convinced that dwelling on conflicts is the best way to get the team ready to perform. In reality, storms occur because the team is not focused, the mission and goals are ambiguous, the roles are confusing, or the operating principles and procedures are dysfunctional. These problems don't disappear by arguing or by ignoring them. Focusing a group requires a concerted effort to answer, "What is the team expected to do?" and "How are the team's efforts going to be coordinated to meet those expectations?"

• *Distortion 4:* Performing is the endpoint of a team's development. Teams often go beyond performing to a point at which their performance levels off (or even declines) because they get complacent, start to burn out, get defensive, or try to preserve the status quo. These symptoms will likely arise if groups are put on "autopilot" once they have hit the performing stage. But, if leaders don't assume that performing is the endpoint, they can avoid static or declining performance by refocusing and revitalizing the teams' efforts.

A new business-oriented, reality-based model of group development can overcome these misleading notions. The four real stages of group development are forming, focusing, performing, and leveling. The leadership strategy for navigating these stages is as easy as "1-2-3."

A team orientation requires both forming and focusing. In forming, the leader needs to tell the team members their mission and goals; why they have been asked to join the team; and management's expectations (that is, leaders need to use S1, directing). In focusing, the leader needs to use S2, problem solving, to involve the group in determining communication norms, decision-making procedures, roles and responsibilities, how the team is going to achieve the mission, and coordinating mechanisms. This involvement will help the team members buy into the mission.

If a team is properly formed and focused, it can move to the performing stage without conflicts and power struggles. If it doesn't get formed around a distinct mission or if the focus on how to accomplish the mission is unclear, storms might occur. Conflict should be seen as a symptom of being out of focus, not as an inevitable stage of development. If storms arise, the leader needs to use S2, problem solving (specifically, getting team members' input to guide decisions), to clarify what the team is expected to do and reorganize the effort to get it done.

When the group moves to the performing stage, team members are ready for action. The most important part of performing doesn't happen in the meeting room; it occurs in the workplace, where individuals deliver on their commitments to the team. Thus, the leader needs to use S3, developing, to distribute responsibilities among team members, giving each one a level of responsibility that he or she can handle. The leader then has to let each member know what he or she needs to do and make sure that the person gets the support he or she needs from the rest of the team.

To stay in the performing mode, the team leader needs to use S3, developing. The team has to meet periodically so that its members can give progress reports, be updated on changes, identify and solve problems that have surfaced, and capitalize on opportunities that have developed. Team meetings also give the leader a chance to offer recognition and support. Without these meetings, team members will redirect their focus back to their daily assignments, causing the team's performance to level off or decline.

For team meetings to be effective, the leader needs to avoid the "over-accommodating trap" of trying to get the team to make group decisions. This is one of the biggest diseases that infect quality teams. The antidote is the distributed-responsibility approach, in which an individual acts on behalf of the team and makes decisions based on team members' input. This is very different from group decision making.

When a decision needs to be made, the team leader needs to use either S2, problem solving, to make his or her own decision, or S3, developing, to guide a team member who is willing to accept responsibility for making it. The designated decision maker needs to listen to team members and then make a decision. When there is consensus among the team members, the decision is easy. When there is not, the individual must be empowered to make the decision. If every decision has to wait for total buy-in, the team will get bogged down in groupthink.

In summary, the leader needs to use a balance of S1, directing, and S2, problem solving, to take charge of the forming and focusing stages, which will get the group launched. When the group is performing, the leader needs to use S3, developing, to empower individual team members to take action with team support. To avoid the leveling stage, the leader needs to bring everyone together at regular intervals with a balance of S3, developing, to help team members make good decisions and S2, problem solving, when the leader needs to make the decision.

EMPOWERING INDIVIDUAL TEAM MEMBERS

Since individual team members have to be empowered for the group to take action, a team leader needs to know what it means to really empower another person. Even though everyone talks about empowerment these days, it is one of those buzzwords that rarely translates into reality.

It's not that empowerment is a bad idea. It is smart to drive responsibility down the organization, delegating it to team members. But if leaders simply let go of their responsibilities, the result will be abdication, not empowerment. Leaders are abdicating when they don't communicate clear expectations to team members, leave them alone too much, don't provide support when team members need it, or waffle when it's time to make tough decisions. That is what's happening in many organizations under the banner of empowerment.

To truly empower team members, leaders have to:

- Give clear directions and clarify expectations (S1, directing)

- Delegate meaningful assignments (S4, delegating)

- Stay in touch with, and provide support to, team members, helping them make their own decisions (S3, developing)

- If necessary, be prepared to make timely decisions based on team members' input (S2, problem solving)

This 1-4-3-2 approach to empowerment contradicts the conventional wisdom that has been preached for years: that managers must pick the right leadership style for a given situation. In reality, all four styles are needed in most situations. While one style might need to be emphasized, effective leaders use all four styles, carefully following the 1-4-3-2 sequence. This approach enables individuals to perform to the best of their potential.

Conventional wisdom also has preached that the way to develop employees is to shift from S1 to S2 to S3 to S4. The problem with this mind-set is that leaders think they should use one style at a time to gradually let out the kite string of responsibility. Even when the business world was slower and more predictable, that idea only worked on occasion. In today's fast-paced, streamlined, rapid-change environment, this one-style-at-a-time process doesn't stand a chance.

The most successful leaders in today's dynamic environment delegate increasing amounts of responsibility, following the 1-4-3-2 approach. That doesn't mean they treat everyone the same way. When team members take on new assignments, these leaders emphasize the beginning and end of the sequence by:

- Providing explicit, detailed directions and expectations (S1, directing)

- Limiting the time members have to work alone (S4, delegating)

- Limiting the number of decisions that team members must make (S3, developing)

- Concentrating on identifying and correcting problems (S2, problem solving)

In contrast, when team members handle familiar assignments, leaders should emphasize the middle of the sequence by:

- Providing limited directions that give team members more flexibility in how they achieve the mission (S1, directing)

- Giving team members lots of time to work alone (S4, delegating)

- Supporting team members' decision-making responsibilities (S3, developing)

- Rarely making decisions themselves (S2, problem solving)

Too many quality initiatives break down because the quality teams' decisions don't get translated into individual accountabilities. Unless each team member knows what is expected, analysis won't result in action. If team members can't get the support they need or timely decisions made for them when they get stuck, they are not likely to accomplish their objectives. The 1-4-3-2 leadership approach is a team leader's guide to getting team members to take action.

MAKING TEAMWORK WORK

As mentioned previously, a team consists of the individual team members plus the group dynamics that occur when they come together. The key to successful teamwork is to use the power of the group in the beginning, individual empowerment in the middle, followed by the strength of the group. Team meetings are useful at the outset for forming and focusing the whole group on top priorities. They are also an efficient vehicle for ongoing communication that is needed to sustain the performing stage, while avoiding the leveling phase. But in between these group meetings, the work ultimately has to be done by individuals who are accountable for their assignments and supported in their efforts.

When the 1-2-3 group approach and the 1-4-3-2 individual approach are combined, the result is The Leader's Window, a simple four-phase template for getting quality teams to perform. Following this template, the team leader needs to:

• *Start with a team orientation (phase 1).* Form the group by using S1, directing, to tell the team members as much as possible about their mission. Then use S2, problem solving, to focus the group by involving team members in determining the best ways to accomplish the team's objectives. With all of the team members together, be sure everyone is clear about goals and roles.

• *Clarify individual assignments (phase 2).* Use S1, directing, and S4, delegating, to make sure that each team member knows what he or she is empowered to do, what deliverables are expected, and when are they due. Also ask each team member how he or she plans to accomplish the tasks and what he or she needs from the team leader or from other team members to get the work done.

• *Let team members get to work (phase 3).* Use S4, delegating, to give individuals room to accomplish their assignments. Use S3, developing, to check in periodically and offer encouragement. Most important, be responsive when team members need support.

• *Make time for team problem solving (phase 4).* Bring the team together regularly to keep team members informed of progress, to identify and solve problems, and to coordinate each person's efforts. When decisions need to be made, use S2, problem solving, to get input for decisions that the team leader needs to make or use S3, developing, to help team members get input for decisions that they have agreed to make. Always encourage the team to look for ways to work smarter.

Remember the cases cited at the beginning? With The Leader's Window in mind, one can see why the quality teams in the midsize manufacturing firm, the high-tech company, the major oil company, and the bank failed.

At the midsize manufacturing firm, the teams failed at phase 1. Everyone was frustrated because the teams did not form around management's objectives. As a result, they were focused on the wrong mission.

Phase 2 was missing at the high-tech company. The quality initiative only existed in team meetings. The team members never took quality assignments back into the workplace. Hence, analysis never turned into action.

At the major oil company, phase 3 was not occurring. Individuals were not delivering on their commitments. They felt overwhelmed, under-resourced, and unsupported.

Phase 4 was the problem at the bank where quality had become a joke. When the team members came together, group decision making became a contest of second-guessing. As a result, they diverted their energy to other tasks.

If companies don't want their quality initiatives to fail, they should apply all four phases of The Leader's Window. This tool helps capitalize on the power of the group while empowering individuals to perform to the best of their potential. With The Leader's Window, companies can put quality tools to work and make their organizations "teaming" with excitement.

ENDNOTES

1. This nomenclature was first used by P. Hersey and K. Blanchard in *Management of Organizational Behavior: Utilizing Human Resources,* 5th ed. (Englewood Cliffs, NJ: Prentice-Hall, 1988).
2. J. D. W. Beck and N. M. Yeager, *The Leader's Window: Mastering the Four Styles of Leadership to Build High Performing Teams* (New York: John Wiley & Sons, 1994).
3. B. W. Tuckman, "Developmental Sequence in Small Groups," *Psychological Bulletin* 63, no. 6 (1965): 384–99.

Section III

Continuous Improvement

If teamwork is the heart of quality improvement, continuous improvement is undoubtedly the soul. The very essence of quality is so closely intertwined with continuous improvement that it would be almost impossible to separate the two. The articles in this section provide some insight into a handful of the many quality tools available.

In "Telling the Quality Story," Howard Gitlow and his colleagues integrate quality storyboards with the plan–do–check–act (PDCA) cycle. The authors present detailed flowcharts and quality control tools (for example, control charts, Pareto diagrams) that can be used in the PDCA cycle to demonstrate how each phase can be measured and analyzed.

In "Continuous Improvement: Methods and Madness," Alan Peterson and Dan Reid suggest that many managers cannot clearly distinguish between continuous improvement, corrective action, and innovation. They provide clear definitions for each of these terms and present compelling reasons why—from the customer's perspective—these concepts really are different.

Dean Bottorff addresses cost of quality (COQ) systems in "COQ Systems: The Right Stuff." He discusses the historical evolution of cost of quality concepts and some of the rather remarkable results that companies have achieved from COQ reductions. Bottorff clearly defines the four categories of quality costs and describes eight roadblocks to COQ system implementation.

Two of the articles in this section address traditional quality tools that are frequently used today in continuous improvement activities. In "The

Tools of Quality—Part II: Cause-and-Effect Diagrams," Stephen Sarazen provides a succinct overview of this useful quality tool. He identifies three types of diagrams—dispersion analysis, production process classification, and cause enumeration—and provides clear directions about their uses and development. Sarazen concludes with some helpful hints for cause-and-effect diagram construction. "The Tools of Quality—Part IV: Pareto Charts," by John Burr, addresses the development and use of Pareto diagrams. Burr provides several examples of Pareto diagrams and discusses how to collect data for use in these diagrams.

The final article in this section, "Benchmarking: Achieving the Best in Class," by Lynn Kaemmerer, discusses the general concept of benchmarking. Kaemmerer provides succinct definitions of various types of benchmarking (internal, competitive, and best-in-class) and presents a four-step model of the benchmarking process. The article concludes with a candid discussion of some of the pitfalls of benchmarking.

11

Telling the Quality Story

Howard S. Gitlow, Shelly J. Gitlow,
Alan Oppenheim, and Rosa Oppenheim

The quality improvement (QI) story is an efficient format for presenting process improvement studies to management. QI stories standardize quality control reports, help avoid logic errors in analysis, and make reports easier to understand. QI stories can also be used to facilitate the transition to a style of management that focuses on continuous improvement.

There are seven steps in constructing a QI story, as shown in Figure 11.1. They follow W. Edwards Deming's cycle of plan–do–check–act (PDCA):

PLAN

1. Select a theme for the QI story and obtain all the background information necessary to understand the selected theme, including a process flow diagram, the reason for selecting the theme, and the organizational and departmental objectives that will be influenced by the theme.

2. Understand the present situation.

3. Analyze the present situation to identify appropriate actions—called countermeasures—to change the process (that is, construct a plan of action).

1. Select a theme
2. Understand the present situation
3. Analyze the present situation to identify countermeasures
4. Set the countermeasures into motion
5. Determine the effectiveness of the countermeasures
6. Revise the standard operating procedures
7. Plan for future actions

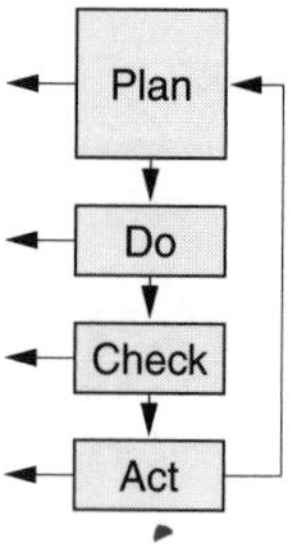

Plan → Do → Check → Act

Figure 11.1   Relationship between the QI story and the PDCA cycle.

DO

4. Set the countermeasures into action on a small scale so that the process improvement actions can be tested on an experimental basis.

CHECK

5. Collect, analyze, and creatively think about the data on the effectiveness of the experimental countermeasures. Determine whether the countermeasures reduce the difference between customer needs and process performance. Make before-and-after comparisons of the effects of the experimental countermeasures on the targeted departmental and organizational objectives.

ACT

6. Determine whether the countermeasures were effective in pursuing departmental and organizational objectives. If not, go back to the plan stage to find other countermeasures. If the countermeasures were effective, either go to the plan stage to seek the optimal settings of the countermeasures or formally establish revised standard operating procedures based on the data concerning the experimental countermeasures. Take steps to prevent the countermeasures set into motion from backsliding.

7. Identify remaining process problems, establish a plan for further actions, and reflect on the positives and negatives of past countermeasures.

These seven steps form the basis of a standard operating procedure for a QI story. All organization personnel must adhere to them. All sections of a QI story must be clearly numbered and labeled so that each section correlates to one of the seven steps.

Employees might encounter two difficulties when using QI stories. First, they might have to work with qualitative (non-numerical) themes. Themes that are hard to describe with numerical values (for example, improvement of presidential reviews) should be analyzed by focusing on the magnitude of the gap between actual and desired performance. Second, employees might encounter exogenous problems. If the primary cause of a problem is beyond the control of anyone in the organization (for example, cold weather, no rain), employees should not conclude that it is impossible to take countermeasures. Exogenous problems cannot be ignored. Instead, employees need to think about why there are so many more occurrences of the problem in area A than in area B, given that both areas have equal opportunities for the problem to arise.

PURSUIT OF OBJECTIVES

Initially, QI stories will be selected because they are near-complete resolutions of departmental problems and will not relate to broader objectives. As employees gain experience with QI stories, however, they will want to select themes related to organizational and departmental objectives. Consequently, quantitative measures that clearly recognize the relationship between these two types of objectives must be established.

For example, the purchasing department might aim to reduce the processing time for purchase orders. The department might contend this goal is related to the organizational objective of creating a great workplace free from system impediments. However, there is no quantitative measure that shows such a relationship. These quantitative relationships must be shown in the QI story. If QI story activities are not consistent with departmental objectives and organizational objectives, there is the distinct possibility that quality improvement efforts will not be in line with organizational goals.

QI STORY CASE STUDY

The experience of a data processing department demonstrates the role of QI stories in an organization's improvement efforts. The department started with the question "Why do data entry personnel produce such a high percentage of nonconforming data entries?" The theme, then, was to reduce the number of operator data entry errors.

In the theme's background were organizational and departmental objectives. The organization's mission statement said that all employees must base their decisions and actions on five objectives. The four most relevant in this case were pursuing improvement in customer satisfaction, improvement in customer satisfaction, respecting and continuously improving all employees, and establishing long-term, trusting relationships with suppliers.

Based on the organization's objectives, the data processing department set these goals:

- Recognize that there are internal and external customers in the organization and continuously strive to improve data processing services for both

- Identify areas in which employees can improve and establish training programs to effect the identified improvements

The department wanted to achieve the first objective by entering all data exactly as they appeared on the source documents and by continually reducing the amount of time it takes to process a data entry job. Obviously, the theme selected by the department was directly affected by organizational and departmental objectives.

The department manager included all of the information just described on a QI storyboard under the "plan" phase. In addition, a process flow diagram was developed for the plan storyboard, as shown in Figure 11.2.

A second storyboard showed the steps by which the department manager obtained a grasp of the present situation. Her intuition that too many nonconforming entries were found during verification led her to conduct a survey to determine customer satisfaction, that is, how satisfied other departments were with data entry capabilities. She put together a list of the department's customers (administration, production, marketing, and so on) and constructed a questionnaire to determine customer satisfaction.

The surveyed departments were asked whether the data processing error rate was unsatisfactory, satisfactory, or excellent. The departments were also asked to estimate the percentage of data entries containing errors attributable to the data processing department. The storyboard for this part of the cycle included an example of the survey form used.

When the responses were analyzed, it was found that 72% of the departments rated the data entry error rate as unsatisfactory and only 8% considered it to be excellent. The departments also reported that 2% of the data entries contained errors attributable to the data entry department.

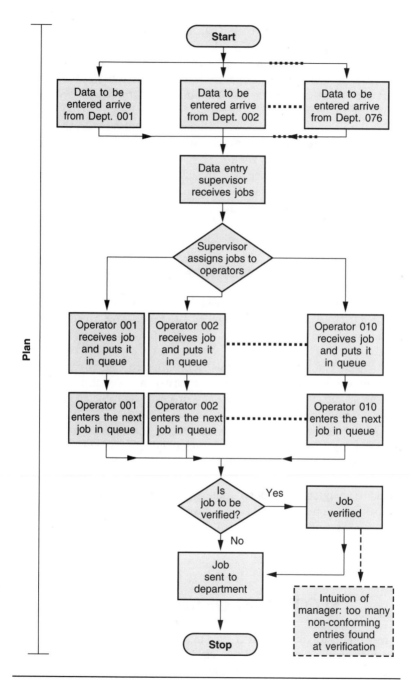

Figure 11.2   Reason for selecting the theme.

The manager decided to collect data concerning the daily proportion of nonconforming entries. The data, plotted on a control chart, revealed that the data entry process was in a state of chaos. It was producing an unknown proportion of nonconformances each day. The data record and the control chart were part of the second storyboard used to report this quality improvement case.

A third storyboard, which was also part of the plan phase, showed the analysis of the present situation. The data revealed that on days 8 and 22, the process had been out of control, producing substantially more nonconformances than on any other day. To stabilize the process, the causes of problems on those two days had to be found and a policy established to prevent the problems from recurring.

The manager reviewed her daily log sheets of unusual events on the two days in question. Her notes revealed that untrained operators were used for rush jobs on both days. She planned to solve that problem by establishing a policy that required training for new operators used in rush jobs.

In the "do" step of the PDCA cycle (fourth storyboard), the manager set the countermeasures into motion and tested them. She established a policy on a trial basis, then collected more data to see if the process was stable and improved.

In the "check" phase, the effectiveness of the countermeasures was determined. The storyboard for this step compared control charts before and after the change in policy. That comparison revealed that the countermeasures were effective. The data entry process was stable and producing fewer nonconformances.

As part of the "act" step (fifth storyboard), the manager established a new standard operating procedure for training data entry personnel. Furthermore, the manager decided that a random sample of 200 entries would be drawn every month from every operator's output. The sample would be analyzed so that appropriate actions could be taken to prevent any backsliding in areas that had been improved.

A sixth storyboard was used to show the plan for future action, which is part of the "act" phase. That storyboard showed the schedule for carrying out the new plan.

SECOND SET OF STORYBOARDS

A new set of storyboards was created to show the new PDCA cycle, which focused attention on individual data entry operators. This theme was selected because the data processing manager realized that future process

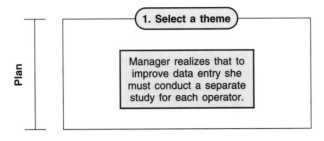

Figure 11.3   Storyboard 1: selecting a theme.

improvements required her to identify and train operators whose performance was out of control (Figure 11.3). As shown in Figure 11.4, the manager determined that the performance of data entry operators 004 and 009 was out of control; she also discovered the reason for operator 004's poor performance. An analysis of the present situation (Figure 11.5) identified the countermeasures necessary to improve operator 004's performance. The manager set the countermeasures into motion, as shown in Figure 11.6. The effectiveness of the countermeasures on operator 004 and on the organizational and departmental objectives was confirmed (Figure 11.7). A new standard operating procedure was set that formalized the countermeasure for all operators to prevent backsliding (Figure 11.8). Finally, a plan for future actions was specified (Figure 11.9).

IMPROVEMENT OF THE QI STORY PROCESS

The QI story process is subject to improvement efforts just like any other organizational process. These efforts must focus on reducing the differences in QI story objectives between QI story presenters and QI story reviewers. The following PDCA cycle must be continuously performed to improve the QI story process.

Plan

A list of QI story presenters and QI story reviewers must be constructed for each level of QI story presentation in the organization. A survey instrument must be developed to gather data for each of these levels in respect to QI story variables. The goal is to determine whether QI stories are being

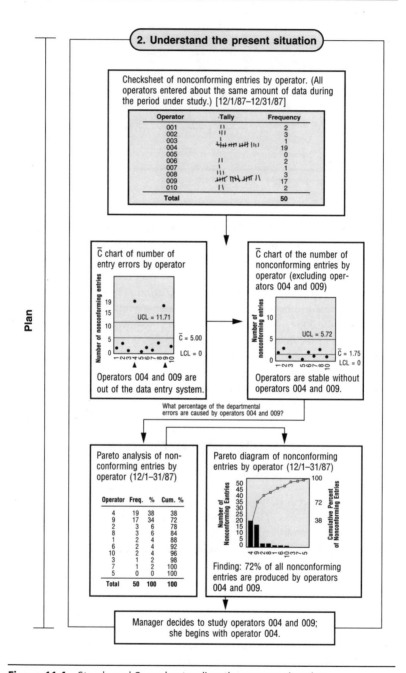

Figure 11.4   Storyboard 2: understanding the present situation.

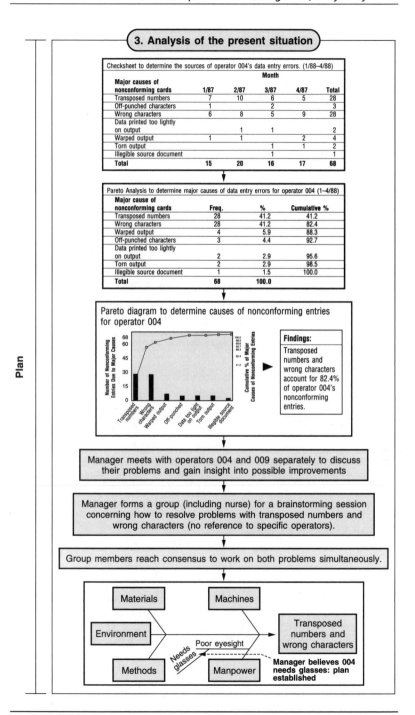

Figure 11.5   Storyboard 3: analysis of the present situation.

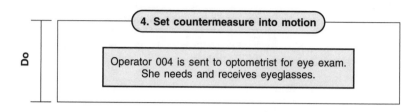

Figure 11.6 Storyboard 4: setting countermeasure into motion.

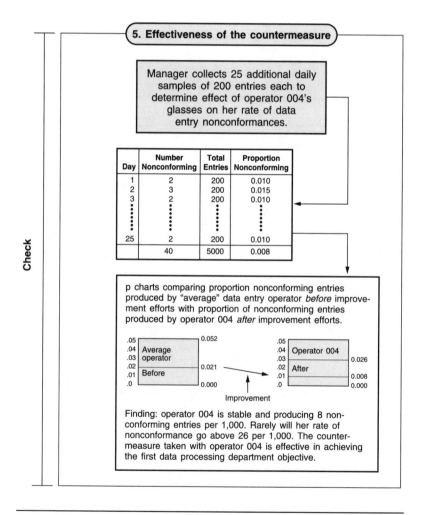

Figure 11.7 Storyboard 5: effectiveness of the countermeasure.

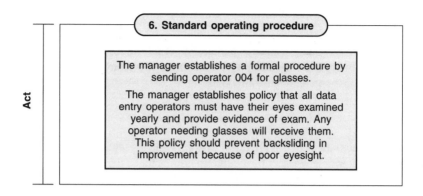

6. Standard operating procedure

The manager establishes a formal procedure by sending operator 004 for glasses.

The manager establishes policy that all data entry operators must have their eyes examined yearly and provide evidence of exam. Any operator needing glasses will receive them. This policy should prevent backsliding in improvement because of poor eyesight.

Act

Figure 11.8 Storyboard 6: standard operating procedure.

7. Plan for future actions

Act

		When Future Plan Will Be Carried Out					Who Will Carry Out Plan
		5/88	6/88	7/88	8/88	9/88	
Phase 1	Work with operator 009	←——→					Manager and operator 009
Phase 2	Check progress of entire dept.			←——→			Manager and operators 001 to 010
Phase 3	Survey customers re satisfaction with dept.					←→	Manager

Figure 11.9 Storyboard 7: planning for future actions.

viewed similarly by QI story reviewers and presenters (positive correlations). Next, a sampling plan must be established for the survey. The sampling plan must consider non-response bias. The survey must be administered in strict accordance with the sampling plan.

The survey must be analyzed so that the correlations between QI story variables can be examined. Countermeasures can then be examined. Countermeasures can then be used to decrease the difference in objectives between presenters and reviewers (that is, to create strong, positive correlations). Proposed countermeasures should be a direct result of this survey.

Do

The proposed countermeasures should be set into motion on a trial basis. The trial could involve a sample of subcomponents from the entire organization or just one pilot subcomponent.

Check

The correlations between QI story reviewers and presenters must be examined to determine whether the countermeasures made the correlations more positive and, therefore, decreased the difference in QI story objectives between presenters and reviewers.

Act

If the correlations between QI reviewers and presenters became more positive, then formal changes must be established in QI story standard operating procedures. Of course, appropriate training must precede implementation of the new procedures to prevent backsliding. Next, a return to the "plan" phase of the PDCA cycle is required to search for new countermeasures to further improve the QI story process.

WORTH THE EFFORT

QI stories can be used to get management to manage with data instead of opinion and guesswork and to think in terms of the PDCA cycle. QI stories take time to construct; however, the time spent is well worth the payoff of increased likelihood of process improvements.

BIBLIOGRAPHY

Deming, W. E. *Out of the Crisis* (Cambridge: M.I.T., Center for Advanced Engineering Study, 1986).

Gitlow, H., and S. Gitlow. *The Deming Guide to Quality and Competitive Position* (Englewood Cliffs, NJ: Prentice-Hall, 1987).

Imai, M., *Kaizen—The Key to Japan's Competitive Success* (New York: Random House, 1986).

12

Continuous Improvement: Methods and Madness

Alan J. Peterson and R. Dan Reid

SUMMARY

No matter who you talk to, everyone (or so it seems) has a different interpretation of continuous improvement. From supplier organizations to the auditors that assess them, the definitions vary widely. It's almost enough to drive a sane person mad.

To get a handle on the basic concept of continuous improvement (and a grip on our sanity), it makes sense to define continuous improvement by demonstrating how it can be differentiated from corrective action and innovation, the two concepts with which it is most often confused.

Why is this differentiation important? Improvements in quality, service and price can, and do, take place as the system corrects problems; corrective actions eliminate special causes and thereby stabilize processes. But once the processes (a process) have achieved stability (and acceptable capability and performance), the process (or system) has only achieved a minimum, or what is considered to be the expected, quality level for any process or system. By achieving a stable process along with acceptable capability and performance the customers' needs have been met. Trouble is, customers want their expectations to be exceeded and, in fact, they want to be delighted! Corrective actions do not produce delight. Only innovation and continuous improvement produce results that exceed expectations and may lead to delight.

Innovation has drawbacks for the supplier. Yes, it can produce delight, but it is reliant upon capital expenditures, specialists, research and development, and is most often sporadic in producing outcomes.

Continuous improvement is characterized by having all employees involved, producing daily improvement, focusing on product characteristics, and by being evolutionary rather than revolutionary.

KEY WORDS

Continuous improvement, corrective action, innovation.

INTRODUCTION

To get a handle on the basic concept of continuous improvement, it makes sense to define continuous improvement by demonstrating how it can be differentiated from corrective action and innovation, the two concepts with which it is most often confused. This paper discusses each concept and illustrates through applications and examples how they differ. The focus, of course, is to set continuous improvement apart from the other two; particularly to set it apart from corrective action.

There is a sense of frustration felt by the groups (and individuals in those groups) who concern themselves with developing effective and efficient supplier quality systems. The frustration stems from the misunderstandings that surround continuous improvement. Managers in charge of supplier development often observe that corrective action is thought to be synonymous with continuous improvement. Though this observation is anecdotal, the perception is that the misunderstanding is prevalent in supplier organizations, and, compounding the situation, the outcome of the misunderstanding is often accepted by the auditors who assess the suppliers' quality systems. Consequently, the misunderstanding is not corrected.

SO WHAT?

Though some may argue, the main problem with not being able to differentiate continuous improvement from innovation and corrective action is that the organization may never really systematically improve. They may very well continue to fight fires, which is the modus operandi of corrective action and/or they will, in all likelihood, wait for the magic pill of innovation. Either way, the chances for measured, systematic improvement are nonexistent.

So what's the big deal? Some improvement will take place if one mixes all quality improvement concepts in one big definition; after all, the problems are getting fixed and ways of getting faster, bigger, better are being looked into. But that is exactly the problem; to correct only, means that the process will only reach stability, it will not truly improve. Stability is not improvement; stability is (and should be) the baseline expectation of any customer. Customers of an airline expect (and rightly so) that the process of getting them from one destination to another is stable; particularly, the stability of the part of the process where they are 30,000 feet from terra firma.

Imagine for a minute that you are a maker of a complex gadget that is highly scrutinized by both consumers and lawmakers. The gadget is subjected to the fickleness of the buyer as well as the restraints of the regulators. Changes have to be made often to keep the buyer buying and to keep the regulators happy. And you are not alone; many other groups are producing the same gadget, trying to entice the same buyers and trying to please the same regulators.

As the maker of this complex gadget, you have found, after years of experience, that you simply cannot make all the things necessary to build the gadget in one building or even one group of buildings, nor is it a good idea that you do. You need to have groups with their own buildings, independent of your group, make 70 to 80 percent of the things that, when assembled by you, form the final complicated gadget; the final complicated gadget that you must sell and warranty.

You are dependent upon the consistent quality of the parts assembled by you, the timeliness of their arrival, their conformity to your specifications, and the price required for each. For you, the group responsible for the entire gadget, to improve each part of the system you first must have a stable process. As long as there are fires to put out, they will require the most attention and energy by you and the rest of the system. The gadget, and the process of making it, will not improve, at least in any consistent and predictable manner; you and the system will struggle simply to not lose any ground.

SO WHAT NEEDS TO BE DONE?

Corrective Action

The first necessary component of establishing a system that knows, understands, and does continuous improvement, is to be sure what continuous improvement is not. Continuous improvement is not corrective action.

True, there is a continuum of quality improvement that includes corrective actions and continuous improvement, but one stops where the other starts.

According to ANSI/ISO/ASQC A8402-1994 the definition for a corrective action is, "action taken to eliminate the causes of an existing nonconformity (a nonfulfilment of a specified requirement), defect (nonfulfilment of an intended usage requirement of reasonable expectation, including one concerned with safety) or other undesirable situation in order to prevent recurrence."

Corrective actions concern themselves with nonconformities and defects. Corrective actions deal with those things that are not acceptable. Corrective actions move the system toward where it should be as a minimum expectation. Corrective actions work to eliminate special causes, which must be eliminated before a process is considered stable.

INNOVATION

Innovation is something newly introduced: a new method, custom, or device, or perhaps a change in the way of doing things. Innovation is generally considered to be on the opposite end of the continuum from corrective action, but it does hold some of its key characteristics. Like corrective action, innovation's intended outcome is to improve quality. Like corrective action, it can cause a variable amount of improvement, from small to huge improvements. And, like corrective action, it can make you feel like you are making efforts toward improvements, and are actually improving to some extent; but, at the end of the day, you did not get where you wanted, or needed, to go.

CONTINUOUS IMPROVEMENT

Continuous improvement is perhaps most succinctly described in the Quality System Requirements QS-9000 Third Edition, element 4.2.5—Continuous Improvement (1998). The third note of the section states: "For those product characteristics and process parameters that can be evaluated using variable data (data where measurements are used for analysis), continuous improvement means optimizing the characteristics and parameters at a target value and reducing variation around the value. For those product characteristics and process parameters that can only be evaluated using attribute data (data that can be counted for recording and analysis—attributes data are usually gathered in the form of nonconforming units or of nonconformities), continuous improvement is not possible until characteristics are conforming. If attribute data results do not equal zero defects, it is by definition nonconforming product. Improvements made in these situations are by definition corrective actions, not continuous improvement." Continuing in that same element, it is stated, ". . . continuous improvement [shall be undertaken] in processes that have demonstrated stability, acceptable capability and performance."

CONCLUSION

Table 12.1 compares and contrasts the three concepts discussed in this paper: continuous improvement, corrective action, and innovation. The table provides a good summary of the discussion.

Quality improvement, if it is to take place in a system, must have all three processes in place. But each must be understood and differentiated if the system is to reach a state of consistent and predictable improvements.

Continuous improvement is the tool that delivers the most bang for the buck. It does not require the specialized resources required by both corrective action and innovation and it does produce results.

Table 12.1 Improvement.

	Improvement Activities	**Examples/Intent/Characteristics**
	Innovation	Capital expenditure R&D Relies on specialists Sporadic breakthroughs Revolutionary Project-based
OK	Continuous improvement	Product (part) characteristics, especially special characteristics (within specifications) Variable data are mandatory Small increments All employees are involved Evolutionary May be project-based Daily improvements
Not OK	Corrective action	Problem resolution (4.1.4.1.1) Product characteristics are out of specifications Assigned case by case as required Improvements that lead to product and process conformance Attribute data

Whether you manage a QS-9000 compliant system or are part of a TQM implementation, you need to understand that continuous improvement is not corrective action. Affordable improvements can be achieved to the delight of the customer with properly focused continuous improvement efforts.

REFERENCE

ISO 8402:1994 "Quality Management and Quality Assurance Vocabulary." *Quality System Requirements QS-9000,* 3rd ed. Southfield, MI: Automotive Industry Action Group (AIAG), March, 1998.

13

COQ Systems:
The Right Stuff

Dean L. Bottorff

Of the numerous quality tools that have come and gone, cost-of-quality (COQ) systems have stood the test of time as a bona fide tool for managing quality improvement in an organization. For thousands of companies, including many Malcolm Baldrige National Quality Award recipients, COQ systems marked the beginning of their prosperous journeys into quality.[1]

By combining a powerful philosophy with a practical technique, COQ systems make quality improvement justifiable for just about every business organization, regardless of size, because such systems do not require a major investment of resources. In a typical midsize company, representatives from three or four departments, including a key representative from the accounting department, can establish a COQ system after about 20 to 30 hours of meetings, if approached properly. Once established, one person only has to spend about 20 to 30 hours per year to maintain the program (this is exclusive of the quality improvement program).

When many companies begin their quality journeys, it is not unusual for them to discover COQ estimates averaging between 20% and 35% of sales revenue. Likewise, it is not unusual for them to lower their COQ by 10% per year or, as a percentage of sales, by as much as 2% per year.[2] Year after year, managers with relatively little formal training in quality deliver significant quality improvements and cost savings with their COQ systems.

Eventually, a COQ program's success creates the need for advanced quality techniques if the same pace of improvement is to be maintained. Nonetheless, the COQ system's effectiveness to jump-start other quality improvement efforts justifies its continued use.

COQ systems' longevity as a proven quality management tool cannot be attributed to their ease of use. Implementing COQ programs is one of the most difficult and critical undertakings in the quality journey. While there have been many successes, there have also been many failures. Two common reasons for failures are:

• *Relying on an individual rather than on a team.* The skill set required to implement a COQ system generally exceeds the individual skills of most managers because COQ is not about individuals. COQ is about working effectively in teams, approaching problems conceptually, building a common language, developing common measurements, and supporting cross-functional solutions. Any organization that attempts to implement a COQ system exclusively through an individual will most likely find its system unsuccessful.

• *The culture of an organization does not support teamwork.* Some organizations foster environments where teams can thrive; others do not. In this way, COQ has served as a cultural litmus test for many companies. Those culturally able to support COQ teams continue on their quality journey while those culturally unable often abandon the journey altogether.

Whether an organization is just getting started in its quality journey or renewing its commitment along the way, an understanding of COQ's historical context, current relevance, technique, skill requirements, and broader process requirements will help it improve its chances of success and help employees effectively rise to the challenges.

THE HISTORICAL CONTEXT

COQ systems measure the cost of poor quality in an organization. Developed in the early 1950s by J. M. Juran and other leaders in the quality profession, the technique was widely published in quality literature by 1960.[3] ASQC's Quality Costs Committee was formed in 1961 to formally develop the technique and to promote its use in industry. By 1963, the U.S. Department of Defense demonstrated its commitment to COQ when it issued MIL-Q-9858A, a military standard that required many contractors to formally measure their quality costs.

Today, COQ systems are regarded as an essential tool in managing quality. In fact, COQ has been incorporated into the bodies of knowledge of the certification programs of such professional societies as ASQ, the Institute of Management Accountants, and the American Production and Inventory Control Society. In addition, numerous business and engineering graduate schools worldwide have integrated COQ into their curricula.

CURRENT RELEVANCE

COQ is a quality performance measure. Similar to other quality performance measures (such as failure costing, nonfinancial process control, Six Sigma conformance, and customer satisfaction measures), it can be linked directly to the success of an organization. There are three empirical yet robust sources of evidence from the quality field that support this claim:

1. Performance measures help justify continuing investments in quality improvement programs. Performance measures do not measure promises. They measure facts about what a program has delivered. The ability to deliver results, especially when backed up by facts, is the key to winning renewed funding for a program in most organizations.

2. A solid history of sustained investments in quality improvement appears to be a universal trait among firms recognized for their world-class quality. Most of the Baldrige Award winners, for example, have been on their formal quality journeys for more than 10 years and most have several quality performance measures.[4]

3. The quality level associated with that of companies winning the Baldrige Award has been linked to superior business performance. In his article "The Baldie Play," B. Ray Helton showed that Baldrige Award winners, on average, experienced sales growth, market share growth, improved earnings per share, and significantly higher stock valuations than companies in the Standard & Poor's 500 as a whole.[5] Consequently, COQ or other kinds of quality performance measures can help companies ensure long-term financial well-being.

THE TECHNIQUE

COQ systems measure total quality costs, which can be broken into four components:

- *Prevention costs.* These discretionary costs are the costs incurred to keep appraisal and failure costs to a minimum—in other words, they lead to the reduction of the other three quality cost components. Prevention costs are associated with such activities as quality planning, training, supplier reviews, statistical process control, and corrective action.

- *Appraisal costs.* These discretionary costs are the costs incurred to determine the degree of conformance to quality requirements. Appraisal costs are associated with such activities as inspections, tests, audits, process data collection, and outside certifications or endorsements.

- *Internal failure costs.* These costs are related to the defects that are caught and corrected before the customer receives the product or service. Internal failure costs are associated with such activities as redesign, scrap, rework, repair, troubleshooting, extra operations, and downgraded product values.

- *External failure costs.* These costs are related to the defects found after the customer receives the product or service. External failure costs are associated with such activities as complaint investigations, returned goods, retrofit costs, penalties due to nonconformances, warranty claims, lost customer goodwill, and lost sales.

The idea that failure costs can be reduced through marginal, discretionary investments in prevention and even appraisal activities is largely what makes COQ accounting so meaningful to an organization. The ratios between the four cost components, total quality cost, and total sales provide management with two valuable insights. First, these ratios reveal how much opportunity exists for quality improvement. Second, they help steer ongoing quality improvement efforts toward the greatest possible economic payoff. Part of what makes steering so critical to the quality program is its link to management's ongoing financial commitment to quality.

SKILL REQUIREMENTS

The COQ technique in and of itself is not complicated. The theory of COQ can be learned and understood by just about anyone. The challenge lies in its implementation.

One common problem in implementing a COQ system is finding individuals with sufficient accounting skills, quality management skills, and interpersonal skills. Accounting skills are needed to gain credibility with the controller and upper management. Quality management skills are needed to coordinate the COQ system with a broader quality improvement process. Interpersonal skills, perhaps the most challenging of the three, are necessary if compromise and consensus on cost items are to occur.

While COQ systems have been implemented by many nonaccounting individuals, the issues of consistency and credibility have often plagued their efforts. Gaining credibility with all participants (especially upper management) and providing sufficient consistency are more important to the success of the COQ process than theoretical correctness. An abundance of literature from both the quality and accounting professions recognizes that COQ efforts are generally best served when the accounting department and the controller are heavily involved.[6]

BROADER PROCESS REQUIREMENTS

Implementing a COQ system requires more than simply applying a new technique because it is a demanding management process. The COQ leader must implement the system within the time and resource constraints outlined by upper management while meeting the requirements of not only the COQ system but also those of the quality management system. While trying to achieve these objectives, the COQ leader often discovers that it is insufficient to function just as a technician within the COQ process. For the process to succeed, the COQ leader must facilitate a high degree of participation and support from all parties involved. The leader must have the ability to:

- Work with cross-functional teams

- Gain consensus on which direct and indirect quality cost items should be included in the system

- Develop reporting methods that meet the specific needs of the information users

- Earn the trust and support of all management levels toward the COQ and quality improvement systems

Those who have successfully implemented COQ systems will attest that it is an extremely challenging undertaking requiring a high degree of motivation and personal commitment.

AVOID THE ROADBLOCKS AND REAP THE BENEFITS

As just shown, implementing COQ systems is not an easy task. Roadblocks frequently encountered include:

- Management does not allocate sufficient time and resources.

- Since the COQ system is usually not entirely compatible with existing product costing systems, it often requires the administration of a separate system.

- The "softness" of indirect quality cost data makes using those data controversial.

- Using only out-of-pocket, or direct, quality costs can result in management investing too little in prevention activities. This generally results in lower reductions in quality costs than was expected, causing management to lessen its financial support for the COQ and quality improvement systems.

- Lack of training in quality concepts and group facilitation methods makes it difficult to lead or participate in cross-functional teams.

- Quality concepts are often inhibited by financial concepts. For example, quality costs are not budgeted, but rather managed and reduced by investing in prevention activities.

- When subjected to the pressures of the budgeting process, harmful quality cost trade-offs are hard to resist without a strong commitment from upper management.

- If a controller lacks the training or commitment to quality management concepts, he or she might allocate fewer resources to the COQ system, eroding the accounting department's critical role in COQ.

If companies can avoid such roadblocks and implement successful COQ systems, the benefits are numerous. The advantages of having a COQ system include:

- Quality data are more readily accepted because they are gathered and analyzed with the accounting department in a team environment.

- The COQ system aids in the evaluation of capital investment alternatives.

- The COQ system helps justify and steer investments in prevention activities, which lowers quality costs. It also helps justify and steer other quality improvement efforts and investments.

- The COQ system leads to the development of more advanced performance measures in the areas of customer satisfaction, production, and design to better target indirect quality costs.

- Return on investment and sales are improved while reducing costs.

A COQ system is a relevant quality management process that organizations can use to initiate and sustain their quality improvement efforts. The system's success should not be judged by traditional cost accounting standards nor by newer performance measurement technologies. Instead, its success should be judged by quality cost reductions over time and by management's commitment to it and other quality improvement initiatives.

ENDNOTES

1. L. Carr and T. Tyson, "Planning Quality Cost Expenditures," *Management Accounting* (October 1992).
2. P. B. Crosby, *Quality without Tears* (New York: McGraw-Hill, 1984): 85–86, 149–54, and J. M. Juran, editor, and F. M. Gryna, associate editor, *Juran's Quality Control Handbook,* 4th ed. (New York: McGraw-Hill, 1988): 4.2–4.29.
3. J. Campanella and the ASQC Quality Costs Committee, *Principles of Quality Costs,* 2nd ed. (Milwaukee: ASQC Quality Press, 1990), and Juran and Gryna, *Juran's Quality Control Handbook.*
4. L. Carr and T. Tyson, "Planning Quality Cost Expenditures," and K. Bemowski, "1994 Baldrige Award Recipients Share Expertise," *Quality Progress* (February 1995): 35–40.
5. B. R. Helton, "The Baldie Play," *Quality Progress* (February 1995): 43–45.
6. T. Pyzdek and R. Berger, *Quality Engineering Handbook* (Milwaukee: ASQC Quality Press, 1992); T. Tyson, "Quality and Profitability," *Management Accounting* (November 1987); and Campanella and the ASQC Quality Costs Committee, *Principles of Quality Costs.*

BIBLIOGRAPHY

Boer, G. "Making Accounting a Value Added Activity." *Management Accounting* (August 1991).
Cupello, J. "New Paradigm for Measuring TQM Progress." *Quality Progress* (May 1994).

Edmonds, T. "Analyzing Quality Costs." *Management Accounting* (November 1989).

Freedman, J. "TQM Applied to Financial Management." *Management Accounting* (October 1992).

Godfrey, J. "Controlling Quality Costs." *Management Accounting* (March 1988).

Rose, K. "A Performance Measurement Model." *Quality Progress* (February 1995).

Roth, H. "What Are the Costs of Variability?" *Management Accounting* (June 1994).

Sellenheim, M. "Performance Measurement." *Management Accounting* (September 1994).

Shea, J. E. "TQM: Are Cost Accountants Meeting the Challenge?" *Management Accounting* (April 1994).

Zangwill, W. "Ten Mistakes CEOs Make About Quality." *Quality Progress* (June 1994).

14

The Tools of Quality

Part II: Cause-and-Effect Diagrams

J. Stephen Sarazen

"Quality begins with education and ends with education." These words, attributed to the late Kaoru Ishikawa, sum up a principal philosophy of quality. To improve processes, you must continuously strive to obtain more information about those processes and their output.

One unique and valuable tool for accomplishing this goal is the cause-and-effect diagram. This tool was first developed in 1943 by Ishikawa at the University of Tokyo; he used it to explain to a group of engineers from the Kawasaki Steel Works how various factors could be sorted and related.

The cause-and-effect diagram is a method for analyzing process dispersion. The diagram's purpose is to relate causes and effects. It is also known as the Ishikawa diagram and the fishbone diagram (because the completed diagram resembles the skeleton of a fish). Whatever it's called, the tool is certainly one of the most elegant and widely used of the so-called seven QC tools.

It has been my experience that this tool is not only invaluable for virtually any issue requiring attention, but can be easily learned by people at all levels of the organization and applied immediately.

There are three basic types of cause-and-effect diagrams: dispersion analysis, production process classification, and cause enumeration. Figure 14.1

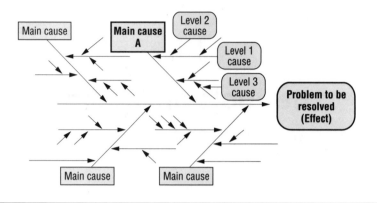

Figure 14.1 The basic cause-and-effect diagram.

depicts the basic format for the cause-and-effect diagram. Note the hierarchical relationship of the effect to the main causes and their subsequent relationship to the sub-causes. For example, main cause A has a direct relationship to the effect. Each of the sub-causes is related in terms of its level of influence on the main cause.

While a cause-and-effect diagram can be developed by an individual, it is best when used by a team. (Considering how well suited this tool is for team applications, it is not surprising that Ishikawa is the father of quality circles.) One of the most valuable attributes of this tool is that it provides an excellent means to facilitate a brainstorming session. It will focus the participants on the issue at hand and immediately allow them to sort ideas into useful categories, especially when the dispersion analysis or process classification methods are used.

DISPERSION ANALYSIS

Let's assume you are having difficulties with customer complaints. Let us further assume that you are able to pull together about seven individuals from various functions throughout the organization. Each of these individuals has sound knowledge of the overall business as well as an area of specific expertise. This team will provide a good example of the way to construct a cause-and-effect diagram using the dispersion analysis methods. There are three steps:

Step 1. It is quite simple to construct the diagram. First, determine the quality characteristic you wish to improve—perhaps customer satisfaction. You must be certain there is consensus when you write the problem statement. For example: "customers are dissatisfied."

Write this brief statement of fact on a large sheet of paper, a white board, or similar area. Write it on the right side, center of the page, and draw a box around it with an arrow running to it. This problem statement constitutes the effect.

In a manufacturing process, you might use a specific characteristic of a product as the effect, such as a problem with paste thickness in a surface mount line, poor paint coverage, or welding errors. In an administrative or service area, you might use customer complaints, decreased sales volume, or increased accounts receivable past due.

Step 2. Now the team must generate ideas as to what is causing the effect, contributing to customer dissatisfaction. The causes are written as branches flowing to the main branch. Figure 14.2 shows the main cause headings resulting from an actual session in a service/distribution business. In this case, the team determined five areas—product quality, service, order processing system, distribution system, and order fulfillment—as the main potential causes of dissatisfied customers. If there is difficulty in determining the main branches or causes, use generic headings—such as method, machine, people, materials, environment, or training—to help start the team.

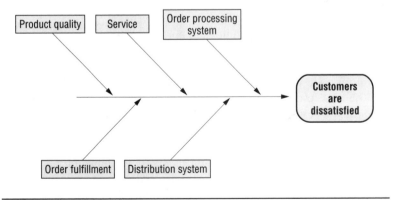

Figure 14.2 The main cause headings.

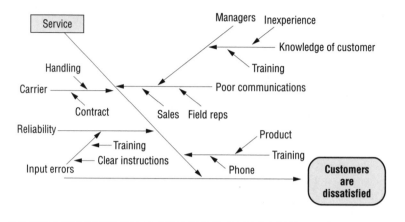

Figure 14.3   A detailed look at one main course.

Step 3. The next step is to brainstorm all the possible causes of problems in each of the major cause categories. These ideas are captured and applied to the chart as sub-causes. It is important to continually define and relate causes to each other. It is acceptable to repeat sub-causes in several places if the team feels there is a direct, multiple relationship. This effort will ensure a complete diagram and a more enlightened team.

Returning to Figure 14.2, you can see that the team identified five main causes of customer dissatisfaction. Now the team members must ask themselves, "What could contribute to each of these five main causes?" Once several sub-causes have been identified, the team continues asking the same question until the lowest-level causes are discovered.

Figure 14.3 shows the completed portion of the diagram for one of the main causes: service. The team identified reliability issues, carrier issues (for example, a trucking company), poor communications, and lack of, or poor, training.

The next level of causes is identified by asking the question "What could cause a problem in these areas?" In the case of the poor communications, the team focused on functions and jobs—salespeople, field representatives, and managers—as potential causes. You can see that lack of knowledge of the customer can cause managers to communicate poorly. Subsequently you can see that inexperience and training can be two key contributors to a manager's lack of customer knowledge. Thus, there are six levels of causes in this example.

PROCESS CLASSIFICATION

Another type of diagram is known as the process classification diagram. I prefer to eliminate the word "production" from the chart title because it has a manufacturing ring to it. From my experience, this tool is as valuable in service-based businesses as it is in manufacturing companies. After all, every product or service is the result of a process.

Although the basic process for constructing this type of diagram is similar to the one used for dispersion analysis, there are some differences. These differences are driven by the application. For the process classification method, you identify the flow of the process you wish to improve and then list key quality-influencing characteristics at each of the steps.

Step 1. Identify the process and develop a flow diagram of the primary sequential steps. For example, in a generic selling process, the following steps might be identified: make initial customer contact, develop an understanding of customer needs, provide information to the customer, follow up, close the sale, and follow up on the sale.

Step 2. Now add all the things that might influence the quality of each step. Use the method described in the previous section. Brainstorming with a team of knowledgeable people will make the finished diagram more like the actual process.

Figure 14.4 is an example of a completed process classification diagram. As you can see, the intent is to take the cause and effect to the lowest level to understand all the contributing factors to improve the process.

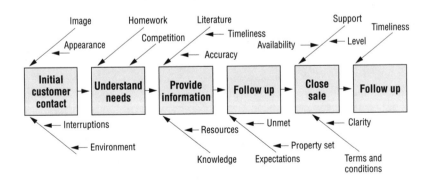

Figure 14.4 A completed process classification diagram.

It is also advisable to consider the connecting steps from process step to process step. Everywhere there is a handoff from one step to the next, there are likely to be possible causes of dispersion. Many opportunities for improvement can be found in these areas.

CAUSE ENUMERATION

The cause enumeration method involves simply brainstorming all possible causes and listing them in the order they are offered. Once the brainstorm has exhausted itself, the team begins the process of grouping the causes as it did for the dispersion analysis diagram. The end result looks exactly the same.

I have found this process can be enhanced dramatically using the affinity diagram process. It is a valuable method for gaining insight and organization of ideas. Basically, the brainstorm is conducted by capturing all ideas on cards or sticky notes. Each card should contain only one idea. The cards are then arranged in groups and subgroups. Cards that have an affinity for one another are placed together. Once it is completed, the affinity diagram provides the basis for the cause-and-effect diagram.

FILLETING THE FISH

Understanding processes, using teams, and identifying areas of opportunity are excellent ways to move toward continuous improvement while solving some of today's tough issues. But they are only the beginning. To obtain the full value from the cause-and-effect diagram, it must be turned into action. It is therefore wise to quantify the problem and as many of the causes as possible. Once this has been done, the business can determine the priority areas to be addressed and can track improvements.

In the earlier example, the business was able to quantify the problem of customer dissatisfaction by measuring several key parameters, including number of calls about problems, number of requests to return material for specific reasons, and receivables aging.

In the areas where sub-causes were identified, various parts of the organization were surveyed to determine the primary areas of opportunity for addressing the causes identified by the cause-and-effect diagram. For example, one need was for training in simple statistical problem-solving methods. This need was quantified not only by the number of people needing training, but also by the results of the training applications.

As the team and business move to quantify the causes, other tools play key roles. Pareto analysis, histograms, control charts, scatter plots, and multivariate analysis might be particularly valuable.

HINTS AND CREATIVE USES

Here are some helpful hints for facilitating or participating in a cause-and-effect exercise.

1. *Consider the big picture.* When constructing a cause-and-effect diagram, think about the issue at hand in its broadest sense. Consider the environment, inside the business and externally; politics, including government policies if appropriate; employee issues; and external factors, such as the local or national economy. Granted, some of these areas are well beyond the control of the team. Nevertheless, there is a benefit to understanding the impact of such factors.

2. *Facilitation.* Facilitating a cause-and-effect session is very challenging. It is similar to facilitating any brainstorming session except that the thoughts must be written in a particular place as opposed to being listed. The facilitator must listen to the ideas of the participants, capture those thoughts in only one or two words, and write them in the appropriate position on the chart. This last step is the tricky part. My recommendation is to have the participants decide where the cause should be written. This approach helps ensure that the correct location is chosen and removes some of the burden from the facilitator.

3. *Review and embellishment.* To ensure that the diagram is complete, have each member of the team review it the next day or have them show it to one or two additional people to obtain their opinion. Use your discretion in deciding whether to use second parties on very technical issues or problems unique to a particular job or area.

4. *Broad-based participation.* If you want to add a creative flair to your development effort and, at the same time, encourage broad-based participation from your group or organization, try this. Hang a large white board or sheet of butcher paper in an accessible location. Ask the group or a manager to identify a problem that needs to be addressed. Write that problem statement in the "head of the fish" and draw the arrow to it. Now invite the entire organization to participate in developing the diagram over a certain time frame—say two weeks. You will be amazed how many people will really get into working and understanding the process.

THE BENEFITS AND WEAKNESSES OF EACH CAUSE-AND-EFFECT DIAGRAM

- **Diagram type: Dispersion analysis**

  Key benefits:
  1. Helps organize and relate factors.
  2. Provides a structure for brainstorming.
  3. Involves everyone.
  4. It's fun.

  Potential drawbacks:
  1. Might be difficult to facilitate if developed in true brainstorming fashion.
  2. Might become very complex; requires dedication and patience.

- **Diagram type: Process classification**

  Key benefits:
  1. Provides a solid sequential view of the process and the factors that influence each step.
  2. Might help determine functional ownership for the work to be done in improvement.

  Potential drawbacks:
  1. It is sometimes difficult to identify or demonstrate interrelationships.

- **Diagram type: Cause enumeration**

  Key benefits:
  1. Easy to facilitate.
  2. Provides in-depth list of all possible causes.

  Potential drawbacks:
  1. The added step of creating an affinity diagram might add time to the process.
  2. The final diagram might be difficult to draw because of the random output of the brainstorming session.

The obvious drawback to this approach is that you miss the brainstorming opportunity. However, reading what others have written in the diagram will generate ideas. The commitment that must be made is to take the input and act on it.

While this might sound a little out of the ordinary, I can tell you from firsthand experience that it works. I trained a vice president's staff in the use of cause-and-effect diagrams several years ago and suggested this approach. We hung a large white board outside his office and began writing a new issue on it every couple of weeks. Some of his people had been trained in the technique; many had not. The end result was that more than 100 people contributed to the first few diagrams and his staff was provided with invaluable information, insight, and suggestions for improving processes.

5. *Working toward the desired result.* I have found it very useful to state the desired result—rather than a problem—in the head of the fish. For example, instead of writing "customers are dissatisfied," write "100% customer satisfaction." The exercise now focuses on finding means to achieve this goal rather than working the problem. Many of the findings will be the same but some unique approaches might find their way onto the chart.

The work could also be stated as "how to" arrive at some desired result. A few years ago, I trained a group of elementary teachers in the use of cause-and-effect diagrams. They needed to get students to perform as a team. Rather than trying to solve the problem of why students didn't perform as a team, we developed a cause-and-effect diagram using the statement "What makes an effective/winning team?"

Many of the teachers returned to their classes and used this exercise with students. The students wanted to be winners. Now they were asked to identify all the attributes of a winning team, and they were able to do so. They learned that it takes a lot of hard work and dedication.

The teachers then posted the completed diagram every day and, when the students did not demonstrate the behavior required to be a winner (in their own words), the diagram served as a reminder. This process has also worked for business issues such as how to improve competitiveness and how to ensure statistical process control (SPC) applications will follow training.

UNDERSTANDING PROCESSES

In the past decade, quality has gained recognition as the competitive imperative for all businesses. The root of all quality improvement lies in understanding processes. Many existing tools assist managers, engineers, and others in this work. You need not always look for the newest tool, software, or management theory to construct a sound foundation on which to build improvements. If you are looking for a tool that fosters teamwork, educates users, identifies lowest-level issues on which to work, helps show a true picture of the process, guides discussion, can be used for virtually any issue your business might face, and is fun, look no further than this 46-year-old tool called the cause-and-effect diagram.

BIBLIOGRAPHY

Ishikawa, K. *Guide to Quality Control*. Tokyo: Asia Productivity Organization, 1986.

Wadsworth, H. M., K. S. Stephens, and A. B. Godfrey. *Modern Methods for Quality Control and Improvement*. New York: John Wiley & Sons, 1986.

15

The Tools of Quality

Part IV: Pareto Charts

John T. Burr

The Pareto principle is several things. It is a state of nature, the way things happen around us. It is also a way of managing projects. Finally, it is a process—a way of thinking about problems that affect us.

STATE OF NATURE

The Pareto principle was first defined by Joseph Juran in 1950.[1] During his early work, Juran found that there was a "maldistribution of quality losses." Not liking such a long name, he named the principle after Vilfredo Pareto, a 19th-century Italian economist. Pareto found that a large share of the wealth was owned by relatively few people—a maldistribution of wealth.

Juran found this was true in many areas of life, including quality technologies. In 1975, he published a retraction of his use of Pareto's name in an article called "The Non-Pareto Principle; Mea Culpa."[2] Nevertheless, the term "Pareto principle" is here to stay.

In simplest terms, the Pareto principle suggests that most effects come from relatively few causes. In quantitative terms, 80% of the problems come from 20% of the machines, raw materials, or operators. Also, 80% of the wealth is controlled by 20% of the people. It is well known that 80% of the funds contributed to charity come from only 20% of the possible sources. Finally, 80% of scrap or rework quality costs come from 20% of the possible causes.

In the quality technologies, Juran calls the 20% of causes the "vital few."[3] He originally called the rest of the causes the "trivial many." However, he and other quality professionals came to understand that there are no trivial problems on the manufacturing floor and that all problems deserve management's attention. Juran has since renamed the trivial many the "useful many."[4,5] But no matter the labels, the Pareto principle is one of the most powerful decision tools available.

A MANAGEMENT TOOL

Data can be collected on the state of scrap, rework, warranty claims, maintenance time, raw material usage, machine downtime, or any other cost associated with manufacturing a product or providing a service. In the case of providing a service, for example, data can be collected on wasted time, number of jobs that have to be redone, customer inquiries, and number of errors. The data should be organized as illustrated in Figure 15.1. The most frequent (highest cost) cause is placed on the left, and the other causes are added in descending order of occurrence.

Figures 15.2 and 15.3 are examples of the Pareto diagram. It is quite obvious which causes or problems have to be reduced or eliminated to have any real impact on the system.

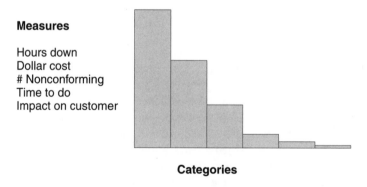

Measures

Hours down
Dollar cost
Nonconforming
Time to do
Impact on customer

Categories

Causes, Products, Manufacturing lines, Operators,
Administrative areas, Equipment, Cost centers

Figure 15.1 Generalized Pareto diagram.

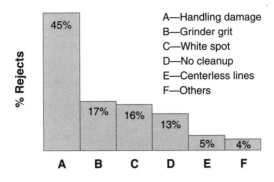

Figure 15.2　Strut rod rejects.

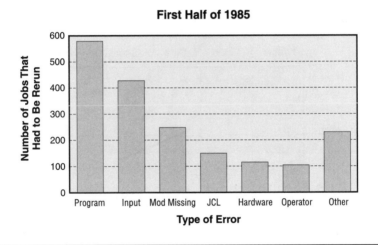

Figure 15.3　Information systems.

A double Pareto diagram, as in Figure 15.4, can be used to contrast two products, areas, or shifts, or to look at a system before and after improvement.

In 1984, Jeffery Kalin, the manufacturing manager of a Hewlett Packard plant in Colorado Springs, stated that no one in his plant worked on a problem until they had developed a Pareto diagram. The diagram had to show that the problem being worked on by the team or the supervisor was the most important one at that time.[6]

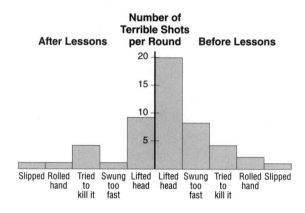

Figure 15.4   Poor golf shots.

Product	Problem					
	Labels	**Liner**	**Glue**	**Score**	**Warp**	
Box A	2		8			10
Box B	1		4			5
Box C		1		7	28	36
Box D		2			4	6
Box E	3		11			14
Box F	1				1	2
Box G	1					1
Box H				2		2
Box I	2					2
	10	3	23	9	33	

Figure 15.5   Problems with supplied boxes.

A WAY OF THINKING

Figure 15.5 is not a Pareto diagram, but a set of data on problems encountered with boxes used to package a number of different products. The most
frequent problem is on only one of the box types. Talking to the supplier
about the specific problem (warping on box C) will solve almost half of the

difficulties. This would also probably lead to less warping of box D, particularly if the boxes are made on the same line.

The next most frequent problem is glue. The problem occurs over several box types. Are they made on a common line? Is the glue or glue lot the same among these? If so, then a common cause has been identified and should be eliminated. The "mess" of incoming box supply problems will be reduced 80% by solving the two problems that have the most impact on quality. Of course, the improvement process is not stopped. The box manufacturing process should be continually analyzed using the Pareto diagram and the other tools of quality.

GETTING DATA FOR A PARETO DIAGRAM

American industries, manufacturing or service, are some of the greatest collectors of data in the world. Computers store vast amounts of data. Wastebaskets receive data daily. Data are there for the asking. The trick is to recognize what data are useful.

Occasionally data are not available. The situation might come up, for example, when a group must define a problem or look for a cause. With a process flow diagram and a cause-and-effect diagram visible and understandable to the group, each member must identify what he or she feels are the most important causes of the problem. This can be done in three ways:

1. Each person votes on the major categories in the cause-and-effect diagram. It might also be helpful to have each person explain why he or she is voting for a particular category. Often, consensus can be quickly reached; otherwise, a Pareto diagram of the votes should be made.

2. Each person has five votes and can place them anywhere on the cause-and-effect diagram. It is good to do this in conjunction with a break so that each person has time to come to the diagram to make the marks. By the way, a person could give all five votes to one cause if he or she felt very strongly about it. A Pareto diagram of the results should be made.

3. There is a nominal technique that is more involved, and particularly useful when there is a large number of possible causes and a good deal of uncertainty of which is important. This technique requires a large supply of 3 by 5 cards. All members get 10 cards (or five for shorter lists of causes). They write each of their top 10 choices on separate cards. They then pick the most likely cause. This card gets a 10. Next they pick the least likely cause and give it a 1. Then the next least likely cause is selected, a 2. Then the next most likely cause, a 9. This process is repeated back and forth until

all the causes are ranked. (It is easier to select the most and the least likely causes than to distinguish among the ones in the middle.) The numbers are then compiled for each cause and a Pareto diagram is constructed. This same technique can be used giving each person 100 points to distribute among the ranked cards. The same process of compiling is then used.

The Pareto principle describes the way causes occur in nature and human behavior. It can be a very powerful management tool for focusing personnel's effort on the problems and solutions that have the greatest potential payback.

ENDNOTES

1. J. M. Juran, "Pareto, Lorenz, Cournot, Bernoulli, Juran and Others," *Industrial Quality Control* (October 1950): 5.
2. J. M. Juran, "Then and Now in Quality Control," *Quality Progress* (May 1975): 8.
3. J. M. Juran, editor, *Quality Control Handbook*, 4th ed. (New York: McGraw-Hill, 1989).
4. J. M. Juran, *Juran on Planning for Quality* (New York: The Free Press, 1988).
5. J. M. Juran, *Juran on Leadership for Quality* (New York: The Free Press, 1989).
6. J. Kalin, Presentation to the Rochester Section, ASQC, on September 6, 1984.

16

Benchmarking: Achieving the Best in Class

Lynn Kaemmerer

ABSTRACT

Often times, people find the process of organizational benchmarking an onerous task, or, because they do not fully understand the nature of the process, end up with results that are less than stellar. This paper presents the challenges of benchmarking and reasons why benchmarking can benefit an organization in today's economy.

INTRODUCTION

This paper will explore three areas with regard to benchmarking: (1) what is involved in the benchmarking tool, including a formal definition of the process; (2) definitions for the various types of benchmarking (internal, competitive, and best-in-class); and (3) a discussion of how "formal" the study must be to be considered benchmarking.

WHAT IS BENCHMARKING?

In 1989, Robert Camp introduced a new tool called benchmarking into the total quality management world, it was quickly adopted by industrial organizations and also became a part of the Malcolm Baldrige National Quality Award (MBNQA). (In the 1996 criteria, competitive comparisons and benchmarking is worth 15 of the 75 points in Section 2.) Many organizations have used the tool to improve performance and, in some instances, to help win the MBNQA; these organizations include Xerox, L.L. Bean, IBM, Boeing, and Johnson & Johnson. However, Xerox has emerged as the leader in the benchmarking process. Therefore, as defined by Xerox:

> *Benchmarking is the continuous search for the best practices that lead to superior performance. It is a systematic way to measure performance capabilities of competitors or recognized leaders and then develop plans to meet or exceed these levels* (Steeples 1993, 268).

In layman's terms, it is the process of continuously measuring an organization's processes and methodologies against those of other organizations, with the challenge of improving its own performance. This includes identification and possible adoption of "best practices" both within and outside the organization's industry. This leads to benefits such as increased customer satisfaction, enhanced business performance, strengthened goal-setting, quality improvements, streamlining the business, and a stronger organizational culture. It provides an organization with a measurement system that fosters improvement.

Those of us in the quality profession recognize that our quality initiatives should spur the organization to a higher level of performance. We must set our sights on goals that stretch beyond the typical achievement and always strive for continuous improvement. Benchmarking can lead to dramatic gains (by helping an organization move beyond the traditional incremental improvements) and stimulate innovative thinking. In our present era of reengineering, the emphasis must shift away from just cost reductions and move toward evaluating organizational processes; this involves identifying and enhancing those processes that work and eliminating those that do not.

Peter Senge says that "learning organizations" (such as Xerox) are doing more than just copying practices used by others (Senge 1990, 11). Merely learning from the best practices does not necessarily institute learning as an event inside the organization. There must also be stimulation for those within the organization who are unable to see that there might be a different, better way of doing business. The first step in this process is accepting that change is needed and that benchmarking might possibly be a tool to assist an organization in achieving that goal. But, there is more to it than just the tool—it must go beyond information exchange to include effective change management. It goes deeply into the organization and the employees and helps create the motivation for change that then delivers the dramatic improvement the organization is seeking. It must drive the organization toward improvement because the current processes are not good enough!

Constant change is now regarded in the marketplace as a stimulation for the continuous improvement necessary for our organizations and, indeed, our economy, to endure and succeed in the coming century. Benchmarking can introduce a healthy uncertainty into the organization about the wisdom of sticking with the status quo, and can help the organization set the stretch goals that will lead it into the next century.

THREE TYPES OF BENCHMARKING

Internal Benchmarking

Many times this is used as the first step in the external benchmarking exercise. Internal benchmarking can provide a clear picture of the organization's problems, which then leads to proper identification of practices or processes to benchmark externally. It can be especially useful in organizations with two or more locations performing the same type of function.

McNair and Leibfried define internal benchmarking as "The comparison of similar operations or functions across a company, or with associated companies, in order to identify the level of service that is best practice within this common setting" (McNair and Leibfried 1992, 54).

Another way to view internal benchmarking is in terms of "baselines." In other words, establishing an internal benchmark means defining a process clearly and understanding the performance parameters of the process. It is crucial that an organization do internal benchmarks prior to doing benchmarks with other organizations. Failure to do this results in wasted time during the benchmarking process. Also, there is no normalized, common measure when comparing processes with the benchmarking partner. Failure to benchmark internal processes is one of the most common problems associated with benchmarking activities.

Competitive or Industry Benchmarking

This method prioritizes aspects of the business that are underperforming the competition. It looks for trends or patterns in the way specific resources are deployed for that specific industry. Competitive benchmarking looks outward to see how competitors are doing and compares itself to what it finds. It can help rank the areas for improvement as customer expectations are analyzed and current performance is measured against them.

Best-in-Class Benchmarking

This is the type of benchmarking most commonly referred to in the many articles and books written about benchmarking. It is focused outside the organization's specific industry and usually is only concerned with one function or role. Best-in-class benchmarking is always looking for new, innovative practices to model.

HOW FORMAL MUST THE PROCESS BE?

While there are many models for benchmarking with a multitude of process steps, I will briefly review the four phases that Camp, and McNair and Leibfried recommend (Camp 1989, McNair and Leibfried 1992). The experts in this field also state that the benchmarking study should meet a defined set of criteria and comparability (against the best-in-class). Validation by the benchmarking team is critical to the success of the study. Objectivity is important also, in that the instrument design, analysis, and implementation, and measures chosen must be done with rigor. When this is not done, the benchmark will fail.

Phase 1

This consists of an internal assessment of existing practice/process and sets a baseline for the benchmarking study. The identification of the organization's critical success factors is the first step in this phase. The benchmarking team should focus on identifying and understanding the drivers of the various processes—or what causes work to occur in the organization—which leads to understanding of the current process or practice. Above all, the team must be given the authority to implement the changes that its benchmarking study determines to be necessary.

Some questions to ask in Phase I are:

- Where are our performance gaps and what contributes to them?

- How good do we want to be?

- What do we need to do to surpass our best years to date?

Phase 2

Once a definition of the project is verbalized, baseline measurements are identified, and resources are distinguished, the team moves on to the instrument it will actually use. This is not only the data-gathering step, but also where the team identifies the outside organizations it will study. A logical starting point is with those organizations receiving industry or quality awards such as the MBNQA. Also, professional associations or The International Benchmarking Clearinghouse at The American Productivity and Quality Center in Houston can provide assistance.

Questions to ask in Phase 2 are:

- What will the organizational team study?
- What does the survey tool look like?
- How well are we doing compared to others?
- Who is the "best" at a particular practice or process?
- How do they do it?
- How can we adapt what they are doing to our organization?

Phase 3

A detailed analysis is done in this step. The benchmarking team must now scrutinize the information collected and determine where the performance gaps exist (that is, what does our organization do right or wrong?). This is where the real learning begins (Senge 1990). The team now must determine the differences between the baseline and the factors contributing to the benchmarked organization's excellence. And, in perhaps the most difficult step of the entire benchmarking exercise, the team must accept the realization that real change is needed and must begin here.

Phase 4

By this step in the process, the team has identified its own organization's success factors, analyzed the differences between internal processes or practices and those of best-in-class, and, ideally, spread the word throughout the organization that things need to be done differently. At this point, it is vital to implement methods of change that are capable of being measured objectively and that will spur continuous improvement and stretching the organization to be its best. Of course, monitoring the progress, communicating, recalibrating, and staring the benchmarking process once again occur within this step.

POSSIBLE PITFALLS

Many times, an organization's representatives will try to begin the benchmarking process before they are ready. Their belief is that once they have targeted the organizations they wish to benchmark, they merely set an appointment and visit the organization, asking for guidance about how to proceed. They talk about whatever their host wishes to discuss, or they only do a comparative analysis. While this is certainly a component of benchmarking, comparison alone will not drive change or focus on processes.

Another pitfall is when the organization's representatives are poorly prepared and are not able to ask the proper questions that will allow them to transfer the knowledge back to their organization. They may identify a few ideas that they come back and implement, but no measurements of success or improvement mechanisms are put into place. This is not to mention that the hosting organization's staff is generally willing to commit time to the endeavor with the goal of learning more about the visitor's processes—and with the possibility of adopting some ideas themselves! If the visitors are ill-prepared, the host staff will quickly recognize that, and the benchmarking effort will be a waste of both organizations' resources.

The organization's benchmarking team must be able to identify internal strengths and weaknesses, and recognize the processes that need special attention. If the parameters are too broad, the team will lose sight of the process that is critical to competition or the performance metrics that drive that particular process.

The team will need to communicate regularly with management and staff regarding its findings and progress. The importance of management's commitment to implementing the necessary changes cannot be overstated. Once benchmarking is underway and the organization's resources have been spent on the process, management support for the team's recommended changes is clearly the best practice.

CONCLUSION

The role of benchmarking in the quality process is to help organizations learn from a path that has worked for others and gain insight into ideas for combining existing resources. It has the potential to move an organization at a pace unmatched by any other quality tool. However, this is a process that, once started, is without end. It is a continuous journey to be the best.

REFERENCE LIST

Camp, R. C. *Benchmarking: The Search for Industry Best Practices That Lead to Superior Performance.* Milwaukee: ASQC Quality Press, 1989.

Lincoln, S., and A. Price. "What Benchmarking Books Don't Tell You." *Quality Progress* 28 (March 1996): 33–36.

McNair, C. J., and K. H. J. Leibfried. *Benchmarking, A Tool for Continuous Improvement.* New York: HarperCollins Publishing, 1992.

Senge, P. M. *The Fifth Discipline: The Art & Practice of the Learning Organization.* New York: Currency Doubleday, 1990.

Spendolini, M. J. *The Benchmarking Book.* New York: AMACOM Publishing, 1992.

Steeples, M. M. *The Corporate Guide to the Malcolm Baldrige National Quality Award.* Milwaukee: ASQC Quality Press, 1993.

Section IV

Integrated Case Studies in Quality Improvement Applications

I f we lived our lives in a silo, this book would have ended with the previous section. Rarely do we get the chance to do just one thing—to use just quality basics, to use teams for the sake of teams, or to use continuous improvement tools with no other goal than to use the tool. So this section ties it all together.

Whereas the articles in the previous sections addressed, for the most part, a single concept or tool, the articles in this section integrate a number of different facets of quality improvement. From this section, we can see how many different types of firms have used different approaches to quality improvement. This is, so to speak, where the rubber hits the road for the quality improvement journey!

In "More, Better, Faster from Total Quality Effort," David McCamey, Robert Boggs, and Linda Bayuk discuss how Proctor & Gamble used strong system leadership, customer focus, and the plan–do–check–act (PDCA) cycle to achieve dramatic cycle time reductions. Their article addresses specific actions that were undertaken in each phase of the PDCA cycle and discusses how those actions differed from traditional ways of doing business. The authors use a control chart to depict what the effect of these improvements looked like at various phases of implementation.

Timothy Clark and his son Andrew Clark discuss how the plan–do–study–act (PDSA) cycle was used to reduce variation on the basketball free-throw line in "Continuous Improvement on the Free-Throw Line." Their improvement process—documented in control charts and cause-and-effect diagrams—delightfully demonstrates that the PDSA cycle has applications that reach far beyond the workplace.

"Hospital Sets New Standard as Closure Approaches: Quality is Continuous," by Martha Dasch, discusses continuous improvement in the same-day surgery unit at a Naval hospital in Orlando, Florida. Dasch describes the improvement process, presents flowcharts of the before and after processes, and describes implementation pitfalls. This article drives home the point that continuous improvement is especially important in environments in which downsizing is a virtual certainty.

In "Quality Quest: One Company's Successful Attempt at Implementing TQM," Robert Drensek and Fred Grubb discuss one manufacturing firm's strategy for implementing Total Quality Management (TQM). Their approach, based on Crosby's four absolutes of quality, is an interesting case study about the different types of training that were conducted to ensure successful TQM implementation. Drensek and Grubb identify several barriers that arose and offer solutions to overcoming those barriers.

Art Davis provides a model for continuous improvement and customer satisfaction in "Continuous Quality Improvement at Williams-Bally Midway Games." Davis discusses how this international manufacturer of pinball and video entertainment games focused on improving customer satisfaction as a means to reducing cycle time, improving quality and reliability, and fostering a sense of continuous improvement throughout the company. He concludes with a discussion of numerous quality benefits that were realized as a result of the company's improvement activities.

In "Teamwork Brings Breakthrough Improvements in Quality and Climate," Steven Crom and Herbert France discuss the process one U.K. company used to reduce scrap by over 70 percent and realize almost a $1 million dollar annual cost savings by doing so. This company utilized a team-based approach to structured problem solving to transform their culture from a traditional, hierarchical one to one that fosters employee involvement. Crom and France identify several obstacles that were encountered during this transformation and discuss ways these obstacles were overcome.

Mary Murdock discusses how Mary Washington Hospital (Virginia) implemented a continuous improvement program in "Continuous Improvement of Emergency Care and Services." Murdock describes a comprehensive model that integrates a variety of quality improvement activities including brainstorming, assessing customer satisfaction, setting a quality agenda, and developing a training program. The article concludes with a thoughtful list of "lessons learned" during implementation of the continuous improvement program in the emergency department.

In "Continuous Improvement in College Teaching: An Application of Statistical Tools," Zhiming Xue and Charles Gulas describe how continuous improvement techniques can be used to improve the quality of classroom instruction at the university level. They present a matrix of improvement approaches and implementation procedures for seven teaching processes. Control charts, Pareto diagrams, and regression analysis are all used as improvement tools. The authors conclude with a discussion of measurable benefits of the improvement activities.

James Gelina and Marty Schildroth, in "Systematic Problem Solving: A Cornerstone for Quality," discuss how various problem-solving tools were used to reduce costs at EMCI Specialities, a Des Moines, Iowa manufacturer. Useful examples of check sheets, Pareto diagrams, histograms, flowcharts, and cause-and-effect diagrams are all depicted in this article.

In "Quality Audit: Tool for Continuous Improvement in Disability Claim Operations," Illona Dubaldo and Jeffrey Nogas describe how Metropolitan Life Insurance Company (MetLife) utilized quality audit principles for continuous improvement in one of their claim operations. The authors define quality and address differences between manufacturing and service industries. Then, Dubaldo and Nogas describe each aspect of the internal quality audit program that was implemented. This article provides an excellent example of a service industry audit program.

The final article in this section, "Can Benchmarking for Best Practices Work for Government?" by Patricia Keehley and Sue MacBride, provides an interesting discussion of benchmarking in the public sector. Purposes, advantages, and disadvantages of benchmarking are discussed and specific guidelines for implementing a benchmarking program are provided.

17

More, Better, Faster from Total Quality Effort

P&G Achieves a Breakthrough in Clinical Study Cycle Times

David A. McCamey, Robert W. Boggs,
and Linda M. Bayuk

The value of total quality principles and methods is well known when applied to manufacturing and other business settings. Procter & Gamble's (P&G) healthcare over-the-counter (OTC) clinical division found the same approach produced breakthrough results in its system of conducting human clinical research studies.

In three years the OTC clinical division reduced the time required for planning, initiating, and reporting clinical studies by over 80% (this excludes time when test subjects are on a drug or treatment during what is called the in-life part of the clinical). Additionally, the level of data quality, measured by reduction in findings from quality assurance audits, improved by 60%.

More importantly, the OTC clinical division improved its capability to support new healthcare product development for business success. Achieving these results required strong leadership working on the system, a focus on delivering critical customer needs, an involved and empowered organization and disciplined use of the plan–do–check–act (PDCA) learning cycle with associated tools and methodologies.

P&G moved into the healthcare business by merging several organizations, including Norwich Eaton Pharmaceuticals, Richardson-Vicks, parts of G. D. Searle and the P&G oral care business. Each clinical group from these organizations had its special way of doing work. Conflicts, rework, and delays were common. The new organization needed a better way. This was especially true in the OTC pharmaceutical business, where work demanded flexible and responsive clinical capability.

WHAT IS A CLINICAL STUDY?

A clinical study is what the healthcare industry calls the testing of drugs, healthcare products, or treatments in humans. This testing follows the scientific method and includes careful and rigorous design, conduct, analysis, and summary of the data collected.

Work on a clinical study begins with the development of a protocol, or specific test plan. Next, physicians or clinical investigators who will actually conduct the study are contacted.

Because these studies deal with the health of human subjects, third parties review and approve the study. These parties include government agencies, such as the Food and Drug Administration (FDA) in the United States, and institutional review boards associated with each study location or site.

Products to be tested and data collection forms must be prepared and distributed to the investigators. Volunteers who meet the specific study requirements are recruited to participate, and the study is carefully conducted according to the approved protocol.

The data are gathered from the clinical study, data errors are corrected, and statistical programs are run. Finally, medical and statistical experts summarize the results in a final report. A clinical study may involve dozens of experts, dozens to thousands of subjects, and tens of thousands to millions of data points.

Given the many steps and people involved in conducting clinical studies, it is easy to see how different organizations could develop different approaches to doing this complex work. P&G had at least four different ways to do a clinical study and needed to find the best way to meet its healthcare research and development (R&D) needs.

P&G wanted its OTC clinical organization to be more effective. It could have just focused on quality of the clinical work or on agreeing to operate only one system. Instead, it focused the improvement on significant reductions in clinical cycle time. This focus on time savings captured the attention of management and the imagination of the organization, creating the foundation for breakthrough change. This effort was a major undertaking involving the entire 100-plus person organization and three years of work in three phases of improvement. Learnings from previous improvement efforts in an upstream R&D organization were built on.[1]

The approach was simple: P&G's OTC clinical division applied the PDCA cycle to its overall improvement effort.

PLAN

The overall plan had four key elements: build on sound total quality principles, have the right leadership structure, understand the work, and enroll the organization. To build on sound total quality principles, the division adopted and applied the following total quality principles in designing its work:

- *Focus on the customer.* The division focused on two key customers for its clinical work: consumers and product development teams. For consumers, it needed to organize clinical systems to deliver safe and effective new healthcare products to them as fast as possible. To do this, it needed to provide product development teams with sound data quickly so these teams could use the data in making the best possible development decisions.

- *Do the right things right.* This meant being clear on objectives and desired outcomes before starting any clinical work. Doing things the right way required simple, effective and efficient work systems and fact-based decision making.

- *Continual improvement.* The division found that struggling for perfection slowed it down. To address this problem in improvement efforts, it constantly applied J. M. Juran's 80/20 principle of "the vital few and the trivial many."[2]

For this improvement effort, that translates to the fact that 80% of the value is achieved through 20% of the work. When the clinical group obtained the 80% improvement value, it stopped the improvement effort and implemented the designed change. It would then study the results and improve again. It also avoided endless debates over what total quality methodology to use at each step by using a published improvement approach that specifically focused on cycle-time reduction.[3]

- *Empowerment.* Leaders and steering teams set clear direction, then got out of the way of the creativity and energy of the people in the organization. The division instituted approaches to remove barriers for teams so they could implement their ideas.

- *The right leadership structure.* There is nothing more fundamental to success in organizational improvement efforts than sound leadership. The director of the clinical organization, Robert E. Boggs (co-author of this article), personally led this work. He chose to break the overall improvement into three phases.

Phase one began in 1993 and focused on reducing cycle time in half from historic levels. Phase two began in 1994 and focused on a further 50% reduction in cycle time from the successful phase one levels. Phase three began in 1996 and focused on maintaining the improvements achieved to that point. However, the organization found other cycle-time reduction opportunities as it had developed a new capability—the capability to continuously improve.

Boggs chartered steering teams for each of the three major phases of the improvement effort and personally led these teams. The teams also recognized that they needed expert resources to advise, facilitate, and manage this major undertaking.

To meet these needs, the steering teams established three roles: a project leader, who managed the improvement project as a whole; a quality improvement manager, who provided day-to-day counsel on total quality methodology; and an external consultant, who regularly advised on overall approach, pitfalls, and success models.

- *Understand the work.* In order to make changes that would truly result in improvements, the teams realized they had to understand how the work was really done. They found the best way to understand the work as a group was to map the process. They first mapped how the work is done. In fact, once a small group had sketched out what they believed to be the current process, it held an event during which the entire center staff literally walked through a maze of tables on which the process map was displayed.

The steering team made sure it gathered everyone's comments on exactly how work was or was not currently being done. From that beginning, they then mapped how work "should" be done. These "is" and "should" maps proved invaluable in clarifying where the division really was adding customer value and where work could be streamlined.

To illustrate the use of process maps, Figure 17.1 shows simplified "is" and "should" maps used to improve the preparation of final reports. The improvement team for this part of the clinical process found that final reports took months to prepare. Only by mapping the process as it really existed did the improvement team fully understand how much work was done sequentially and the frustrating amount of rework and recycling done during review and sign-off.

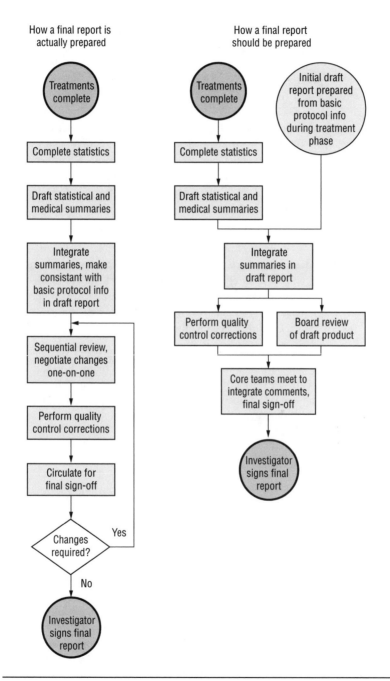

Figure 17.1   Final report "is" and "should" map example.

The improvement team was able to simplify the process and move several activities from sequential work to parallel work. As a result, the OTC clinical division is now able to complete reports in four weeks or less. More important, experts are spending more quality time understanding the data and results and less time arguing over wording and format.

The division also used the process maps to determine the critical few measurements that needed to be tracked to ensure the process was working as desired. The steering team spent a surprising amount of energy and resources on the measurement system because its experience had been that you indeed do get what you measure. The key was to get the information to the workers so they could make the necessary adjustments. The steering team was careful not to use these measurements as new tools for management to punish the organization.

- *Enroll the organization.* Many improvement efforts end with exciting designs that are never implemented. The steering team avoided that pitfall by chartering improvement teams to tackle specific improvements. These improvement teams were composed of people who really understood the work and were credible to the rest of the OTC clinical organization.

The improvement teams not only created new process designs, but stayed in place long enough to actually implement them. Further, each improvement team developed a communication or enrollment plan, ensuring that the organization was aware of the changes and understood why the changes were made.

DO

Every improvement team planned and executed a pilot test of its system improvements. These pilot tests led to practical process changes and drove out the theoretical or nice-to-have design elements that did not demonstrate true value or were too difficult to implement. In addition, by asking teams to pilot test their work, the fear of making a systemwide change that would not work was reduced. This led to more creative and out-of-the-box thinking and system designs.

For example, analysis of sources of delay pointed to use of contract laboratories as a potential system improvement. Labs that provided clinical chemistry and other biological measurements were meeting quality standards, but not all labs were meeting data transfer and timing requirements. The improvement team assigned to this problem developed a list of laboratories that claimed to be able to meet quality and timing requirements.

Before asking all clinical groups to use these laboratories, the contract laboratory improvement team qualified each lab by running a study and evaluating the lab's performance. It approved a short list of preferred laboratories that successfully demonstrated they could meet the division's data handling and timing requirements while maintaining its high quality standards.

In parallel with the pilot tests, the improvement teams developed implementation plans. These plans identified what new equipment, procedures, training, forms, measurements, and so forth must be in place before instituting the changes.

The team that identified the preferred contract laboratories prepared standard forms and ongoing monitoring systems and then trained the entire organization on how to work most effectively with these laboratories.

CHECK

Once the pilot test results were in, the improvement teams decided whether the changes delivered the desired improvement. If so, they implemented the changes. If the improvement was not sufficient or the changes proved to be too cumbersome, they cycled back to the beginning of the PDCA cycle and evaluated other options.

At this point, an issues team was established. This group of managers regularly met with the improvement teams to help resolve issues that were identified in the pilot tests or early in implementation. Many times issues that appeared to be roadblocks to the improvement teams were quickly and easily dealt with by these experienced managers.

ACT

When system changes were found to be true improvements from the pilot tests, the steering teams moved to implement these improvements across the entire division. Aside from effective training and measurement to ensure specific changes were implemented properly, the division learned it needed to do a few other things to make sure continuous improvement became a way of life in the organization.

First, the division made changes to its reward and recognition systems. The management team adopted continuous improvement in clinical cycle time as a recognized contribution to the business. In other words, individuals would see a benefit in their compensation and career progress when they helped make significant achievements in this improvement work.

The old reward system had stressed individual outcomes (such as analyzing data from a key clinical study), not team-based improvements to the way work was done. Management publicly recognized the work of improvement teams in its regular business meetings. Also, the division held several special recognition events celebrating cycle-time improvement milestones and team or individual achievements.

Finally, the steering teams found some of the improvement work was not being implemented quickly or rigorously because middle management was not providing full support for the work. Senior leadership and the workers had been involved, but the steering teams did not establish a clear path for middle managers to participate in the improvement effort.

This problem was tackled openly, and the right answer was found in concert with these managers. Cross-functional leadership teams were instituted that were delegated responsibility for achieving cycle time targets. These middle management teams were then enrolled completely in how to track progress and sponsor the improvement efforts themselves. The director was then able to move into the role of coach and advisor.

The most important thing done to instill the new habit of continuous improvement in the organization was not to stop. After each system change was implemented, the steering teams immediately moved on to the next improvement opportunity.

When major cycle-time targets were reached, new targets were set and new steering teams were chartered. It did not take long for the organization to realize cycle-time improvement was here to stay. And, as a result, work system changes achieved improvements in both overall clinical cycle time and in the quality of clinical data.

WORK SYSTEM CHANGES

Major system changes were implemented during each of the three phases of improvement. The nature of the changes, however, progressed as improvement work matured.

In phase one, the steering team found important improvement in cycle time over historical performance as it focused on implementing a cycle-time measurement system and standardizing work.

By simply agreeing on the current best approach to its most important tasks, it eliminated the constant negotiations, guesswork, and rework that existed because everyone had a favorite way of doing things.

To achieve targets in phase two, the steering team identified what it came to call low-hanging fruit—the systemic changes that were most obvious.

WHAT WORKED AND WHAT DIDN'T

The results of this effort were dramatic and surprising, even to those leading this total quality effort. In reflecting on this work, the team asked itself: What did we learn? What worked? What would we have done differently?

The first significant reduction, phase one, was achieved predominately by communicating what was important and documenting the work. To an extent, this result probably reflects the well-known Hawthorne effect: by simply focusing management's attention on the organization, the organization responded with improved performance. However, the level of improvement was not sufficient, and there was a strong possibility that the improvement would be fleeting.

A more influential and lasting reduction in cycle time was achieved through creative system changes identified and implemented in phase two. However, these improvements only really stuck when middle management enrolled during phase three.

Clearly, although the division did a good job of involving senior leadership and empowering the organization, it probably would have seen better results earlier if it had truly involved middle management directly as the steering team for the improvement work.

The division found it achieved its biggest improvements when it crossed functional boundaries (for example, involving the statisticians in improving database design). In the same way, it found tremendous insights when it brought product development teams into the improvement of its planning processes. In future improvements, it would begin by extending the scope of its improvement work to include the broadest system and crossing the broadest functional boundaries possible.

Faster clinical studies by themselves mean little to anyone. However, P&G's healthcare OTC clinical division is now able to run more studies in a given time period, the clinical data are of even higher quality, and systems are much less cumbersome and costly.

These included operational changes such as setting up and testing the database and statistical programs prior to receiving the real data.

The steering team also made administrative improvements such as changes in the review and approval approach that allowed it to reach closure on clinical protocols using focused, one-day work sessions, as opposed to endless cycles of review and revision.

System changes from the third phase of improvement work can be characterized by improvements in leadership and planning systems, innovative parallel work systems and technical innovations that allowed the division to move from paper-based data gathering systems to real-time data gathering and error correction.

One of the most important changes was to involve the clinical supplies group early in the development of the clinical plan and protocol. This provided enough lead time so it could begin preparing the medicines or devices to be tested in parallel with the work others were doing to prepare data-gathering forms, train the investigators, and so forth.

In a simple example of using technology to improve cycle time, the division used a desktop publishing group to transform its study protocols into first-draft clinical reports with placeholders for the actual results and analysis sections. When the study was finished, the group could quickly update the draft report to reflect the actual results and specific conclusions.

In another example, the division began using fax technology to continuously feed data from physicians or clinical investigators into its database. The division was able to rapidly determine if there were errors and fax questions to the investigators, who made the necessary corrections. It was thus able to prevent these errors from being reproduced in future forms.

CLINICAL CYCLE-TIME REDUCTION

Figure 17.2 shows the overall non-in-life cycle time for all clinical studies run from 1993 through 1997 using an individual's moving range (XmR) control chart, as described by, for example, Kaoru Ishikawa[4] and Donald J. Wheeler.[5] From an extensive sampling of previous studies, the historical or baseline performance of the organization was estimated to be a median of 82 weeks and is illustrated on this same figure.

While the division calculated and used averages for analyzing cycle-time progress, it chose to compare these averages to the median of the historical clinical cycle times. It used the median of the historical clinical cycle times because some of these older clinical studies were exceedingly

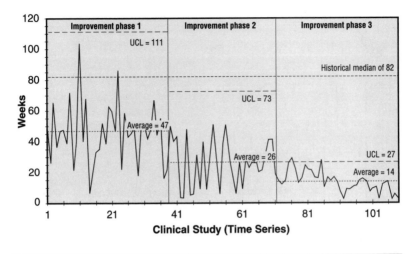

Figure 17.2   Non-in-life clinical cycle time control chart (individuals or x-chart).

long and would force the average value for this historical baseline to be too high for useful comparisons.

The historical cycle time seemed lengthy until the division learned of the results of a study done by S. T. Barnett and J. A. James.[6] Those authors had surveyed pharmaceutical companies and found an average of about 150 weeks for the non-in-life components of clinical studies conducted in these companies. This information gave the center even more confidence that its baseline value was a reasonable estimate.

Three separate means and upper control limits (UCL) are plotted to correspond with the three phases of the improvement work. (The lower control limits were all less than zero weeks and are not shown in the graph.) The initial phase gave an average cycle time of 47 weeks, representing a 43% reduction in cycle time from historical performance levels.

A second improvement phase resulted in an average cycle time of 26 weeks, which was another 44% reduction from the 47 weeks in the first improvement phase. Finally, the last improvement phase achieved an average clinical cycle time of only 14 weeks, which was a 46% reduction from the second improvement phase.

Overall, the division achieved an 83% reduction from its historical levels. The last improvement phase cycle time of 14 weeks also represents a

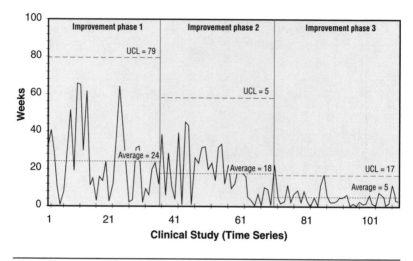

Figure 17.3 Moving range chart.

90% reduction from the industry non-in-life cycle times found by Barnett and James.[7]

A corresponding reduction in the variation in clinical cycle times was also observed. In Figure 17.3, the variation in cycle times is represented by graphing the moving range, where the moving range is the difference between clinical cycle times from one data point to the next. The average moving range was 24 weeks in the first phase. The variation improved to an average moving range of 18 weeks in the second phase and, finally, to an average moving range of five weeks in the final improvement phase. The moving range UCLs for each improvement phase are also illustrated.

DATA QUALITY IMPROVEMENT

Clinical studies involve thousands of data points collected over long periods of time by many different people. All these data are entered into huge computerized databases and are then analyzed by statisticians, leading to study conclusions. It is not surprising that data errors creep into this process—for example, parts of forms not properly filled out, transcription errors, and illegible entries. So, it is common practice in the pharmaceutical industry that all clinical studies be carefully audited and the data corrected prior to any report being finalized.

Data correction takes time, adds cost, and is frustrating rework. Although the division's data quality was consistent with industry standards and practices, it did not meet internal improvement needs. Data correction steps were found to be an important cause of significant delays in reaching study conclusions and completing final reports.

Because measures were set so a clinical study was not complete until the data and report were error free, the division expected the amount of required corrections to decrease dramatically as a result of improvement efforts. Therefore, the cycle-time improvements automatically led to data quality improvements.

As an example, quality assurance audit results from the beginning of the improvement work (October to December 1993) were compared with those from a similar time period in the final improvement phase (October to December 1996). The measurement of data quality used was "audit findings," defined as errors or inconsistencies in the data or draft clinical report that required correction prior to report finalization. (No errors were found in any study that would have compromised subject safety or study outcome.)

The rate of clinical study draft reports that were completely free of audit findings improved to 25% in the 1996 period, compared to only 10% in the 1993 period. Importantly, even for those draft reports with audit findings, the rate of findings per report decreased from 7.6 findings per report in 1993 to 3.0 findings per report in 1996. These comparisons represent a 60% improvement in data quality.

The objective findings from these audits substantiate the following observation made by an external auditor:

"On the basis of my observations across the industry, I am confident that the quality of these operations in your organization is not only outstanding, but is well above the industry average."

More, better, cheaper—these are the benefits to the business. The people in the organization are more empowered and excited about their work. Consumers get new and improved healthcare products that are proven to be safe and effective and are presented on the market at the earliest possible timing. Total quality, even applied to unusual work processes like the conduct of clinical studies, can truly benefit all stakeholders.

ACKNOWLEDGMENTS

The authors gratefully acknowledge R. M. Siconolfi for his assistance in analyzing the data from the quality assurance audits. We also appreciate J. H. Thompson's advice on the appropriate statistical process control methodology.

ENDNOTES

1. L. V. Wood and D. A. McCamey, "Implementing Total Quality in R&D," *Research-Technology Management* 36, no. 4 (1993): 39–41.
2. J. M. Juran, *Juran on Quality by Design* (New York: The Free Press, 1992).
3. C. Meyer, *Fast Cycle Time* (New York: The Free Press, 1993).
4. K. Ishikawa, *Introduction to Quality Control* (Tokyo: 3A Corporation, 1990).
5. D. J. Wheeler, *Understanding Variation: The Key to Managing Chaos* (Knoxville, TN: SPC Press, 1993).
6. S. T. Barnett and J. A. James, "Measuring the Clinical Development Process," *Applied Clinical Trials* (September 1995): 44–54.
7. Ibid.

18

Continuous Improvement on the Free-Throw Line

Timothy Clark and Andrew Clark

In 1924, Walter Shewhart developed a problem-solving method to continually improve quality by reducing variation (the difference between the ideal outcome and the actual situation). To help guide improvement efforts, Shewhart outlined a process referred to as the plan–do–study–act (PDSA) cycle. The PDSA cycle combined with the traditional concepts of decision making and problem solving are what my son and I used to continuously improve his basketball free-throw shooting.

RECOGNIZING THE PROBLEM

Identify the Facts

I had observed over a three-year period from 1991 to 1993 that in basketball games, my son Andrew's free-throw shooting percentage averaged between 45 percent and 50 percent.

Identify and Define the Process

Andrew's process for shooting free throws was simple: go to the free-throw line, bounce the ball four times, aim, and shoot.

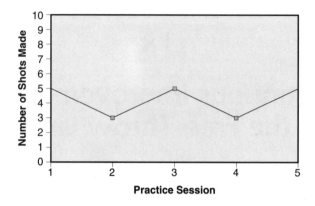

Figure 18.1   Free-throw shooting run chart.

The desired outcome was a higher free-throw shooting percentage. An ideal outcome, or perfection, would be one in which 100% of the shots fall through the middle of the rim, land at the same spot on the floor every time, and roll straight back in the shooter's direction after landing.

Plot the Points

To confirm my observations on the results of the current process, we went to the YMCA and Andrew shot five sets of 10 free throws for a total of 50 shots. His average was 42%. Results were recorded on a run chart (see Figure 18.1). Based on this information as well as on past observations, I estimated the process was stable.

DECISION MAKING

Identify the Causes

Causes of variation in any process can be identified through the general categories of people, equipment, materials, methods, environment, and measurement. A cause-and-effect diagram is used to graphically illustrate the relationship between the effect—a low free-throw shooting percentage—and the principal causes (see Figure 18.2).

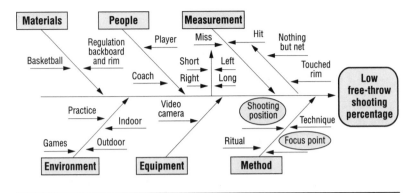

Figure 18.2 Free-throw shooting cause-and-effect diagram.

In analyzing my son's process, I noticed that he did not stand at the same place on the free-throw line every time. I believed his inconsistent shooting position affected the direction of the shot. If the shot goes left or right, there is a smaller probability that the ball will have a lucky bounce and go in. I also noticed that he didn't seem to have a consistent focal point.

Develop, Analyze, and Select Alternatives

The alternatives selected for Andrew, a right-handed shooter, were for him to line up his right foot on the middle of the free-throw line, focus on the middle of the front part of the rim, and visualize the perfect shot before he released the ball. The modified process is:

1. Stand at the center of the free-throw line.

2. Bounce the ball four times.

3. Focus on the middle of the front part of the rim, and visualize a perfect shot.

4. Shoot.

Develop an Action Plan

The course of action at this point was for Andrew to shoot five more sets of 10 free throws to test the effectiveness of the changes.

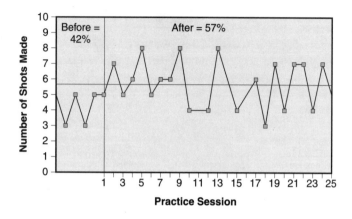

Figure 18.3   Free-throw shots made before and after implementing the PDSA cycle (March 17, 1994, to November 23, 1994).

PROBLEM SOLVING

Implement the Selected Alternative and Compare Actual with Expected Results

The new process resulted in a 36% improvement in Andrew's average free-throw percentage at basketball practice, which raised his average to 57% (see Figure 18.3). The new process was first implemented in games toward the end of the 1994 season, and in the last three games, Andrew hit nine of his 13 free throws for a free-throw shooting average of 69%.

During the 1995 season, Andrew made 37 of his 52 free throws in games for an average of 71%. In one extremely close game where the other team was forced to foul Andrew's team in an effort to get the ball back, Andrew hit seven of his seven shots, which helped his team win the game. In team practices, the coaches had the players shoot two free throws and then rotate. For the entire season, Andrew hit 101 of 169 of his team practice free throws for an average of 60%.

As we monitored Andrew's process from March 17, 1994, to January 18, 1996, we plotted the total number of practice shots made out of 50, using Shewhart's number-of-affected-units control chart (see Figure 18.4). A control chart is a trend chart with upper and lower control limits. If all of the data points fall within the control limits, the variation in the process is due to normal or common causes of variation, and the conclusion can be made

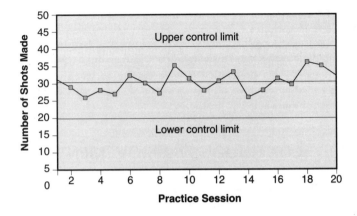

Figure 18.4   Determining whether the free-throw process is stable (March 17, 1994, to January 18, 1996).

that the process is stable or predictable. In other words, if you always do what you always did, on average, you will usually get what you always got.

If any points fall outside the limits, the variation is due to a special cause that makes the process unstable or unpredictable. A special cause might represent a temporary or fleeting event and might require little or no action to resolve. Variation due to a common cause requires a permanent change in the process. In this case, the process is stable, which will make it easier to validate future improvement efforts.

In the late summer of 1995, Andrew went to a basketball camp where he was advised to change his shooting technique. This change to his process reduced his shooting percentage during the 1996 season to 50%. This caused him to lose confidence in his shooting ability, and consequently, he took fewer shots. We then reinstalled his old process, and his shooting percentage returned to its former level. In one series of 50 practice free throws, he hit 35 of 50 shots for an average of 70% and in another set, he hit 32 of 50 for an average of 64%. During the remaining team practices, Andrew hit 14 of 20 of his practice free throws for an average of 70%. During the final three games, he hit two of three free throws for an average of 67%.

During the 1996 and 1997 seasons, Andrew was a point guard and was responsible for controlling and distributing the ball. In this position, he had fewer opportunities to shoot free throws. Therefore, during the 1997 season, he had the opportunity to shoot only 12 free throws, but he made nine of them for an average of 75%.

Overall Benefits

In addition to the tangible results, such as improved free-throw shooting, the intangible benefits were also significant. For example, Andrew's confidence improved, and he learned how to determine when changes to his shooting technique resulted in improvement. W. Edwards Deming referred to this type of knowledge as profound.

CONTINUOUS IMPROVEMENT

Take appropriate action based on study results. In preparation for the 1998 season, Andrew's priorities for improvement are to continue to monitor his free-throw shooting to ensure it remains stable and to work on improving the shooting percentage of his two- and three-point shots.

KNOWLEDGE CHANGES HOW PEOPLE LOOK AT THE WORLD

Shewhart's methodology represents a problem-solving or decision-making process that requires a fundamental change in thinking. Traditionally, people are trained to make decisions based on gut feelings or on relatively few facts. The PDSA process requires people to first determine if the process outcome is due to a common cause or a special cause. This knowledge becomes the foundation for making decisions, which can only be developed by plotting points. Developing a knowledge and understanding of variation will change the way you look at the world forever and can lead to unprecedented levels of quality.

BIBLIOGRAPHY

Deming, W. E. *Out of the Crisis.* Cambridge, MA: Massachusetts Institute of Technology, 1986.

Small, B. S. *Statistical Quality Control Handbook.* Indianapolis, IN: AT&T Technologies, 1985.

Total Quality Tools for Education. Dayton, OH: QIP Inc./QP Systems, 1995.

19

Hospital Sets New Standard As Closure Approaches: Quality Is Continuous

Martha L. Dasch

C ontinuous improvement in a medical facility can occur at any time, even when it is scheduled to close its doors. This is what happened at Naval Hospital Orlando in Florida. Although its staff was aware of the hospital's impending closure (the hospital was notified officially on July 1, 1993, that it had to close), it saw a need to improve and decided to do what was necessary to make it a better, more efficient medical facility. Specifically, a self-directed team was interested in improving its same-day surgery (SDS) unit. The improvement plan that it developed faced some rough spots, but in the end, not only did SDS procedures dramatically improve, an ambulatory procedures unit under the SDS unit was established as well, making the hospital more efficient and patient-friendly.

NAVAL HOSPITAL ORLANDO

Naval Hospital Orlando, built in 1982, was a four-story, 153-bed facility with five operating rooms (OR). It provided healthcare for the Orlando Naval Training Center's military members and their families. The hospital had an outpatient clinic that covered most specialties, and it provided ancillary services to support inpatient and outpatient needs. When it was built, however, it was not constructed with an SDS unit. Because of an increasing need for a unit of this kind, the hospital converted 2,200 square feet of the third-floor surgical ward into an SDS unit in 1990. The 10-bed unit combined preoperative teaching, staging, recovery, and administrative services all in one area. The surgery was performed in the OR on the second floor.

SDS SATISFACTION SURVEY

In 1993, the SDS unit conducted a satisfaction survey of its internal and external customers. Patients were asked to rate and comment on areas such as the care they received, time it took to check in, and staff helpfulness. The staff received a different survey that asked them to rate and comment on such items as the timely receipt of patient information, patient notification, and the check-in process. The results revealed several areas that could be improved. First, the results indicated that patients were dissatisfied with the disorganized preadmission process. While it only took two hours for some patients to complete the process, it took others up to two days. Because the unit did not specify a time for completing the preadmission work and did not schedule appointments for patients, long delays occured, particularly in anesthesia. If patients became impatient with the long delays, they took their preadmission packages home. When they returned to the hospital, information inevitably was lost or out of order, forcing the SDS administration to reorganize the paperwork, resulting in further delays. In addition, preadmission was not located in a single area. Elderly patients, sick patients, and those with disabilities had to visit three different floors to complete the process.

Second, because patients did not have appointments, the OR unit was not able to schedule its staff appropriately to conduct preoperative sessions. Before a surgical procedure, patients are provided with information explaining the procedure and what they can anticipate prior to, during, and after the surgery. Patients are also given a list of instructions about how long to fast before surgery, how to physically prepare before coming to the hospital, and when to arrive. Patients with additional questions or concerns can be reassured by the staff prior to the day of the surgery.

Third, because there was not a dedicated SDS staff, but rather a staff that rotated from the surgical ward, there was a lack of commitment and poor follow-through in the SDS unit.

Fourth, each of the seven clinical services that referred patients to the SDS used different preadmission packages. Preadmission packages consist of the doctor's orders; the patient's medical history; authorization for surgery; ancillary service information, such as lab, X-ray, and electrocardiogram (EKG) test results; progress notes; nursing assessment forms;

and admission authorizations. The variety of preadmission packages created confusion, and errors resulted when patients were prepared for the SDS unit.

Fifth, the SDS unit received late or incomplete preadmission packages from clinical services, which caused delays or surgery cancellations.

Sixth, the SDS unit's physical layout was stressful for patients. The preadmission and recovery areas were side by side; prospective patients who were participating in the preoperative sessions could observe post-surgical patients coming from surgery.

SDS IMPROVEMENT TEAM

In June 1993, a group of concerned staff members got together to review the results from the SDS satisfaction survey. This multidisciplinary group included a surgeon; the associate director of surgical nursing; an OR nurse; a nurse anesthetist; and representatives from patient administration, the laboratory, EKG, and the nursing staff. Scheduling clerks from the seven clinical services that used SDS also participated.

The group's meetings weren't highly productive at first. Comments such as, "you don't understand how our service does this" or "this won't work" showed a lack of understanding and trust. But, as the meetings continued and the different departments of the hospital explained their particular needs, the group agreed that there had to be a better way. The group came up with a plan to chart patient flow from the day surgery was deemed necessary to the day of the surgery. Figure 19.1 illustrates the many steps a patient had to complete during the preadmission process.

The initial plan was to analyze the flowcharts of the seven clinical services and then develop a single admission procedure that all could follow. It was hoped that this would decrease the preadmission time for patients.

The group analyzed the flowcharts, used Ishikawa diagrams, and brainstormed in order to develop a list of improvement opportunities. About six months later, the group prepared to implement several of its improvement solutions. While some could be implemented immediately, others were considered long-term improvements. The improvements for immediate trial included the following:

- Schedule pre-admission appointment times for patients to eliminate "walk-ins"

- Combine preoperative teaching, laboratory blood tests, and admission authorization to decrease the number of stops patients must make (see Figure 19.2)

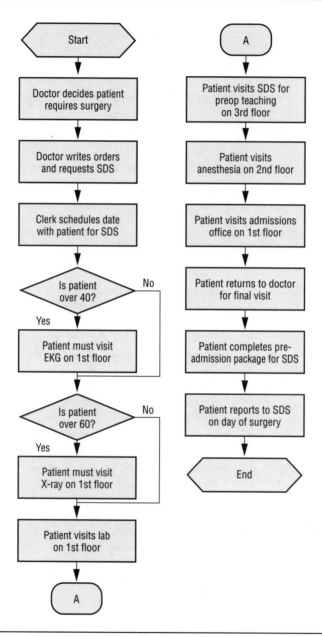

Figure 19.1 Preadmission process for SDS (before improvements).

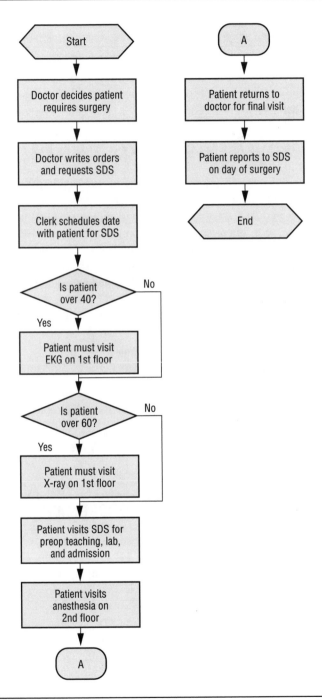

Figure 19.2 Preadmission process for SDS (after first improvement change).

- Implement a single preadmission package and checklist for use by all seven clinical services to reduce confusion and increase efficiency

- Centralize the processing, storage, and retrieval of preadmission packages by moving responsibility for completion to the SDS unit

IMPROVEMENTS SPARKLE THEN FIZZLE

At first, success seemed certain. After polling the hospital staff, results indicated that the implemented changes had reduced patient preadmission time and had increased staff satisfaction. However, no timeline had been established for long-term improvements, and the group stopped meeting. With no meetings, communication channels began to close. Instead of fine-tuning improvements when questions arose, old methods were reinstated.

In early 1994, the group realized what was happening and began meeting again to adjust the short-term improvement plan and develop a long-term improvement plan. After carefully evaluating the problems that were occurring, the group decided on the following:

- Assign permanent staff to the SDS unit to facilitate cross-training in administrative, laboratory, and EKG duties

- Relocate the SDS unit to the second floor to allow for greater space and collocation of the unit with the OR and anesthesia staff

- Provide the capability for patients to complete all preadmission work in one place, with the exception of X-rays

DOWNSIZING CLOSES OBSTETRICAL WARD, BUT PRESENTS SDS OPPORTUNITY

As part of the Base Realignment and Closure Commission process, the hospital closed its obstetrical ward in June 1994. This closure enabled the improvement group to implement its long-term improvement efforts. The SDS unit moved to the second-floor obstetrical and nursery ward. The unit now occupied 4,000 square feet and took advantage of the 12 beds, two delivery rooms, and four labor rooms. The nursery area was converted into an administrative preoperative area where all preadmission work except X-rays could take place. It also separated the preoperative patients from patient staging and recovery. Most of the preadmission procedures now were taking place in one area on one floor, greatly improving the pre-admission process for patients (see Figure 19.3).

The second-floor location was more convenient because the administrative preoperative area now was located across the hall from the OR and anesthesia staff. In addition, permanent staff was assigned to the SDS unit and cross-trained so that personnel could handle SDS, preoperative teaching, and admission responsibilities.

The increased space motivated the group to expand on their improvement vision. With the additional space now available, why not create an ambulatory procedures unit (APU) under the SDS unit? Nurses in the APU unit could be trained to give intravenous medication, known as intravenous conscious sedation (IVCS), and assist in the performance of endoscopies (the insertion of a lighted tube down the throat of a patient for diagnostic purposes) and other minor procedures. This would free anesthesiologists from having to be present for every minor procedure and allow them more time for the major OR surgeries. Patients could be treated on an outpatient basis in the APU or be brought in from the inpatient nursing department. Centralization of these capabilities would enable providers to do more procedures more efficiently with dedicated staff.

On June 24, 1994, the SDS/APU unit began initial operations. The labor and delivery rooms were easily adapted to perform ambulatory procedures under IVCS, such as endoscopies, formerly performed in the surgery clinic area. Also performed in this area were uncomplicated ear, nose, and throat procedures formerly performed in the OR. Many clinical areas came to the APU with suggestions of procedures that could be performed in the new space.

A number of efficiencies resulted from combining the SDS and APU units:

- The anesthesia staff was used more effectively.

- All minor-procedure and endoscopy equipment was located in the APU area, which expedited its use and assignment.

- Nurses' professional capabilities were enhanced because they were cross-trained in IVCS skills. Credentials for clinical competency in IVCS were instituted.

- The main OR was made more available for complicated cases.

- The APU's capacity for procedures increased due to quicker turnaround time and the ability to stage and recover patients outside the procedure room.

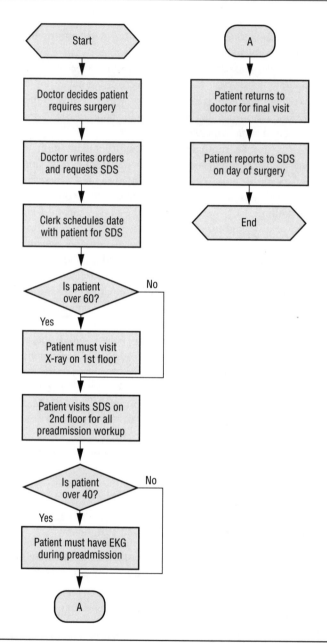

Figure 19.3 Preadmission process for SDS (after final improvement change).

LESSONS TO BE LEARNED

The group at Naval Hospital Orlando achieved improvements by trial and error. The lessons it learned may be of value to others wishing to make similar improvements in a healthcare facility:

- Be persistent. Don't give up when it seems as though nothing will happen. In this self-directed team, there was no just-in-time training or quality advisor, which led to some initial frustration and floundering.

- Don't stop meeting after you think you have the improvements in place. The group stopped meeting in late 1993 after implementing initial improvements, and it provided no communication channel for clinical services that had changes that needed to be made. Again, a quality advisor may have advised the group to continue to meet in order to perform all steps in the plan–do–check–act (PDCA) cycle. Once the group made improvements in the "do" phase, they needed to monitor and "check" to ensure that the improvements produced the gains anticipated.

- Ensure that the improvements are continued after initial implementation so there is no regression. The organization must take steps to institutionalize changes. Since the change in procedures had not been institutionalized, when clinical services ran out of the new preadmission checklists, they reverted to their old forms and methods. Again, PDCA would have assisted in institutionalizing this change.

- Continue to expand your vision and your opportunities to improve. When you begin to reach your goals, look around for other opportunities. The group experienced a significant breakthrough in developing the APU as part of the SDS improvement effort.

- Improvement efforts should not be a short-term investment; they need top-level support and multidisciplinary collaboration with the intent to improve patient care. They are time-intensive and can be frustrating, but they are ultimately worth the investment.

CONTINUOUS IMPROVEMENT
LASTS FOREVER

Improvements are worthwhile in any organization, regardless of the time it has left. Because of the changes that were made at Naval Hospital Orlando, patients' quality of care and employees' quality of work life improved, even if only for a while. Although the Naval Hospital Orlando has closed and ceases to function, the SDS unit stands as a benchmark for others to emulate. The members of the improvement team will take their planning, team, and communication skills to other facilities. Physically the doors have shut, but in the minds of those who made the change, the improvement will last forever. Continue improvements as long as you have an organization to improve.

20

Quality Quest: One Company's Successful Attempt at Implementing TQM

Robert A. Drensek and Fred B. Grubb

Once senior management is committed to starting a total quality management (TQM) process, your work has just begun. Whom do you train first? What are your goals? How will you know if you are successful?

The authors have been involved in a TQM implementation at a $140 million manufacturer of consumer products. What follows is a nuts-and-bolts discussion of the implementation, with both the successes and the stumbling blocks they encountered along the way.

To implement TQM, the company used a total quality strategy called the Quality Quest, which is based on Philip Crosby's quality philosophy and incorporates his four absolutes of quality.[1] Crosby's four absolutes of quality are:

- The definition of quality is conformance to requirements

- The system of quality is prevention

- The performance standard of quality is zero defects

- The measurement of quality is the price of nonconformance

TRAINING MANAGEMENT AND ALIGNING ITS COMMITMENT TO THE PROCESS

Senior management was trained over a three-month period in Crosby's four absolutes so that it fully understood them and was aware of the changes needed for these absolutes to be fully internalized within the company. Naturally, unresolved problems encountered during these instruction sessions reflected what management was to encounter in later training.

The senior staff members had varying levels of commitment to the process, and the rest of the organization could not be trained until the senior staff was fully committed. The content of the training was threefold. First, it was necessary to help the staff work together as a team. The training began with an analysis of how the rest of the organization perceived the senior staff. Many structured interviews were conducted with employees at all levels of the organization prior to the training, and the results were presented anonymously during the sessions. The results revealed that the employees saw the senior staff members as fighting among themselves and at cross purposes with each other a great deal of the time. Therefore, several team-building and strategic planning activities were designed to help the senior staff work as a team. These activities were so successful that many were used in later training sessions.

Second, the senior staff needed to fully understand the four absolutes and 14 steps of Crosby's process. Since they were skeptical of the process, the president, his staff, and the three plant managers visited several companies that had successfully implemented this process.

The first company they visited was Milliken, which started using the Crosby process in the late 1970s and is still devoted to the quality process. After the visit, however, those who were predisposed to total quality found much at Milliken to support their ideas, while those who were skeptical said things such as, "Milliken is different from us," and "what works there won't work here."

The skeptics remained wary even when other, more similar companies were visited. But these visits solidified the president's opinion that TQM was critical to the company's long-term growth and profitability and that the company should move forward with the process.

Third, a structure needed to be set up under which TQM would be carried out. This meant more than just setting up quality improvement teams at each facility. A great deal of time was spent discussing the responsibilities and priorities of each member of the team. In the early stages of TQM, managers wondered, "where will we find the time for this?" Before teams could be set up, this question had to be answered by the senior staff. The answer: "you have nothing more important to do." It is amazing, though, how long it takes managers to recognize this.

Once senior staff went through the training, quality improvement teams were set up at each of the three main facilities. The teams consisted of department heads who were direct reports to the senior staff. During the training of these teams, each of Crosby's 14 steps was discussed in great detail over a four-day, off-site training session.

TRAINING THE MASSES

The next step was to train the rest of the company. A training strategy was set up so that in a year every employee in the 800-person company would be trained in the following:

- *The four absolutes.* All employees needed to understand the philosophical underpinnings of the TQM process.

- *Opportunities for improvement.* This is the company's employee suggestion program, which was styled after Milliken's model.

- *Customer-supplier training.* Employees met with their internal customers and suppliers to ensure a good understanding of each other's requirements. While the process was focused on internal customers, teams that met with external suppliers also had good results.

To train 800 employees in these areas and make sure that everyone received the same message, members of the quality improvement teams were paired up to teach 40 training sessions, with approximately 20 employees per session. For step one of the training, the company put together a four-hour module on Crosby's four absolutes, which included a discussion of each absolute, a videotape regarding the relationship between the company and its customer, and a time for questions from the participants.

The question-and-answer period usually turned out to be a gripe session, and many of the participants commented, "we've heard all this before," and "we don't believe you." It was important to have this discussion in all of the training sessions, because if people are continually asked for their feedback, sooner or later they will stop griping and understand that you really want their opinions. It took several grueling months, however, before getting to that point.

Step two was training in opportunities for improvement. Since merely handing out suggestion pads to employees and telling them to fill them out is a prescription for failure, they needed to be trained. The same basic procedure in step one was followed: the pairs of quality improvement team members trained each of the 800 employees in an opportunities module. During this module, a senior staff member was present at each session to talk about how important it was to the company that employees fill out their opportunities-for-improvement cards, and then 30 minutes was allotted for the employees to fill them out. This proved to be a very successful module. First, it let people know how serious senior management was about needing their suggestions. Second, it immediately gave senior management hundreds of opportunities to work on.

The opportunities for improvement were prioritized, and safety-related issues were tackled first. Problems that had multiple opportunities for improvement were then worked on. In almost all cases, the people who originated each of the opportunities for improvement were involved in the problem-solving effort.

Opportunities for improvement were sorted by area and given to the appropriate area supervisor, and the supervisors grouped these opportunities together according to each problem in their area. Thus, fixing one problem might address 12 opportunities for improvement.

This first round of improvement opportunities served as a great boost to the TQM process because the employees saw that management was serious about listening to their concerns. Also, several problems were solved that related to safety, product quality, and production efficiency.

EMPLOYEES LEARN CUSTOMERS' REQUIREMENTS

Step three, customer-supplier training, has been the cornerstone of the company's TQM process. The quality improvement teams believed that many departments in the company did not know their internal customers' requirements, the logic being that if everyone knew what was expected, they would stand a much better chance of doing it right the first time. But the problem was how to get more than 600 factory employees to know and understand their internal customers' requirements. To get everyone in the company to understand their customers' requirements, each department was split into teams based on common work tasks. These teams scheduled meetings with their customers to learn their requirements and established performance measures for self-assessment.

Clearly, training in this process could not be accomplished in just a four-hour module. A completely different format for accomplishing the training objectives needed to be developed. It was determined that approximately 50 people were needed to guide the small groups through the process steps.

This process met two of the company's goals for the year: 100% participation in Quality Quest and the reduction in the price of nonconformance. In trying to devise a simple process that could be followed, one issue that kept coming up was how to prioritize the teams' efforts to make use of limited resources. In understanding customers' requirements, it seems natural to ask them, "How am I doing at activity X?" This approach, however, assumes that one has a good understanding of customers' internal processes, their current performance levels, and an idea of what is important to them. Thus, in the company's first attempt at customer-supplier requirements training the following four-step process was proposed:

1. Refresh employees' memories regarding the four absolutes and internal and external customer relationships.

2. Conduct a brainstorming session focusing on barriers to zero defects.

3. Have employees conduct a meeting with their internal customers or suppliers to resolve barriers and requirements.

4. Use problem solving to meet the requirements.

EMPLOYEES CAN SOLVE THEIR OWN PROBLEMS

In the pilot run of the process, it became apparent that all of the teams believed they could achieve zero defects only if the parts they received had zero defects. The teams reported that they had to perform rework on the materials they received before they could carry out their part of the process. (The company produces more than 2,000 different products with more than 50 unique parts per product.) Management thought this was an excuse from the union employees and they were not taking responsibility for their work. There might have been an element of truth in that statement, but the employees had pride in their abilities. From the point of view of processes, the employees were saying that if they were given the right tools and materials, they could do their jobs right.

This is the real heart of the TQM philosophy as it pertains to manufacturing. The employees had been conditioned, through the organizational structure and union contract, to believe that they could not and should not resolve their own problems. This was the key part of the company's culture that needed to be changed. Employees need to feel responsible and actually be accountable for producing zero defects. This problem cannot be solved if management requires supervisors to handle all issues. This formed the basis for the rest of the training.

Employees are in a better position than their supervisors to see and measure the defects coming to them, and they can communicate that information to their suppliers. By measuring their problems, work teams can focus on the most frequent or most expensive problem using Pareto analysis.

This method seemed to have more potential than the first proposed process, especially due to the large volume of unique parts. In fact, in most companies' purchasing departments, when ordering parts from a supplier, the customer specs out the parts and then compares the incoming parts to that specification. Each team has expectations of the quality of inbound parts (requirements) and an opportunity to check conformance (measurements). In time, a supplier certification can be earned, which minimizes the need for inbound inspection.

TEAM WORKS WITH ITS SUPPLIER TO SOLVE PROBLEMS

An important part of the pilot run was step three. Although the team wanted to work with its supplier to correct the problems identified in step two, it realized that it could not just meet with the supplier without data. Further, since the tendency among employees is to believe that their own issues are important and relevant to the rest of the company, training was needed to develop a broader focus. Team members prioritized the largest barriers to zero-defect performance, and a simple tick sheet system to gather data was established to determine how severe these barriers were, how often they caused problems, and to what extent they were problematic.

After gathering data for a couple of weeks, the team found that it actually caused some of its own problems, which it fixed quickly. The team then went to its supplier, which was another small manufacturing team, and presented its data. Some members were concerned that this meeting would become adversarial; however, the supplier said that it had been unaware of some of the problems and was willing to help fix them. The group then went through the same process cycle with its other barriers. The new process reflects the modifications made by the team:

- Provide quality training explaining the four absolutes and internal and external customer relationships

- Conduct a brainstorming session focusing on barriers to zero-defect performance and create a measurement system to track problems so they can be prioritized and communicated to the supplier

- Perform a data review to determine requirements and appropriate suppliers

- Have a meeting with the suppliers to resolve requirements on the most frequent or costly barrier, and start problem solving

The flowchart in Figure 20.1 details the steps in the process. Some teams accomplished the steps in an hour, while other teams needed several meetings to get through just the measurement step. Some teams solved a half-dozen quick and easy internal departmental problems before starting on the barriers external to their departments.

POSSIBLE BARRIERS AND RESISTANCE TO CHANGE

Since there were a number of potential barriers to the process, the following responses were developed to answer common objections:

Barrier: Meetings will cause lost production time.
Answer: World-class organizations have at least 40 hours of training per employee per year and many have more. Relative to that standard, the amount of time spent in meetings is small. If the teams succeed in problem solving, the dollars saved will more than offset the dollars spent.

Barrier: Union workers do not have experience in problem solving.
Answer: They can be trained in a problem solving methodology that has been proven to work.

Barrier: Problem solving is the job of supervisors.
Answer: True, but so far supervisors have been more successful at putting out fires than eliminating problems.

Barrier: The customer–supplier meeting will get out of control.
Answer: Supervisors and facilitators will be trained to handle the meeting, and for the first few rounds of the process, someone from management will be present as a facilitator to maintain control.

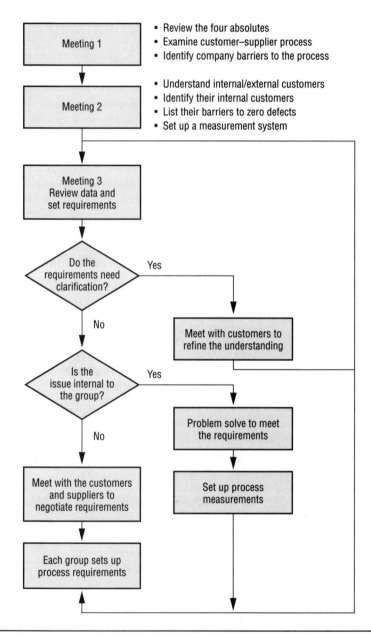

Figure 20.1 Customer/supplier requirements process flow.

Barrier: This is the third program in 10 years, so why should we bother?
Answer: Ultimately, actions will show that Quality Quest is not going away. The company has already been involved in it for two years—longer than any previous attempt—and has achieved positive results. The marketplace is becoming increasingly more competitive, and the company needs to become more efficient just to survive.

Barrier: Problem solving and setting requirements is management's job.
Answer: The union members are the experts at their jobs, and solving all problems is too big a task for management to do by itself. It will take everyone's involvement to succeed. This is an opportunity to join the team for everyone's mutual benefit.

Barrier: Management does not care, so why should we?
Answer: Management's actions over time will ultimately be the only way to break this barrier. Management has already provided the resources for training, which shows a level of support that has not been seen before.

Resistance to the process was still encountered from middle and senior managers. They were threatened by the process because it did not conform to their paradigm of how a company should be run. Great efforts were expended to win them over; in the end they were either incorporated into the ranks or worked around as necessary.

FACILITATORS RECEIVE INTENSE TRAINING

The plan then called for training 50 facilitators, who would each guide two teams of five to eight people. The facilitators would be responsible for leading the union workers through the process, particularly the problem-solving portion, since formal problem-solving training for the plant would not be online for some time.

The facilitator training was an intense four-day program focusing on the following:

- Quality, including Crosby's four absolutes and 14 steps (day one)
- The customer–supplier process and the facilitator's role in it (day one)
- Problem-solving methodology (day two)
- Measurement and measurement systems (day two)

- Facilitation and presentation techniques (day three)

- A sample presentation from the material facilitators are required to present to their teams (day four)

While a four-day seminar could not make them experts, the objective of the training was to give facilitators enough knowledge and experience so that they would not go into the process cold. For the first round or two of the process, they would receive assistance, and after that they would be left alone; further assistance would be available if needed. The seminar was a good introduction; the real learning, however, would come on the job.

VALIDATING THE NEW PROCESS USING A PILOT

Before the company's new TQM process could be implemented, a pilot had to be conducted. The pilot was tested at the customer–supplier negotiation meeting. In fact, four of these meetings were conducted during the pilot, and all of the participants were pleasantly surprised by the positive results. In the meetings, the customers focused on the objective data. They were instructed before the meeting not to make accusations about how well others did or did not do their jobs but to just tell their story, which was supported by data. The suppliers were informed before the meeting that the other team wanted to talk to them about specific problems.

During the meetings, all parties were very interested in bringing the issue to a satisfactory conclusion. Everyone listened to each other and offered their opinions, and each problem was negotiated without incident.

At this point, the quality improvement team was informed of the progress made to date, with the recommendation that it proceed even though the problem-solving method had not been used on the new problems. The quality improvement team was also told that everyone involved believed the issues could be resolved, that the selected problem-solving methodology was in use at several other companies, and there was no reason not to expect it to work in this company as long as management supported the process.

Some people recommended that the team wait to fully test the problem-solving method, but the president overruled the objections and gave orders to proceed. The first group of facilitators selected received four days of training.

Now, there are approximately 30 facilitators leading the process in the plant, which has led to many successes and a real culture change in areas that are actively participating. So many barriers have been removed that in the past year worker productivity has risen greatly, the amount of product produced with zero defects has increased by 20%, the price of nonconformance has decreased by millions of dollars, and product returns have been reduced by 50%. All this has been accomplished without any new capital expenditures, which demonstrates that quality actually puts money in companies' pockets.

PROCESS HITS SOME BUMPS

The entire process wasn't always smooth. Senior management suffered many stinging comments when they explained the concept of zero defects to employees who had assumed for years that anything other than defective work is impossible. The most difficult problems, however, have come from middle management, and they all center around the pace of change. The pilot actually took several months because the plant managers were reluctant to let their people off the floor to attend meetings. The company's president actually had to force them to let employees attend. Once the process was underway and they were able to see the positive changes, however, the plant managers became supportive.

Several important lessons were learned throughout this process. First, management was the biggest barrier to implementation; the easiest part of the process was dealing with the union workers. Since the managers are the people who have typically been promoted based on their success in the current system, it is difficult to get them to see a need for change. This makes the front-end work of getting management buy-in even more important. Although much time was spent making sure that senior management was committed to the process, relatively little time was spent at the beginning getting the middle managers to actively support the process. Active participation in Quality Quest should have been made part of the managers' and supervisors' regular performance reviews and compensation processes.

The most troublesome problem was that the manufacturing management team tended to view the whole process as training and, therefore, the trainer's total responsibility. Because managers were being taught a new way of doing business, it was a mistake to allow the plant managers to play a passive role in the implementation of this process. When managers turn most of their responsibility over to the trainers, their employees get confused about whom to take direction from—the manager or trainer. This is just another way middle management expresses its reluctance to change. These roadblocks must be dealt with out in the open because training is merely the first step in the process.

SUCCESSFULLY IMPLEMENTING TQM IN THE WORKPLACE

One solution to the roadblocks is to use a mission statement that everyone in the company believes in. If a company works to live up to a mission statement, then management can work on defining strategies, company values, acceptable behaviors, and the systems to support and reinforce the new culture. Establishing this framework up front can go a long way toward removing roadblocks on the journey to a TQM workplace.

Key points for a successful TQM implementation effort include:

- Visible and active commitment from top leadership is essential to success

- Top leadership commitment must be used to rally middle management

- The process must be led by management without the option of opting out

- The process must be understood and accepted by management before employees are involved

- Involve employees because, as a rule, they want to be involved

Pursuing the implementation of a TQM process for your business is a valuable experience both personally and financially, but as with most things of value, it comes at a price. The barriers encountered in this company are not unique to its business or industry and seem to be universal. They can be overcome with diligence and effort (the price of success in TQM). The methodology presented here isn't the only one available or the only successful way to go; in the end, each organization needs to find its own way to do it.

ENDNOTE

1. P. Crosby, *Quality Without Tears* (New York: McGraw-Hill, 1984).

21

Continuous Quality Improvement at Williams-Bally Midway Games

Art Davis

SUMMARY

The presentation will explain how the Williams-Bally Company imple-mented its continuous quality improvement (CQI) process. This team pre-sentation will describe how it evolved its plan and used its total quality approach to achieve record performance in boosting customer satisfaction and service level, while reducing product lead time and costs. Training was the "launch vehicle" to foster involvement of employees in "speeding-up" cycle time throughout the organization.

KEY WORDS

Team building, culture change, total quality management, quality training.

INTRODUCTION

Williams-Bally is the premier manufacturer of electromechanical pinball, video amusement, and video lottery terminals. It commands over 75 percent of the world market for this type of product. The company was founded 65 years ago in Chicago and is recognized for its leadership in developing clever and creative game product designs.

The product is technically very sophisticated. It marries computer technology with robotics and electromechanical animation. The product is complex and labor intensive in its assembly. The opportunities for error in overall manufacturing are very high. Product quality and reliability were often compromised much to the dismay of their customers. Therein lay a good part of their problem.

The continued business success and growth of the company is tied to increasing customer satisfaction primarily through: 1) improving product quality/reliability, 2) reducing overall business cycle time, and 3) instilling a continuous quality improvement culture throughout the organization.

In the early 1990's, the company experienced significant business growth—on the order of 30 to 40 percent per year. As a result this significantly strained systems then in place. Internal coordination and communications suffered. Business cycle time, from inception of customer order to receipt of payment, became painfully elongated. See Figure 21.1.

This spawned product and manufacturing quality problems as employees struggled to overcome the obstacles of rework loops and information disconnects. This increasingly led to product quality problems in final assembly and delayed shipments. Senior management increasingly

% of Time	Activity
0–13	Design concept
27	Design requirements
34	Development
58	Design complete
61	Support pre-production
64	Test
68	Administration get order
	Order entry
	Planning/get parts
	Quality assurance
79	Produce game
95	Game shipped
100	Accounting expedites payment

Figure 21.1   Cumulative business cycle time.

recognized that this situation was untenable. It needed to be corrected if continued business success was to be assured. Management recognized that much, if not all, of the business problems encountered were related in some way to quality deficiency.

Management therefore set out on a process of self-introspection. Working with their newly hired director (now VP) of quality and an outside consultant, they assessed various aspects of the organization. This involved evaluating what was good and bad with the ways business was conducted. The results of this assessment revealed that the various departments in the organization were unfocused and functioned as independent entities. Coordination between groups was frequently lacking or non-existent. Employees often did not understand the "big picture" and how or what their contribution to it was.

Management concluded that a strong customer focus was lacking throughout the organization. What was needed was a process that would help all employees adopt a culture of serving the customer. Working with their consultant, they adopted the Customer–Supplier Methodology (CSM). The CSM became the core of their quality and business-cycle-time improvement intervention. See Figure 21.2.

The management group formulated the policy that quality and cycle time improvement begin with the idea that any work function can be viewed as a process to be managed and improved to benefit customers (internal and external) and the business. Particular emphasis was given to the concept that each department and employee has customers (that is, the receivers of department/employee outputs and suppliers [providers of input]). The challenge now was how to get the message across to the employees of the company.

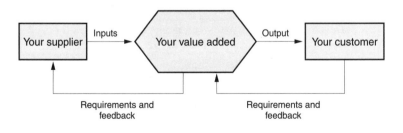

Figure 21.2 Customer/supplier model.

Behaviors needed to be changed if not the basic culture of the organization. To help with this task, the firm decided it required a complete, corporate-wide approach. They adopted and formalized a strategy they called continuous quality improvement (CQI). Working with their consultant they developed a unique, highly interactive training process and implementation plan.

To address the behavioral and culture change issues, they developed a special role-play simulation workshop. The training was designed and delivered over 16 hours. The first 10 hours involved doing the simulation followed by study and application of the tools for continuous improvement. The remaining six hours involved starting the CQI implementation intervention while in the workshop. Because of this, participants were required to attend together with natural work group(s).

The simulation exercise involved a fictitious company that has problems with systems, communications, and product materials, not unlike their own firm. Participants role-played various functions in the simulation, such as customers, sales, order entry, manufacturing, shipping, management, and staff support. The objective here was to demonstrate the need for cross-functional communication, provide a common quality "vocabulary" for discussion by diverse participant audiences, and to demonstrate the need for the type of improvement that could be accomplished by application of the "customer–supplier methodology."

It also provided "raw material" for subsequent explanation and practice of the tools for continuous improvement. The workshop and simulation was a lot of fun. This motivated the participants to get interested and more involved with instituting improvements in the organization.

Management then articulated its "CQI management strategy" which consisted of the following steps:

- Conducting a senior management overview session

- Establishing a corporate CQI steering committee

  - Developing mission statement, goals, and objectives for overall business and plant-level macro and micro measures of quality performance

  - Designating internal administrator/facilitator—each plant

  - Establishing budget, by plant, for:

    - Formal training of work group teams

    - Internal and external resource support

- Employee communications/awareness campaign

- Employee recognition program

- Conducting CQI communication campaign at each plant

Management developed a "roadmap to continuous quality improvement and customer satisfaction," which they shared with all their employees (see Figure 21.3).

The plan involved training everyone in the organization, from senior management on down to the bottom of the organization. Natural workgroup teams were to be the engine of implementation. They were trained together in the CSM and tools of CQI whose focus in the workshop training stressed the following:

- Customer–supplier trust and respect

- Quality at the source

- Eliminate inspection at the source

- Establish rapid cycle time council
  charter to develop policy to create, foster, and
  ensure application of RCT throughout organization

```
┌──────────────┐      ┌──────────────┐    ┌──────────────┐
│  Executive   │─┐  ┌▶│   Workshop   │───▶│  Normal work │
│  awareness   │ │  │ │   training   │    │  group teams │
│              │ │  │ │   in CSM     │    │              │
└──────────────┘ │  │ └──────────────┘    └──────────────┘
                 │  │                                        ┌──────────────┐
                 ▼  │     • Customer/supplier                │  Continuous  │
           ┌──────────────┐   methodology                    │ improvement  │
           │   Plan and   │                                  │              │
           │organize program│                                └──────────────┘
           └──────────────┘                                         ▲
      • Communicate goals, strategies        ┌──────────────┐       │
        and implementation plan              │   Execute:   │───────┘
                                             │ Implement TQM │
                                             │and problem solve│
                                             └──────────────┘
                                              • Form internal and
                                                external teams
                                              • Define: Customers/suppliers
                                                        Products/services
                                                        Critical requirements
                                                        Processes and measure
                                                        Improve cycle time
```

| Inspiration | Information | Implementation | Institutionalization |

Figure 21.3 Roadmap to continuous quality improvement and customer satisfaction.

- Measure process, not finished items

  - Actual cycle time versus entitlement

- Flowchart process

  - Eliminate non-value work

- Continual effort to reduce variability

  - Pareto, SPC, brainstorming, problem solving

- Set measurable goals for performance

  - DPU/DPM (Defects/unit—million)

- Total company agenda

As mentioned, employee involvement teams were the "prime mover" of the CQI. They are small natural work groups of people doing similar work. They met regularly to reinforce the CSM and to analyze and improve their work process to reduce defects and cycle time.

The objectives of the employee involvement teams included:

- Creating a quality awareness and interest among all employees.

- Tapping a vast resource of expertise in individual processes *(the experts are the employees)*.

- Developing major improvements in quality and cycle time.

- Improving the morale, skill, and motivation of every employee.

- Creating an atmosphere of listening, working together, and responding. Accepting the opportunity to make positive changes.

The initial thrust of the CQI involved training a pilot group of 11 administrative and plant teams consisting of approximately 108 employees as follows:

Administrative/Support	Plant
Purchasing (5)	Final cabinet assembly (55)
Industrial engineering (5)	• Power box team
Material control (6)	• Coin door assembly team
Receiving (8)	• Cabinet subassembly team
Warehouse (20)	• Switch assembly team
Incoming inspection (9)	• Final assembly teams 1 & 2

These pilot teams were enormously successful. They eagerly met the challenge and tackled the vexing problems of internal communications by applying the six-step process of the CSM learned in the workshop.

The teams determined their customer's critical requirements for the product or service output they provided and negotiated to achieve commitment. They also defined their own needs and their requirements for the inputs they needed from their supplier. For most of the employees, customers and suppliers were other internal functions.

By formalizing and then documenting these requirements, employees began to view their jobs as an important process. Attitudes and feelings about their jobs changed. Many teams became entrepreneurial. They also tackled the tough task of changing the old ways work was performed. They analyzed their process, looking for ways to reduce the cycle time. In the training they learned and practiced the technique of flowcharting or "process mapping." They discovered that in a typical process, less than 10 percent of the overall time consisted of "value-added" activities. (See Figure 21.4.)

The teams relentlessly challenged excessive delays, moves, and storages as revealed by their flowcharting of the process. They devised new ways of processing work by combining and simplifying activities. They discovered that by reducing the cycle time of their process, quality also improved. Most of the time was previously expended in various rework loops that added to the cycle time.

By also formally negotiating customer and supplier critical requirements "up front," they focused on doing only those tasks that supported customer satisfaction. The results were impressive. Attitudes and feelings about the work and the company greatly improved. Many of the revised processes of teams resembled the ideal shown in Figure 21.5.

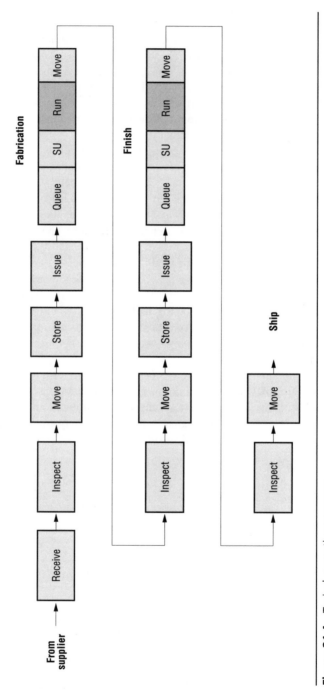

Figure 21.4 Typical operations process.

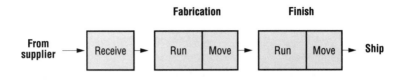

Figure 21.5 Ideal operations process.

CONCLUSION

The benefits and results of their activities are in the numbers as follows:

- Manufacturing cycle time was reduced 100%.

- Overall business cycle time was reduced greater than 30%.

- The focus shifted toward the process versus people problems.

- Much improved communications using the CSM.

- Problem solving was made easier using the tools of CQI.

- Quality performance was up. First pass yield went from < 45% to > 95%.

Based on the results of the pilot team's efforts, the CQI intervention was scaled up and introduced to the rest of the organization. Over 1100 employees in three plants are now actively involved in continuous quality improvement. The journey isn't over. Quality education continues.

The company developed a training curriculum map for all line and staff functions to cover the next three to four years. This involves the intro-duction of more progressive and sophisticated tools and techniques that build upon the foundation they all received in the basic CQI workshop. These courses include SPC, cycle time management, design for manufac-turability, benchmarking, and eventually assessment training for the Malcolm Baldrige National Quality Award (see Figure 21.6).

In summary, the management and employees of the company both feel much more confident about their future. Everyone subscribes to and sup-ports the continuous quality improvement process. They see it as an envi-ronment that needs constant nurturing and development. It starts at the top with management setting the example. Training fosters the culture change necessary for success.

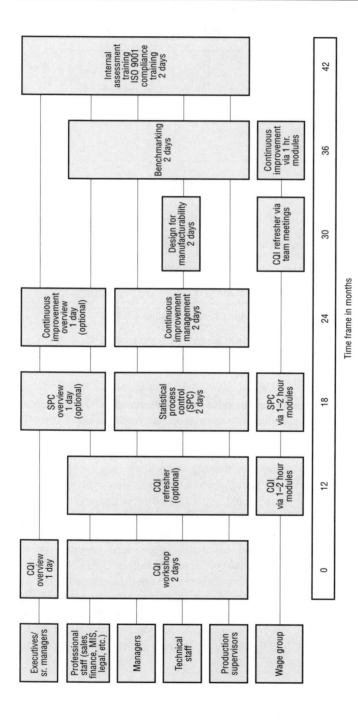

Figure 21.6   Training curriculum map for continuous quality improvement (CQI).

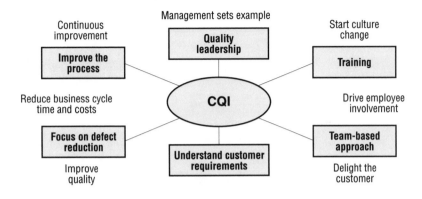

Figure 21.7   Continuous quality improvement environment.

Employee involvement drives the process through teams focused on delighting the customer. They do this by understanding and formalizing customer requirements. Using the six-step CSM methodology, they focus on cycle time and defect reduction by improving their process. The key is that it is a never ending journey (see Figure 21.7).

ACKNOWLEDGMENTS

Dan Galarde
Vice President, Quality
Williams-Bally Midway Games, Inc.

22

Teamwork Brings Breakthrough Improvements in Quality and Climate

Steven Crom and Herbert France

Achieving breakthrough improvements in quality is as much a cultural challenge as it is a technical one. An integrated improvement approach that uses team training, structured problem solving, regular team meetings, clear team leadership, and ongoing management support has helped one U.K. company make impressive improvements: it reduced scrap rates by more than 70%, which translated into an annual savings of $980,000 on $40 million in sales. Moreover, the results have been sustained because the employees have learned how to identify, solve, and prevent quality problems by improving the underlying work practices and processes.

The company, which will be referred to by the fictitious name of Packco, manufactures cardboard packaging for consumer goods. For many years, Packco was a family-owned enterprise until it was acquired by a large multinational company. Now, about 350 employees work at Packco.

HOW IT ALL BEGAN

Well into the mid-1980s, Packco had a traditional corporate culture that reflected its past as a family-owned enterprise. For 12 years, the presiding managing director, Mark Smith, ruled the company with a firm hand. Highly competitive, Smith had no tolerance for mistakes.

As a result, employees learned to keep a low profile. The unwritten rule was "concentrate on your job, do what you know how to do, and let someone else worry about the rest"—which included any problems that appeared later in the manufacturing process of printing, laminating, cutting, creasing, and gluing cardboard packaging.

In short, the climate in this hierarchical, functionally-oriented organization was one of fear—employees were afraid to take risks. Each department worked in its own well-established turf, while the quality department tried to catch quality problems before they got out the door. Although the company maintained a reputation for well-printed packaging, it did so at significant internal cost.

Smith realized that the company's climate and approach to quality had to change. He began by using a process-oriented approach to improve the printing process. One of the biggest challenges to implementing this approach was dispelling the widely held belief that printing is an art, not a science, and therefore cannot be proceduralized.

With input from production director Peter Philips, who came from outside the printing industry, Smith decided to first improve the presses' makeready times, which is the time it takes to set up the presses from one job to the next. Employee teams were formed and were given formal team training and a structured problem-solving approach to use.

Central to the teams' problem-solving approach was the belief that employees (in this case, the equipment operators) have many ideas on how to improve their work processes (in this case, reducing makeready times) and would gladly implement those ideas if given sufficient time, training, and management support. The teams' belief was confirmed; the equipment operators' suggestions enabled the teams to reduce makeready times by 65% to 75% on complex six- and seven-color printing presses. This was the start of Packco's cultural change to a more self-directed work force.

As Smith and Philips had hoped, the machine operators recognized the need for more flexibility in the types of work they performed. In the past, jobs were categorized into two classes of press operators, two classes of assistants, and two classes of ink personnel, each performing specific tasks in accordance with his or her status. The makeready time reduction effort, however, instilled a sense of teamwork. Employees became more flexible, doing what needed to be done. For example, the press operators started helping the assistants clean printer rolls before setting up new jobs.

THE NEXT STEP

Delighted by the improvements in both the makeready operation and in the culture, Smith and the board of directors decided that scrap reduction was the next biggest area of potential improvement. Cost-of-quality summaries estimated that process scrap costs (that is, internal failure costs) accounted for 72% of the total cost of quality in 1992 (see Figure 22.1). This amounted to $1.3 million, or 3.5% of sales. It was believed that true scrap losses were twice that amount because there was incomplete scrap reporting throughout the manufacturing process. Analysis of the limited scrap and processing data revealed that at least half of the identifiable scrap losses ($675,000) could be cut through team problem-solving efforts.

Since most of the scrap originated from three processes—two printing processes and a finishing process—three teams were organized. The teams consisted of process operators; setup and maintenance personnel; and representatives from purchasing, sales, quality, and support functions, as appropriate. While teams should consist of five to seven people to be most efficient and effective, the size of these teams ranged from eight to 10

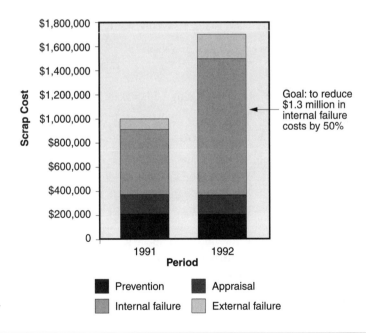

Figure 22.1 Rising scrap costs.

members because of the overriding necessity to have all resources available to solve the scrap problems.

Team leaders were appointed by top management. The individuals selected were relatively young "rising stars" in the organization, who had the respect of team members, had direct access to top management, and shared the drive to improve.

Because of scrap-reporting deficiencies, it was not possible to charge each team with its own mission. So a combined team mission to reduce scrap costs by $675,000 in nine months was set. Translated to percentage of sales, this meant getting the monthly scrap rate down from 3.5% to 1.75%.

All three teams attended training together at an off-site location, which provided an excellent atmosphere for learning, getting acquainted, and relaxing. Over a three-day period, the teams learned about, and practiced, how to work effectively as multilevel, multifunctional teams to identify and solve quality problems. They learned that obtaining breakthrough results is a combination of:

- Adopting new mind-sets about possibilities (that is, overcoming established paradigms)

- Involving those closest to the problems

- Working effectively together as a team

- Using data correctly

- Communicating and coordinating with stakeholders (including upper management)

- Following a structured problem-solving approach

During this training, the teams met with senior management to receive their mission and to hear the declaration of management's commitment and support. Given the employees' past experiences, serious doubts about management's sincerity were voiced. What followed was a healthy, open exchange in which managers challenged the teams to test their sincerity by coming forward with specific requests and by asking for their support on decisions when needed. This cleared the air and set the stage for moving forward.

The team leaders were trained several weeks later. This training focused on team leadership skills and was timed so that the leaders could develop the skills they really needed, based on their recent experiences in trying to lead their teams.

The teams then followed a quality improvement road map to reduce scrap. The road map took into account that:

- The defects most responsible for scrap were appearance characteristics (that is, only visually identifiable).

- Analyzing the defects and the products in which they occurred invariably identified the particular points in the process where the defects occurred. It was even possible to trace defects to a particular machine.

- Special data collection processes had to be implemented. (Up to that point, data were only collected from the 100 percent sorting inspections performed on lots rejected by in-process sampling inspections.)

As he was with the makeready time reduction teams, Philips was involved throughout the scrap reduction teams' efforts because he understood the importance of ongoing management support. Philips provided support by:

- Helping the teams set intermediate goals

- Supplying resources that the teams needed to succeed (such as time on the equipment for experimentation)

- Following the teams' progress by periodically attending team meetings, arranging regular progress reports, and following up on action items

- Constantly asking, "how can I help?"

Philips' actions demonstrated management's commitment to the teams. Above all, his actions let the teams know that it was safe to take risks. The teams knew that Philips was not interested in assigning blame but rather in learning, improving, and reaching goals.

HURDLING OBSTACLES

During their efforts to reduce scrap, teams encountered and overcame several obstacles:

1. *Doubt about management support.* Naturally, doubt about management's support persisted among many team members until experience taught them otherwise. Once the teams' initial requests were approved and other types of top management support were demonstrated, doubts subsided. Changes in the managing directorship and several other management positions further solidified employees' confidence in management's willingness to change and support the improvement efforts.

2. *Differences in terminology.* Analysis of the defects from both printing processes showed that one type of defect, referred to as "marks," was responsible for more than 90% of the scrap in the printing areas and for 65% of all reported scrap. This would have made a great target problem to solve—except for the revelation that, in the two printing areas, there were 18 different kinds of marks that could not be quantified to determine which were the highest contributors to scrap. Furthermore, there were a variety of terms used to describe these marks.

This problem was addressed in two ways:

- Based on the experience of the operators and quality personnel on the print teams, specific types of marks known to be large contributors to scrap were selected as the initial problems to be solved. Action plans were then made accordingly.

- A defect terminology standards committee, consisting of two members from each of the three teams, was set up to standardize the terminology for each defect. In addition to writing the terminology standards, the committee wrote descriptions and provided examples of each defect, provided data processing with additional computer codes for the defects, and trained all relevant personnel in the new standards and codes.

Within three months, data on each type of mark (as well as other defects) were being gathered. The data verified that the initial problems chosen were the correct ones (see Figure 22.2). This information was later used to help the teams track the effects of their corrective actions.

3. *Disagreements on what problems to solve.* Improving processes usually involves solving a series of problems. As is typical in teams chartered to make improvements, the members of the three teams brought with them their opinions on what problems should be solved first. To resolve disagreements, team members were allowed to nominate problems that they would like to solve. Those problems that received the consensus of all team members were worked on first.

While this was a shotgun approach to problem selection, it had several benefits beyond satisfying certain team members:

- The teams captured the "quick" successes, which kept the team members motivated.

- From early on, employees who were not participating in teams saw how the teams' successes benefited them, which encouraged them to support their colleagues.

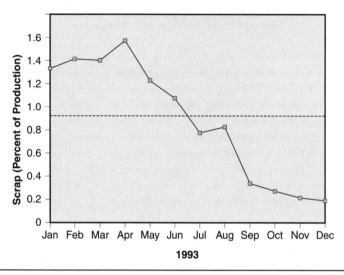

Figure 22.2 Scrap due to mark type AZ.

- Some of the problems selected and solved by the teams were later found to contribute significantly to the overall scrap reduction problem. For example, two major scrap contributors were drastically reduced by overhauling a press and changing printing plate preparation procedures.

4. *An uncooperative team leader.* One team experienced frustration with its team leader, who often changed the solutions that were agreed to by the team. The leader, who was a middle manager and technical expert, would sometimes implement his own solution because he thought his solution would work just as well as the team's but be less costly or easier to implement. Other times, he just sat on actions that he was asked to implement.

The team finally challenged the leader on his actions, which spurred him to ask outside consultants for advice. He was urged to share his view and any relevant information about a proposed solution with the rest of the team, but if the team reached consensus on a solution with which he didn't completely agree (meaning that he could live with the team's solution), he must see to it that the solution agreed upon was implemented. Through this experience, the team leader learned that an idea that could yield an 80 percent improvement and is supported by everyone is worth more than an idea that could yield a 100 percent improvement but only he supports.

THE TEAMS' RESULTS

The quality improvement effort began in March 1993 and was expected to be completed in nine months, but since summer holidays delayed work for a month, the teams' deadline was extended to January 1994. As Figure 22.3 shows, the goal of reducing the scrap rate to 1.75% was reached in November 1993. Continuing efforts brought the scrap rate down even further to 1.3% by January 1994 and to 1% in the months that followed (that rate is still being sustained). The drop in the scrap rate from 3.5% to 1% represents almost a $1 million gain for this $40 million business.[1] Management was very pleased with the results and with the experience that the workforce gained in making improvements.

Early in 1994, the teams paused to be recognized and to celebrate their achievements. They requested, and were granted, permission to continue the investigations and solutions that were still in progress. Packco has also trained a small group of employees in how to assess process capabilities and reduce product variability using statistical process control (SPC) methods. This core group of SPC experts-to-be will teach others how to apply these methods. In addition, Packco plans to make technological improvements in how product and process variables are measured and in

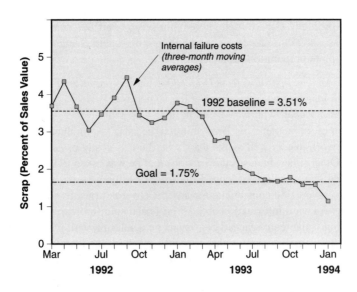

Figure 22.3   Scrap goals met through teamwork.

how parameters for product characteristics are established to ensure functional quality in customers' packaging.

WHAT'S BEHIND EVERY SUCCESSFUL TEAM

Packco's successful efforts to reduce scrap underscore the need for senior management's commitment to achieve breakthrough improvements in climate and quality. Packco's board of directors recognized that the scrap reduction effort was part of a larger strategy that enabled employees to redesign their work processes to better meet the customers' and the company's needs. From the outset, the directors recognized that the existing company culture would work against employees exercising their initiative and being creative in their problem-solving efforts. By attending team meetings and asking team members, "how can I help?" senior management indicated that the improvement effort was taken seriously and was, therefore, worthwhile.

While it's important to develop the requisite technical problem-solving skills for improvement efforts, the people side of the equation cannot be ignored either—otherwise the improvement efforts will never have the effect that they might have had. Teams succeed when they have confidence in themselves and their managers, and the training and opportunity to make changes in the way work gets done.

ENDNOTE

1. This figure is calculated using 1993 business rates.

23

Continuous Improvement of Emergency Care and Services

Marianne Murdock

ABSTRACT

A total quality control/continuous improvement program was initiated in the Emergency Department of Mary Washington Hospital, a 340-bed, not-for-profit, regional hospital in Virginia, because of concerns expressed by care providers and consumers that increases in patient volume and acuity were affecting quality of care and service. A conceptual framework for the program was devised using the Shewhart/Deming quality improvement cycle and the quality contour model, which was developed at Mary Washington Hospital.

The first step in implementing the program was to determine the nature of the quality problems. Brainstorming sessions were conducted with Emergency Department associates to gain their perspective on the nature and type of quality problems. Two conclusions emerged from these problem identification exercises: 1) many of the quality problems arise from the process nature of the work in the Emergency Department, and 2) the Emergency Department is an internal customer of other hospital departments.

The extent of the quality problems was explored by conducting a baseline study to assess customer satisfaction, needs, and expectations and to evaluate process flow. The results of the study indicated that the average turnaround time (from time of arrival to time of discharge) was 150.1±11.4 minutes (mean ± standard error of the mean). More than half of the patients' time was spent waiting for and receiving services from associates in other departments. This result was useful in illustrating to the Emergency Department associates that they were internal customers of other departments. Less than half (43.1%) of the 58 randomly selected Emergency Department customers interviewed for the study said the time their visit required was "acceptable." A majority (67.2%) of the patients indicated that the staff was "very sensitive" to their illness/injury. All the patients indicated that they felt the caregivers had explained the treatment the patients received.

Based on the outcomes of the brainstorming sessions and the baseline study, three general foci for the continuous improvement program were developed: 1) setting a quality agenda, 2) establishing and sustaining quality improvement teams, and 3) training associates in the philosophies and methods of continuous improvement.

The purpose of setting the quality agenda was to give form to the continuous improvement program and to clarify the vision of the program by stating it in terms that everyone understands. A Delphi study was the mechanism used to set the quality agenda in the Emergency Department. Three agendas were set: 1) improving Emergency Department processes for administering care and service (meeting the needs and expectations of the external customer), 2) improving the Emergency Department practice environment, and 3) improving internal customer relationships with other departments.

Quality improvement teams were organized among Emergency Department associates in response to the identification of the three quality agendas. One team was organized to evaluate and improve the work processes using the approach that all work is a process and processes can be improved. A second quality improvement team was organized to monitor and improve relations with internal customers. The practice environment was the focus of the third team, which worked on problems resulting from insufficient staff and high patient volume and acuity.

The continuous improvement training program curriculum included these topics: Deming's 14 points; quality problem identification techniques such as fishbone diagrams, Pareto diagrams, runs charts; and statistical process control methods. The training is being done simultaneously with the activities of the quality improvement teams to give associates experience with the techniques they are learning.

While the total quality control/continuous improvement program is in a constant state of evolution, there are certain lessons that have been learned about the process to date. These include: 1) continuous improvement is hard work, 2) continuous improvement requires an organizational paradigm shift, 3) continuous improvement is everybody's job—in health-care, this includes physicians, 4) continuous improvement training must be made applicable to the nature of the work—training programs designed for manufacturing do not work in healthcare, 5) continuous improvement train-ing must be made applicable to quality problems encountered by the trainees in their work, 6) healthcare quality assurance professionals have a role in continuous improvement programs, 7) continuous improvement is a time-consuming process that is well worth the effort.

The total quality control/continuous improvement program begun in the Emergency Department at Mary Washington Hospital is both revolu-tionary and evolutionary for the organization. The next step in continuously improving the quality program is to expand the program to the entire insti-tution. In five years Mary Washington Hospital will move to a new replace-ment hospital. Embracing and implementing a continuous improvement philosophy and plan now will guarantee that the foundation of that new structure will rest on a base of quality.

INTRODUCTION

The Mary Washington Hospital Commitment to Continuous Improvement

Mary Washington Hospital (MWH) is a not-for-profit, regional, commu-nity hospital serving a population of 170,000 in one of the most rapidly growing areas of the Commonwealth of Virginia. The stated mission of MWH is to provide quality care and service in an environment of respect for all customers. The commitment to continuous improvement (CI) began with an interest by the president and chief executive officer, the chief operating officer, and the senior management staff in W. Edwards Deming's philosophy of continuous improvement in general and his 14 points specifically.

A Conceptual Framework for Continuous Improvement

A conceptual framework for CI was deemed necessary to ensure that the effort had a sound foundation. This framework was a CI-centered model developed at MWH that featured six components: 1) identify the quality concern, 2) recall or review the values, 3) identify the stakeholders, 4) propose several alternative courses of action, 5) form a vision, 6) pledge a commitment.

PURPOSE

The purpose of this paper is to describe the development, implementation and ongoing evaluation of a total quality control/continuous improvement program in the Mary Washington Hospital Emergency Department (MWH ED).

SETTING

The MWH ED is staffed 24 hours a day, every day of the year by an all–board certified group of emergency medicine physicians, registered nurses, licensed practical nurses, a head nurse, a Master's prepared emergency nurse clinician, unit secretaries, orderlies, and a department manager. The ED was chosen as the test site for the implementation of CI at MWH for several reasons: the ED represents a microcosm of the hospital at large; the service volume is rising at a steady rate; and the ED has high visibility in the community. In the last fiscal year (FY 1989) for which data are available, there were over 40,000 visits to the MWH ED. This represented an increase in volume from FY 1986 of 26,000 visits. Physicians, nurses, administrators, and patients have all voiced concerns about the quality of care and service provided patients given the increase in volume. Another factor in choosing the ED was community/customer relations. MWH is the sole provider in a rapidly growing one-city and five-county region. Individuals moving into the area demand a high caliber of healthcare. Similarly, long-term residents of the area expect the MWH ED to provide them with a consistently high level of care and service. In general, customers expect the MWH ED to provide quality care and service while meeting increasing patient volume and acuity demands.

Process Flow in the MWH ED

Patients arriving at the MWH ED are first registered and then triaged so that they will be placed in a queue for treatment. Entry and exit from the queue does not follow a first-in, first-out hierarchy. The order of entering and leaving the queue depends on the severity of presenting condition with life-threatening emergencies always being attended to first. A nurse makes an initial assessment of a patient, documents the assessment, and leaves that documentation for a physician. When a physician becomes available he or she assesses the patient and writes orders either for diagnostic tests or for discharge. If lab tests or X-rays are required, patients must wait for the availability of personnel from laboratory or radiology or both to perform the ordered procedures. Once the results of the procedures are reviewed by the ordering physician, the physician makes the decision to either discharge or admit the patient. If the patient is discharged, a nurse assists the patient in preparing for his departure.

IMPLEMENTING CONTINUOUS IMPROVEMENT IN THE EMERGENCY DEPARTMENT

Identifying the Quality Concerns

The quality concerns in the MWH ED were identified by using brainstorming sessions; nominal group processes; formal surveys of patients; and focus groups with patients and their families, the ED care providers, and ancillary service providers. An Ishikawa fishbone diagram was used to delineate and represent the quality concerns identified by these various groups. ED Personnel thought there were insufficient nurses and support personnel per shift. ED staff members also thought that there was a high volume of acute patients, that the needed supplies and materials were not always available, and that the quality of service provided by other departments was variable. Patients and their families thought that they waited too long for service and that visits to the ED required too much time. All the groups consulted agreed that the ED was dirty and, at times, chaotic.

A formal survey of 58 patients at the time of their discharge from the ED revealed that patients found the staff to be sensitive to their illness or injury and that the appearance of the ED was adequate but could be improved. Of the patients surveyed, 10% said the time their ED visit required as "Not at all acceptable"; only 43% judged the time their ED visit required to be "Acceptable".

Reviewing the Values

The values on which the MWH ED continuous improvement program rest are the quality contour model and the concept of continuous improvement. The quality contour model, developed at Mary Washington Hospital, represents MWH's various customer groups—patients, care-givers, support service providers, and the resident community. The quality contour model features the patient at the center of four concentric circles. The patient is served by a variety of direct caregivers, including physicians, nurses, and allied healthcare providers, who, as a group, comprise the second of the four concentric circles. The direct caregivers are served by support personnel including administration, information services, housekeeping, materials management, and dietary, among others. The outside circle represents the resident community of the institution and includes suppliers, accrediting and regulatory agencies and potential and previous customers and their families. The model affirms that there are many customers and suppliers in the system with patients being the ultimate customers. The model is dynamic and allows consideration of the impact of the forces that perturb and alter the state of the system served by the model. In its ideal state, the equidistance of the four concentric circles represents a balance of forces that alter the system. In its real state, the four circles are not necessarily concentric as forces perturb the system. An understanding of those forces and how they impact on the system enhances one's ability to affect continuous improvement of a system.

The second value consideration is the fit between the quality contour model and the concept of continuous improvement. Continuous improvement has two elements: 1) adding value to the care and services provided by continually improving the process used to provide those products; and 2) meeting the needs, desires, and expectations of the customer. Adoption of the quality contour model leads to advocating the patient as the focus of all activity in a healthcare institution. Continuous improvement sharpens the central focus on the patient by acknowledging the patient's inherent and essential value to the system.

Identifying the Stakeholders

The stakeholders are those persons who are affected, directly and indirectly, by the quality concerns, and who will be impacted by the solutions. The stakeholders in the MWH ED are the patients and their families, physicians, nurses, rescue squad personnel, ancillary support personnel, hospital administration, regulatory and accrediting agencies, and the resident community at large which relies on the MWH ED for care and service. The interests of these stakeholders is delineated in the quality contour model. The importance of the ancillary support personnel to the system was illustrated in the results of a process flow/observational study of 58 randomly selected ED patients. The results of this study revealed that, on average, 58% of the patient's time was spent waiting for or receiving the services of the departments of laboratory and/or radiology. This result mandated the inclusion of ancillary support service personnel as critical stakeholders in the ED system.

Proposing the Actions

The quality improvement plan developed by Florida Power and Light (Stratton 1990) was reviewed in developing a continuous improvement plan for the MWH ED. The three major foci of the Florida Power and Light quality improvement program—quality policy deployment, quality in daily work life, and development of quality improvement teams—were adapted for the MWH ED continuous improvement program. The three components of the MWH ED continuous improvement program are: 1) setting an improvement agenda, 2) developing and implementing improvement teams for the various caregiving stakeholders, and 3) improving the work environment and processes.

An improvement agenda was set in consultation with the various direct caregiving and ancillary support personnel. The items on the improvement agenda are: 1) decrease total turnaround time, 2) decrease waiting time for patients at all activities, 3) become more aware of the needs, desires, and expectations of patients and their families, 4) improve relationships with departments that supply service and 5) modify ED policies and governance rules to support continuous improvement.

The first two items on the improvement agenda are interrelated and were addressed by diagramming the process flow for the MWH ED. Using the patient as the basis for study, a detailed process flow diagram was constructed that tracked the movement of patients through all the various care and service activities of the MWH ED. Taking a cue from simulation modeling, the process flow diagram included queues (where patients waited for care or service), activities (where patients received care or service), source nodes (through which patients entered the ED), and sink nodes (from which patients exited the ED). The patients represented transactions moving through the network and the caregivers and support personnel were represented as resources. Having drawn the ED process flow diagram, process evaluation was performed. Process evaluation involved consideration of five questions about processes: 1) are all the steps currently a part of the process necessary to accomplish the desired outcome?, 2) do the steps occur in the most effective and efficient order?, 3) what steps in the process represent bottlenecks?, 4) are the steps in the process understood by those who execute them?, and 5) what revisions or refinements in the process are suggested by the people who perform the process? The process flow diagram was then evaluated for changes, revisions, and enhancements by ED physicians, nurses, and ancillary support personnel.

Several recommendations and actions have resulted from this analysis of work flow in the MWH ED. First, when the process began it was agreed that there were too many steps and that the process was too cumbersome. A process flow quality improvement team identified bottlenecks and made recommendations to alleviate them. These recommendations did not always involve increasing staff sizes. A detailed work flow analysis was commissioned by the process flow quality improvement team to determine what each of the ED jobs involved and, more importantly, how the job functions were interrelated. The process flow quality improvement team also made recommendations about the physical location of treatment areas and equipment in the ED. As a result of the work of the process flow quality improvement team, processes have been streamlined, physical changes have been made in the work area, and both total turnaround time and waiting times at various activities have decreased.

The process flow quality improvement team has also employed quality function deployment (QFD). Early in the deliberations of the process flow quality improvement team it became apparent that if the customers' interests were to be paramount in the MWH ED, the operation had to be essentially redesigned. The quality function deployment notion of the "house of quality" has been useful in designing a new product and service. In developing the house of quality the quality improvement team first identified the requirements of the various customers. This proved to be a somewhat cumbersome process as there are many customers of the MWH ED. To simplify the process, the external customer (the patients and their families) was chosen as the focus. The Marketing Department was very helpful in the process as they had collected some customer satisfaction and requirement data. The customer requirements were prioritized as: 1) to receive appropriate treatment from competent healthcare professionals, 2) to be treated in a timely manner, 3) to receive high quality care and service at the lowest possible cost, 4) to receive treatment when it is needed, and 5) to be treated with equipment that is accurate, reliable, and used in a safe manner. Having defined the customer requirements, care and service specifications to be optimized to ensure customer satisfaction were delineated. These specifications included sufficient staff in the ED, sufficient ancillary and support staff in other departments, availability of supplies (medicines, dressings, equipment), ability to respond to variations in patient volume and acuity, physical work space, triage of patients, good communication with rescue squads, clinically competent caregivers, and appropriate management of the many demands made on the system. The relationship between the importance of customer requirements and care and service specifications was described by the quality improvement team. These relationships along with the suggestions made in examining the process flow have resulted in changes in the care and service provided to MWH ED patients.

Becoming more aware of the needs, desires, and expectations of patients and their families is accomplished in both formal and informal ways. Scientific surveys of patients discharged from the ED are useful means of obtaining satisfaction information. These are not used exclusively to ascertain needs, desires, and expectations. The ED manager and the hospital quality engineer make routine, random visits to the ED waiting room to ask, "how are we doing?", and "what could we do better?" While this information is not generalizable, it does provide insight into the expectations of the external customer. Formal quantitative data have an important place in continuous improvement. However, the value of less structured, qualitative data should not be minimized.

Improving relationships with other departments is critical to continuous improvement of care and service provided in the MWH ED. The results of the observational study indicated that more than half of patients' total time in the ED is spent waiting for or receiving treatment from other departments. In addition, the direct caregivers in the ED identified their reliance on support departments such as materials management, housekeeping, and engineering. Improved relationships with other departments have been forged through teamwork. Every quality improvement team has membership from a cross-section of direct caregivers and support personnel. In the early meetings of these continuous improvement teams, there was a great deal of finger-pointing and blame being assigned. The opportunity to discuss interdepartmental relationships in a neutral forum has been a useful one. Quality improvement teams have worked and socialized together. These teams have celebrated their successes and learned from their failures.

There are many agencies and organizations that monitor and evaluate the performance of healthcare organizations. These include the Joint Commission on the Accreditation of Healthcare Organizations (JCAHO), the Health Care Financing Administration (HCFA) and their associated peer review organizations (PROs), and third-party payors such as insurance companies. As a result of this scrutiny, healthcare organizations tend to have many policies, procedures, and governance rules that dictate a style of management or a set of behaviors. This myriad of rules and regulations frequently stifles creativity and may be incompatible with continuous improvement. In the MWH ED the policies and procedures were examined by the governance rules quality improvement team to determine which policies and procedures could be changed, streamlined, or eliminated. In an industry where the stakes are high and the decisions are literally ones of life and death, rules and regulations are important. Acknowledging this indisputable fact, the policies and procedures of the MWH ED have not been eliminated but changed to encourage an environment where caregivers provide the best possible care and service to patients.

Realizing the aims of the improvement agenda continues because of the quality improvement teams that have been organized around the work of the MWH ED. The specific membership of the quality improvement teams varies according to the identified quality problem but generally consists of ED physicians and nurses, support personnel from other departments, and the hospital quality engineer. Some of the activities of the quality improvement teams include creating process flow diagrams and recommending changes in the process flow, creating fishbone diagrams to describe the quality problem and to separate causes from symptoms, identifying costs of poor quality, examining treatment processes and their associated patient outcomes, and developing a continuous improvement–centered compensation and performance evaluation system. The quality teams use worksheets based on the six-step continuous improvement framework described above. They develop continuous improvement measurables against which the progress of the team may be identified. This activity does not violate Deming's point 11a, "eliminate work standards (quotas) . . ." (Scherkenback 1988) as these measurables are used as benchmarks and not as standards.

Quality improvement teams have been and continue to be the primary means of doing the work of continuous improvement in the MWH ED. Quality improvement teams require commitment of the members and acceptance that these teams are an essential element of work. Employees must be given time away from the workplace to participate in quality improvement teams. If managers ask their employees to wait for a time when there is less work that time will never arrive and the organization will not have evolved into one that is committed to learning about and satisfying the needs, desires, and expectations of its customers. Sustaining the energy and enthusiasm of quality improvement teams is both difficult and rewarding.

The final element of the continuous improvement program is designed to give employees and managers the tools to enhance the quality of their daily work life. The backbone of this aspect of the program is training. Deming (Scherkenback 1988) indicates that the transformation to continuous improvement requires training on the job and vigorous programs of education and self-improvement. The curriculum includes these topics: continuous improvement philosophy; Deming's 14 points; quality problem identification techniques such as fishbone diagrams, Pareto diagrams, runs charts; and statistical process control (SPC) methods. The training is conducted simultaneously with the activities of the quality improvement teams. This is done to give team members practical experience with the techniques they are learning.

Another important element of the improvement of quality in daily work life is employees being given accountability for and taking responsibility for continuous improvement. A key factor in this is empowerment of employees. In the MWH ED, empowerment has meant that those in management positions be more willing to listen and act as coaches rather than conventional managers. Empowerment has also meant that employees have had to learn to work as members of a team. This has impacted in interesting ways on physician–nurse collaboration. Prior to the implementation of continuous improvement, the physician–nurse relationships were, at times, adversarial. While the physician remains legally responsible and, therefore, in charge of the care of a patient, physicians and nurses have begun to complement each other's roles in caring for ED patients. Improving quality in daily work life is about changing attitudes.

Form a Vision

The vision of continuous improvement in the MWH ED is a simple, yet powerful one: we will act as a team to continually provide patients with the best possible and most economical care and service. That vision is already taking shape as the three skills of continuous improvement are being learned by MWH ED employees: 1) customer skills—learning who the internal and external customers are and what their needs, desires, and expectations are; 2) analytical skills—learning to manage and problem-solve by fact rather than emotion or intuition; 3) people skills—learning to listen rather than talk, learning to empower rather than to dictate, learning the responsibility that accompanies being empowered.

The vision for the MWH ED is that managers will become leaders and coaches. Employees' suspicion of their managers will evolve into trust. An emphasis on quantity will be replaced with an emphasis on quality. Being reactive will be replaced by being proactive. Concern for the financial bottom line will be supplemented with a concern for the quality bottom line.

Pledge a Commitment

Achieving this vision will require a continuing commitment to leadership, process and outcome monitoring, process evaluation, and employee involvement. In emergency medicine the phrase "the golden hour" is used to describe the time that caregivers have to support and sustain the physiological vital signs of badly injured patients to increase their chances of surviving. At Mary Washington Hospital we believe that "the golden hour" is upon our Emergency Department. We have adopted continuous improvement as a means of controlling costs, insuring quality of care and service, and generally doing more with less. The journey on the path of continuous improvement in healthcare is a young one. The trip is fraught with unknowns, excitement, enthusiasm, disappointment, and rewards. Even given our brief experience with continuous improvement we are no longer the Emergency Department we were when the project started. We know, with great confidence, that we will continuously evolve into an Emergency Department and a parent institution that adds values to its care and services and meets the needs, desires, and expectations of the customer.

SOME THINGS WE HAVE LEARNED ABOUT CONTINUOUS IMPROVEMENT

While the continuous improvement program in the MWH ED is still evolving, we have learned valuable lessons about implementing such programs.

1. *CI is hard work.* The hardest thing about CI is setting the agenda and then getting started doing the work of CI. Given the opportunity, CI may get lost in the "firefighting" mentality that pervades many healthcare institutions.

2. *CI requires an organizational paradigm shift.* The new paradigm is that quality must be the engine that drives the organization.

3. *CI is everybody's job.* The success of CI teams is greatest when the membership of the team is a cross section of the organization. In healthcare this includes physicians. Physicians who are advocates of CI are typically the best marketers of the program.

4. *CI training must be made applicable to the nature of the business.* Materials have been developed from the MWH CI program that are specific to healthcare, as it is difficult to get healthcare workers interested in the quality problems associated with tool wear and other manufacturing engineering concerns that are often used in "canned" CI training programs. Developing these materials has required creativity and diligence.

5. *CI training must be applicable to the quality problems encountered by the trainees in their work.* The excitement of CI is infectious when people see that applying the methods makes a difference.

6. *Quality assurance professionals have a role in CI programs.* Many quality assurance professionals in hospitals fear that CI renders their services obsolete. When quality assurance professionals are exposed to CI training they often broaden their own practice to include the concepts of CI.

7. *CI takes time.* Patience and perseverance are rewarded with small victories in improving quality. The program begun in the ED at MWH is both revolutionary and evolutionary for the organization. The next step in continuously improving the quality program at MWH is to expand the program to the entire institution.

REFERENCES

Berwick, D. M. "Continuous Improvement As an Ideal in Health Care." *New England Journal of Medicine* 320, no. 1 (January 5, 1989): 53–56.

Scherkenback, W. W. *The Deming Route to Quality and Productivity.* Washington, DC: CEEPress Books, George Washington University, 1988.

Stratton, B. "A Beacon for the World." *Quality Progress* 23, no. 5 (May, 1990): 60–63.

24

Continuous Improvement in College Teaching: An Application of Statistical Tools

Zhiming Xue and Charles S. Gulas

SUMMARY

This paper identifies seven key teaching processes and examines the usefulness of statistical tools in helping understand and improve both the teaching and learning processes.

KEY WORDS

Continuous process improvement, education, statistical process control, total quality management.

INTRODUCTION

There is a growing view of students as primary customers who are currently being underserved. The implementation of total quality management (TQM) in higher education is expected to provide a potential avenue for improving instruction quality, administrative and operational efficiency, and possibly research quality. While involving faculty in quality improvement efforts in academic settings has been difficult, a few professors across the country are attempting to bring the concept of total quality into the classroom (Bateman and Roberts 1992; Hau 1991; Helms and Key 1994; Milbank 1992). With the goal of satisfying and exceeding student expectations, those pioneering professors have sent us a signal that the conventional approach of "sage on a stage" is being renovated and challenged and that the time has come to practice what we teach.

Our idea of making continuous improvement in college teaching originated from the work of Dr. Shingo, co-founder of the Toyota production system, who codifies three steps for improving manufacturing processes: (1) identifying problems, (2) applying basic approaches to improvement, and (3) making plans for improvement (Robinson 1990). Applying this approach to teaching resulted in the improvement matrix (Table 24.1) which represents seven teaching processes and the three improvement steps. Central to our continuous improvement efforts is the application of statistical tools. Statistical tools have been taught for decades in colleges and universities, but barely practiced there until recently when TQM principles and techniques started to be cautiously but progressively adopted in higher education. To assess their usefulness in improving college teaching, one of the authors of this paper applied such statistical tools as quality control charts, a Pareto diagram, and multiple regression analysis to the teaching of an undergraduate management course. Some interesting results are presented and discussed here.

PROCESS 1: IDENTIFYING STUDENT EXPECTATIONS

There are many concerns for both professors and students in the first-day class. But what concerned us most was student expectations of the course. To understand their expectations, one author prepared three ready-for-class questions for students on the first day: 1) what does the course title mean or suggest to you?, 2) what are the topics that you are interested in or expect to learn from this course?, and 3) what grade do you expect to get from this course and what is your strategy to achieve that grade? The first question is a pre-test for students to assess content knowledge of the course. Their answer to it serves as a speedometer in determining the overall class pace. It is also meant to be used by students as a reference point to see how much progress they have made as the semester develops. The second question is to solicit input from those students who have some content knowledge and to explore their learning expectations. The last question helps understand motivation and the personal strategy that they are going to undertake for their learning task. The original answer sheets of these three questions were

Table 24.1 Improvement matrix for college teaching.

Seven Teaching Processes	Current Problems	Three Steps	
		Improvement Aproaches	Implementation Procedures
Identifying student expectations	Unidentified	Self-declaration and observation	Asking three ready-for-class questions and talking to students at the beginning of the semester
Setting course standards	Unclear	Written policy	Writing grading policies in syllabus and stressing critical thinking and problem-solving skills in class
Gathering timely feedback	Untimely	Student input	Getting written feedback twice and seeking instant feedback in each class
Monitoring the learning process	Loose	Pareto diagram control charts	Digging out the root causes and adjusting teaching activities
Taking corrective actions	Ineffective	Follow-up review	Making a checklist and asking students to monitor the progress of corrective actions
Focusing on individuals	Minimal	Individual talks	Interviewing students and analyzing their academic status
Assessing class performance	None	Regression analysis	Collecting data before the final, establishing the model, and explaining the crucial factors to students

returned to students after being reviewed by the instructor. Students were instructed to use them to measure their progress throughout the semester.

There are two rules that we kept in mind to avoid any potential controversy over the concept of students versus customers. First, students as our primary customers do not always understand what their expectations are, just like consumers do not always know what they need when they go shopping. Therefore, the instructor should play a role of assisting, inspiring, and guiding students to realize what knowledge and skills they need. Second, satisfying and exceeding student expectations should not be at the price of lowering the course standards. Just because students want to have a take-home exam does not mean that such an exam is in the best interest of the class. After all, education differs from manufacturing and service in that learning is not equivalent to buying a product. The determination of the current level of knowledge of a content area and the best way to achieve a higher level can only be accomplished through a student–instructor partnership in which the instructor must have an overall control of the quality of his or her course.

PROCESS 2: SETTING COURSE STANDARDS

The quality of teaching and learning is largely determined by the course standards an instructor uses. Compared to setting the grading rules for homework, projects, and exams in the syllabus, transferring the knowledge outlined there to the mind of students is much more difficult. If grading rules are considered the hard side of the course standards, then the criteria used in transferring knowledge are soft, but crucial. The goal to hold students up to a reasonably high standard can best be attained through a close and friendly cooperation between students and the instructor. Once clear course standards have been established, appropriate strategies can be developed to meet these standards. In our continuous improvement efforts, the student–instructor partnership was addressed in both course preparation and teaching activities. Pamphlets containing the topical material were made available to students prior to each lecture to facilitate their note-taking and after-class review. In teaching activities, attempts were made to create a comfortable learning environment by combining instructor's teaching, group discussions, and teamwork together and, more importantly, developing a class culture in which no questions or answers were considered stupid. Accordingly, students were expected not only to attend class, but also to *think* in the class, particularly to learn critical thinking and problem-solving skills. It was repeatedly emphasized in the class that it is more important to understand the idea of how a particular problem was solved than to remember the detail of it. Such a requirement may be difficult to measure, but students will benefit greatly from it after they graduate.

PROCESS 3: GATHERING TIMELY FEEDBACK

The typical official university teaching evaluation has at least three deficiencies: 1) while the official evaluation does provide valuable feedback, it is usually conducted at the end of each semester, too late for the instructor to make necessary changes to serve the current students; 2) the questions on the evaluation form are often standardized, which does not leave much flexibility for instructors to get the feedback they want; and 3) the evaluation policy often prohibits teachers' presence when students are filling out the forms, which occasionally invites students' chatting rather than focusing their attention on the task.

In our effort to overcome the limitations of the current teaching evaluation system, a simple feedback form was developed in which only two open-ended questions were asked, "what is your positive feedback," and "what is your negative feedback?" This was done about one month after the semester began. Students were not mandated to complete the feedback sheet, but they could have a chance of winning a maximum of six bonus points on the first exam (three points were awarded to three best positive feedback givers and another three points to three best negative feedback givers). The response rate was approximately 60%. For those who participated but were not awarded, some little gifts were distributed in the class to show our gratitude and to share our attitude that every student's work was respected. It is amazing to see how generous students were in giving their opinions to the instructor. Their feedback covered virtually every aspect of teaching, ranging from class materials and organization to instructor's behavior and attitude toward teaching. In addition to the written feedback, in-class communications through question asking and answering were also relied on to seek constant feedback from students. At the end of each semester, students were asked, but not required, to list the most interesting topics of the course. This valuable information may be used to revise the course in future semesters.

We believe in the concept that every suggestion is an opportunity: a good one points out the right direction for improvement, and an inappropriate one indicates the need of help or training for the individual making the suggestion. The feedback sheet itself becomes an open window through which students can make complaints and compliments without feeling too much pressure, and provides an effective structure upon which open communications between students and the instructor can proceed. One of the most rewarding comments that we have ever received is, "if only my other professor asked us for feedback." Above all, getting feedback helps to solve students' problems promptly, which is in our view essential in making college study a pleasant experience.

PROCESS 4: MONITORING THE LEARNING PROCESS

We view learning as a process that can be measured to some degree by sampling variables such as exam grades or attributes such as the number of questions students responded to and asked in each class. The purpose of applying control charts to teaching is to monitor the learning process, to signal the existence of assignable causes when it is out of statistical quality control, and to improve it by identifying and eliminating the root causes. We focused primarily on students' exam grades to see who falls outside the control limits and whether there is anything wrong with the process itself. The control charts for individual measurements were chosen because each exam is only one repetition and the regular X-bar chart and R chart (or S chart) do not apply (cf. Duncan 1965). Montgomery (1991) suggests that the control chart for individual measurements be constructed according to:

$$\text{Upper control limit: } UCL = \overline{X} + 3\frac{\overline{MR}}{d_2};$$

$$\text{Center line: } CL = \overline{X};$$

$$\text{Lower control limit: } LCL = \overline{X} - 3\frac{\overline{MR}}{d_2}$$

where $\overline{MR}$ is the moving average ($MR_i = |X_i - X_{i-1}|$) of n observations and d_2 is a factor for constructing variables control charts (when n = 2, $d_2 = 1.128$). A control chart on the moving range can be similarly established. In the following example, we recorded 31 individual observations, tested their normality by Chi-square goodness-of-fit test at the significance level of $\alpha = 0.025$, which the data did follow, and computed the control limits, along with the centerline. One-sigma was considered since three-sigma control limits gave so little information as to be inappropriate. The complete control chart is shown in Figure 24.1.

The one-sigma control chart indicates that the learning process was "out of statistical quality control" since there were students whose grades

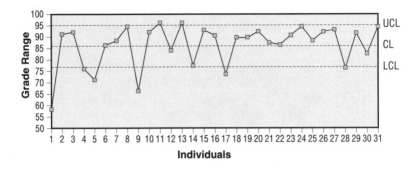

Figure 24.1 Control chart for individual exam grades.

went beyond the upper limit or below the lower limit. It is by this indication that the instructor started to look into the process to figure out the hidden but assignable causes. The same control charts were also drawn for the second and the third (final) exam in which efforts were made to reduce the variation of the difficulty level of each exam to better reflect students' understanding. The approach to identifying and eliminating the root causes is addressed in Process 6. What we found at the end was an improved learning process with less points going out of the control limits, especially the lower control limit. Our ultimate goal was to bring an out-of-control learning process to not only an in-control process but also a new improved zone of quality control. The rationale of this improvement plan has been well explained by Juran's (1989) trilogy.

PROCESS 5: TAKING CORRECTIVE ACTIONS

Taking corrective actions against the teaching problems is a critical step: if students see nothing changed after the feedback has been taken, they will stop participating in the ongoing improvement process, and the whole experiment will be ruined. Therefore all the positive and negative feedback was shared with students. It was presented as valuable information rather than self-congratulation or self-incrimination. All teaching problems were then categorized into ten major areas and prioritized with a Pareto diagram, as shown in Figure 24.2.

The diagram indicates that the "textbook and reading," problem was most critical among the teaching problems. Applying the "five whys" approach (Ohno 1988) to locating the root cause, the instructor found that

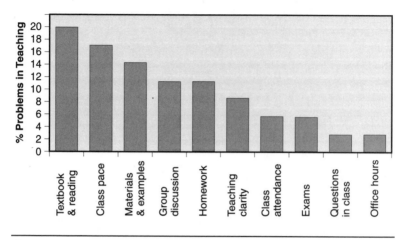

Figure 24.2 Pareto analysis for problems in teaching.

some students became confused when they missed a few classes but tried to complete homework by reading the textbook, and some experienced difficulties in understanding the technical details and examples in the supplementary textbook. These problems were addressed immediately by a) clarifying that teaching and the textbook supplement, but do not substitute, for each other; b) asking students to pay more attention to the lessons that could be distilled from the technical examples; c) showing students some sample questions from previous exams; and d) answering further questions on an individual basis. It turned out that, as many students commented in the second feedback sheet, they learned a lot by reading the "too technical" textbook and some were even going to apply the techniques they learned to their co-op or internship work. To address homework-related problems, it was emphasized that the homework might require more thinking, and might not just be a repetition of what was done in the class. In addition, the instructor wrote the homework assignment and its due date on the chalkboard at the beginning of each class, posted homework solutions afterwards, added more examples to the handout, and discussed the problems in the class that the majority of students had difficulty with. Similar steps were taken to resolve the other problems that emerged in the feedback. This problem-solving example simply shows that teaching and learning processes can be greatly improved if students' problems are carefully addressed, thoroughly understood, and quickly resolved by the instructor.

PROCESS 6: FOCUSING ON INDIVIDUALS

While understanding that too much help from the instructor might be counterproductive toward learning, we adopted an individual focus approach. In the class, we recognized each and every student by their first name. We usually addressed individual questions to the class so that confusion among other students would be cleared up, or further questions might be brought out. However, if we had a reason to believe that the question raised was idiosyncratic, we would work with the individual so that no precious in-class time would be wasted. One student specifically commented on the individual focus approach, writing in her feedback, "that makes me feel like a person and I can relate to you and so I take more interest and pride in my work since I know you will recognize the name and know whose it is!" In particular, individual attention was focused on those students (four here) whose grades fell below the lower control limit, as identified in Process 4. Each of these students was interviewed individually and informally to discuss their problems and concerns, which proved to be worthwhile and productive. Needless to say, their problems could not be solved overnight, but we did point out where they stood and advised them what would be best for them to do at the next step. Their reaction to these discussions was unanimously positive. Among them, three students did quite well on the final as compared to their poor grades on the first two exams. The progress of these students appeared to be mostly attributable to this individual focus approach.

The core of our individual focus approach lies squarely in the belief that it is from the instructor's commitment and willingness to help students that continuous improvement in teaching starts and carries forth. The instructor will probably have to spend additional time in working with students and, in the case of teaching a larger size of class, may have to make necessary refinements. The individual talks, for example, could be replaced by written memos or brief notes, but the key is still the word *individual*.

PROCESS 7: ASSESSING CLASS PERFORMANCE

To examine the statistical causal relationship between student input factors (Table 24.2) and class performance we applied multiple regression analysis. In our study, the dependent variable (variable 0) is the average grade on the three exams. Among the ten independent variables we selected, there

Table 24.2 Summary of variables used in the development of the class performance regression model.

	Variables	Description of Student Input Factors
0	AVEGRADE	Dependent variable, average of the three exam grades
1	ATTEND	The number of class attendance (random sample)
2	HWGRADE	Total grades on the homework (recorded)
3	BYTIMES	The number of times they stopped by during the office hours (self-reported)
4	EXPECT	The degree (%) to which students' expectation is satisfied (self-reported)
5	HWHOURS	The number of hours they spent doing homework per week (self-reported)
6	INTLEVEL	Their interest level in the course (self-reported)
7	KNOW	The level of their pre-course knowledge (self-reported)
8	QUEST	The number of questions they responded to and asked during the semester (self-reported)
9	RHOURS	The number of hours they spent on reading per week (self-reported)
10	UNSTAND	The percentage of class material they understood in each class (self-reported)

are two *objective variables* whose values were recorded during the semester (variables 1–2), and eight *subjective variables* whose values were estimated by students (variables 3–10).

The multiple regression model for class performance, obtained by running the data on the SAS program, is:

$$\text{AVEGRADE} = 48.38 + 1.1359\ \text{ATTEND} + 0.7979\ \text{BYTIMES} + 2.8535\ \text{KNOW} + 0.9120\ \text{QUEST} - 1.2954\ \text{RHOURS}$$

The model suggests that a linear causal relationship exists between the average grade and several student input factors. Input factors such as class attendance, the number of times he/she stopped by the instructor's office, pre-course knowledge level, and the total number of questions responded to and asked in the class have a statistically significant positive contribution to a student's average performance in the course. Surprisingly, the reading hours seem to have a negative effect on the average grade. At first glance this finding is alarming in that it would appear to suggest that optimum grades would be achieved if students spent no time reading. However, we interpreted the finding to imply that good students use time more effectively and that low grades may motivate students to increase time spent studying. Using this interpretation, we emphasized effective ways of reading in class. Interestingly, overall GPAs, when included into the independent variable pool in stepwise regression, would exclude most of the student input factors from the model above. They would not improve the explanatory power of the model significantly. This suggests that the student input factors have roughly equivalent effect in interpreting student performance in a given course. The overall regression model explains 68% of the total variability in the average grade (Probability > F = 0.0001 and the residuals are normally distributed according to Chi-square goodness-of-fit test).

The regression model was derived from the data largely dependent on students' self-estimation, and therefore its accuracy cannot be guaranteed. The main purpose of having such a model, however, is to understand how significant the student input factors are in relation to their achievement in a particular course. The instructors can use it as a quantitative analytical tool to predict students' performance and inform them of the possibilities. Students can then become more knowledgeable in pursuit of their personal goal. In this sense, the model may also be used as a motivational tool.

CONCLUSION

Though the effects of continuous improvement take time to emerge, several positive patterns have taken shape as a result of improving the seven teaching processes discussed above. First, according to the official teaching evaluation results, students' overall satisfaction level with the course and their learning experience has increased, as compared to that of the previous semester with the same instructor. Second, many students felt that they learned a great deal from the course, and more than 70% of the students in one class indicated that their interest in the content had been increased. Third, while learning is intangible, TQM techniques, including statistical tools, provide an organized structure for making continuous improvement in the classroom. For example, by driving out student's fear, as Dr. Deming advocates in his 14-point management philosophy, the instructor can more easily communicate with students.

While statistical tools are found useful in identifying and solving the problems inherent in teaching, it is neither our assumption nor our intent to suggest that the application of these tools be the prerequisite for making continuous improvement in teaching. In fact, continuous improvements take no specific format. Improvement efforts are not limited to instruction in the classroom. They can and should be extended to course design and even curriculum development. The authors of this paper have experimented with such methods as student input into course design, student-written test questions, peer grading, and project "menus" to introduce individual choice, and have had various degrees of success.

It should be noted that the seven processes are by no means complete in describing the teaching process. Where appropriate, a partial combination of them can be considered. To get started in practicing continuous improvement in teaching, benchmarking may be a good and easy way. As TQM expands into many academic institutions, there will be more professors who buy into the concept of continuous improvement, thus more successful lessons can be shared. Student teamwork is another opportunity, which is not fully covered here. When implementing quality principles and techniques in the classroom, professors will have to adjust their role. There are no fixed strategies that we could offer here, but we do know that no evidence has suggested that faculty would lose their power by not purporting to be the smartest person in the classroom when practicing continuous improvement in teaching. Our conviction is that improvement in teaching, as in other areas, never ends if we are committed to it.

REFERENCES

Bateman, G. R., and H. V. Roberts. *TQM for Professors and Students.* Working paper. University of Chicago, 1992.

Duncan, A. J. *Quality Control and Industrial Statistics,* 3rd ed. Homewood, IL: Richard D. Irwin, 1965.

Hau, I. "Improving Teaching in Higher Education." In *Handbook for Productivity Measurement and Improvement,* edited by W. F. Christopher and C. G. Thor. Cambridge, MA: Productivity Press, 1993.

Helms, S., and C. H. Key. "Are Students More Than Customers in the Classroom?" *Quality Progress* 27 (September 1994): 97–99.

Juran, J. M. *Juran on Leadership for Quality: An Executive Handbook.* New York: The Free Press, 1989.

Milbank, D. "Academe Gets Lessons from Big Business." *Wall Street Journal* (December 15, 1992): PB 1 (E).

Montgomery, D. C. *Introduction to Statistical Quality Control,* 2nd ed. New York: John Wiley & Sons, 1991.

Ohno, T. *Toyota Production System.* Cambridge, MA: Productivity Press, 1988.

Robinson, A. G. *Modern Approaches to Manufacturing Improvement: The Shingo System.* Cambridge, MA: Productivity Press, 1990.

25

Systematic Problem Solving: A Cornerstone for Quality

James Gelina and Marty Schildroth

SUMMARY

At EMCO Specialties, Des Moines, Iowa, the application of a statistically-based problem-solving methodology has proven results in bottom-line cost reduction, employee participation in organizational decision making, increased educational level of the entire organization, and an increase in the quality of products manufactured. The following article will detail the systematic problem identification and problem-solving process developed and utilized at EMCO. The development, application, and results of the systematic problem-solving methodology will be discussed.

KEY WORDS

Continuous improvement, systematic process, team approach.

INTRODUCTION

EMCO Specialties is one of the home improvement industry's leading manufacturers of high quality storm and screen doors. EMCO's corporate, manufacturing, and distribution facilities are located in Des Moines, Iowa. EMCO employs 450 associates nationwide.

During the fall of 1994, a need was identified for the development of a team-based problem identification and problem-solving system. The organization was growing at a 15 to 20 percent increase each year and was attempting to accomplish business utilizing the same methods as done in previous years. EMCO was continuing to follow the same paradigms of operations, and as the business grew, more and more associates were added to the organization utilizing the same processes from yesterday. Business was booming; profits were level. Changes to EMCO's business and management paradigms were needed in order to compete in today's very competitive home improvement market.

The continuous process improvement (CPI) methodology in practice at EMCO was developed to provide an opportunity for all associates to participate in the identification, reduction, and solution of problems and constraints within the service, production, and distribution processes. The EMCO CPI methodology was developed by two EMCO associates with the aid of many local and national leaders in the area of quality improvement. The foundations upon which the problem identification and solving process was developed originate from the ideas developed by Kaoru Ishikawa and W. Edwards Deming. Contributions to EMCO CPI methodology were added through the writings of Joseph Juran (1988), Steven Covey (1991), Eliyahu Goldratt (1992), and Peter Scholtes (1988).

The systematic process, applied to problem identification and problem solving, is what allows EMCO to realize the benefits achieved. Many organizations involved in the quality improvement area follow the toolkit approach. In this type of organization, 15 to 20 statistical tools are presented to the teams, and the teams need to pick and choose which tools are correct for the application and then apply these tools. At EMCO, a systematic (step 1, step 2, and so forth) CPI model has been developed and applied. This model consists of six statistically-based tools systematically positioned for each tool to build upon the results of the previous. The systematic model can be applied to all problems encountered, and at the time of this writing, all problems the model has been applied to have been significantly reduced or eliminated.

At EMCO, all associates (organizationwide) will receive 40 hours of application-based education and become a high-performance CPI team member. The 40 hours of education are distributed over 20 weeks of ongoing two-hour classroom sessions. Highlights of the educational process consist of discussion and applications of the following:

1. Variation and the relationship to quality.

2. Identification and elimination of constraints within the system.

3. W. Edwards Deming and the 14 management points.

4. Cost-added versus value-added activities.

SYSTEMATIC THINKING

The CPI model in Figure 25.1 is the cornerstone of the continuous quality improvement methodology that has been implemented at EMCO. The process utilizes six steps that have been selected to work together systematically to help a team identify a problem and then solve it. Ishikawa developed the tools that are used (1986). The tools have been selected for their relative simplicity and powerful results when used together properly. The first four steps (check sheet, Pareto diagram, histogram, and stratification) are problem identification tools that are used to accurately collect the information from a process. The fifth and sixth steps, flowchart and

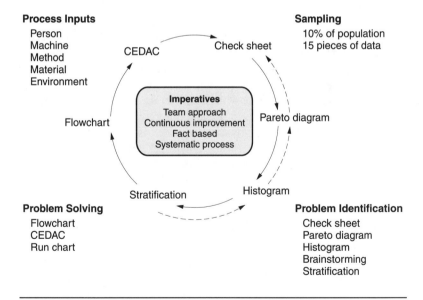

Figure 25.1   CPI model.

cause-and-effect diagram with the addition of cards (CEDAC), are problem-solving tools that are used to solve the problem identified with the first four steps.

The first step in the CPI model is the check sheet. The check sheet is a data collection tool that records information from the process being analyzed. The heading of the check sheet contains the following information: description of the process, name of person collecting the data, dates, and process total. The person performing the operation or function in the process collects the data for the check sheet. Information is collected by writing down the problems or defects encountered with a check or hash mark for each subsequent event.

The second step in the EMCO CPI model is the Pareto diagram. The Pareto diagram is a bar chart that is used to evaluate data collected from the check sheets. Multiple check sheets are combined and the information is transformed into a graphical representation of the process being analyzed. The Pareto diagram is designed to have the most frequently occurring defect (longest bar) on the left-hand side with the remaining bars being graphed in descending order. At this point, the longest bar is typically the problem, which the emphasis of the following tools will focus on. One must be careful to evaluate all of the problems, as there may be less frequently occurring problems that may prove to have a greater impact on the process. Once a problem is defined, the process is ready for the third step.

The third step of the EMCO CPI model is the histogram. In an effort to keep the information at a level at which all associates at EMCO can understand, the tool is used to evaluate how the problem recurs over time. Since the data being collected are typically attribute data (data that can be classified as either yes or no, good or bad, or white or black) the histogram can easily be set up for this. The purpose of the histogram is to determine whether the problem being analyzed has normal variation, which is represented by a bell-shaped curve. By evaluating the histogram shape, center, and variation, the process will yield information regarding repeatability, predictability, and reliability. If the histogram has normal variation, the problem will be easier to solve. If the process does not have normal variation, the next step, stratification, will be necessary to further define the parameters of the problem. The purpose of evaluating the histogram is to reduce the variation of the occurrences and then move the mean of the process in the direction desired. Less variation in the process is an indication of higher quality.

The fourth step of the EMCO CPI model is stratification. Stratification is the process of breaking down the problem into smaller components. For example, in examining tire sales in a discount warehouse, one can break the entire number of sales into the following categories: supplier, size, width, whitewall/blackwall, tread wear, speed rating, and so on. If the histogram does not show normal variation, often the problem that is selected has multiple variables producing difficulty in identifying the root cause. By stratifying the data, the information will become focused in the direction that will allow the data to be properly evaluated. If the problem is to be stratified, usually a brainstorming session will be necessary to start identifying which components of the problem to focus on.

If the problem has been stratified, the process must return to the first step, the check sheet, as the data collected has not been formatted to gather the data now needed for the model. If the data no longer need to be stratified, the process is ready to go to the fifth step.

The fifth tool in the EMCO CPI model, the flowchart, is used to provide a pictorial representation of the process being analyzed. The pictorial representation is used to analyze the process and identify where cost-added and value-added activities are taking place. Construction of the flowchart will use simple rectangular boxes to denote every step in the process.

The construction of the flowchart begins by determining the process boundaries and then identifying the sequence of events between the boundaries. This determination is made through the use of the following activities:

1. High-performance team brainstorming.

2. Actual viewing of the process.

3. Input from the process owners.

The sixth step, CEDAC, is used to identify the relationship between the problem in the process and the root cause(s) of the problem. A CEDAC board is divided into two sections, the effect side and the cause side. Construction of the CEDAC always begins on the effect side, where a team will develop the problem statement, target statement, and a measurement technique derived from information collected from the four problem identification tools.

The cause side of a CEDAC board utilizes Ishikawa's fishbone diagram and the five process inputs—machine, method, material, person, and environment (Deming 1986). The left side of each spine is where team members place cards that identify possible causes to the problem identified on the effect side under the problem statement. Possible solutions, written on cards, are placed on the right side of the spine adjacent to the identified cause. A team selects, implements, and statistically monitors the change to a process as identified on the selected solution card.

The foundation of the CPI methodology has been developed upon the principles of the team approach, continuous improvement, fact-based, and systematic process. These four principles are termed the imperatives to the CPI methodology.

The team approach is the collaboration of an organization's most valuable resource, the people. Through the application of teams, a synergy is created that yields results greater than an individual (Covey 1991). Continuous improvement, the second imperative, is inherent within the teams. Teams focusing on continuous improvement of the processes allow for greater productivity.

The third imperative is operating in a fact-based environment. Teams make decisions based upon the data collected during the use of the previous steps. Dealing in a fact-based environment aids teams in receiving the necessary resources required to continually improve the process.

The final imperative, systematic process, is the application of the CPI model. The methodology begins with the check sheet and follows through until the completion of the CEDAC diagram. The systematic process is the application of all problem identification and problem-solving tools in the proper sequential order.

APPLICATION

EMCO has a distribution center located at 2800 Dixon Avenue in Des Moines, Iowa. A cross-functional team consisting of three fork truck operators, traffic dispatcher, load coordinator, inventory control technician, and warehouse operations manager was formed under the guidance of our CPI leadership team. The team fittingly chose the "Fixen Dixon Pioneers" as a team name. After structured brainstorming and database analysis, it was determined that a possible constraint to the distribution center's operation was a possible problem of product damage. Product damage identified at the distribution center creates the following cost-added activities in the distribution system.

1. Rework, product repackaging.

2. Inefficient order picking and trailer loading.

3. Product damage (scrap).

4. Interruption to fork truck operator work schedule.

The following information details the process the team followed and documents the results the team achieved.

All doors produced at EMCO's manufacturing facility are packaged in a two-piece tray-style corrugated box. The completed door package is a box measuring 40" wide, 85" tall, and 3" thick. Fourteen individually packaged doors are stacked in a horizontal position, stretch wrapped with a poly film, and tilted vertically, creating a shipping package of 18 door packages standing upright. Wooden pallet runners are attached to the bottom of the shipping package. The completed shipping package is then loaded into a shuttle semi-trailer and hauled to the distribution center across the city.

Upon arrival at the distribution center, it was noted that many of the shipping packages were leaning. When the leaning shipping packages were removed from the semi-trailer, these packages would sometimes fall over onto the floor. Leaning shipping packages are termed "leaners." Leaners create the cost-added activities described previously. The team began using the EMCO CPI problem-solving model, beginning with the first step as described earlier in this paper, the check sheet.

The check sheet was used to collect the information needed to determine if leaners were a significant constraint to the distribution operations (see Figure 25.2). The total number of leaning door packages was collected each day. The door model of each of the leaners was also recorded each day. The check sheets were constructed and filled out each day by the fork truck operators at the distribution center.

Upon collection of the leaner information on the check sheets, the data were then used to create the second step of the CPI problem-solving model, the Pareto diagram. The number of leaners per day and the door model information were used to produce the Pareto diagram in Figure 25.3. The Pareto diagram informed the team that the problem of leaners occurred 204 times in a one-month period.

The third step in the CPI problem-solving model is to determine if the problem recurs and if the problem shows a pattern of normal variation. The information on the number of leaners, collected from the check sheets, was then utilized to form a histogram, shown in Figure 25.4. The histogram identified for the team a bimodal distribution, alerting the team to the possibility of two different problems acting upon the process. This bimodal distribution was investigated, and it was determined that two separate fork truck operators were collecting the information for the check sheets on different days. The criteria for determining a leaner was different for each of the operators. A standardized criteria for leaners was developed, and the bimodal distribution was corrected creating a normal distribution. The histogram also identified that the leaners were a repeatable problem and were occurring an average of 9.35 times per day.

The fourth step of the EMCO CPI problem-solving model was applied, stratification. The data collected by door model were determined to be too vague. The information was recollected through the application of a check sheet and was collected to a more detailed level part number. The results of the stratified information identified for the team that the problem of leaners was distributed evenly throughout the entire product line of doors.

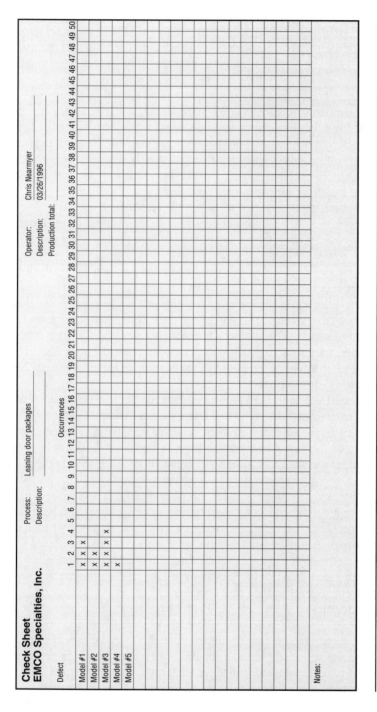

Figure 25.2   Check sheet.

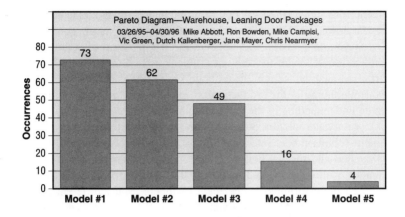

Figure 25.3 Pareto diagram.

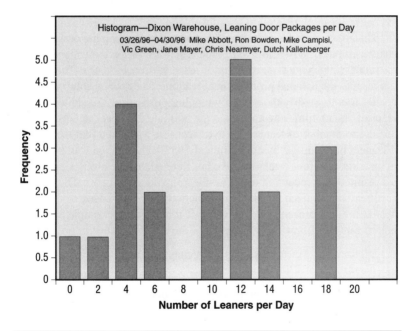

Figure 25.4 Histogram.

The fifth step of the EMCO CPI problem-solving model is the formation of a flowchart. A flowchart, shown in Figure 25.5, of the door packaging and shuttle process was created for the purpose of aiding in the identification of where the leaning problem was being created. The flowchart also aided the team in the reduction of unnecessary cost-added activities, streamlining of the production process, and providing the entire team with an understanding of the process identified.

Upon the completion of a flowchart, the sixth step of the EMCO CPI problem-solving model was applied: CEDAC. The CEDAC in Figure 25.6 was created and the problem statement, target statement, and measuring technique were identified. The potential causes were identified through structured brainstorming by the team members. Many different possible causes to the problem of leaners were written on cause cards and placed on the left side of the spines of the CEDAC. The most significant cause was identified through a consensus-creating technique, then solutions were created for that single cause. From the numerous solutions identified, one solution was chosen through a consensus-creating technique, and then a procedure for implementation was developed.

The solution implemented by the team was changing the design of the wooden runners and corrugated corner sections. After implementation of this processing change, the amount of leaners did not change. The process was reset to the original process specifications. The second solution implemented was to modify the stretch wrapping procedure. An additional four wraps of stretch film were applied to the bottom of the package. After monitoring the number of leaners for two weeks, it was noted that the number of leaners had reduced by approximately 95%. The change was monitored for an additional four weeks and the data defined that the processing change had resulted in a reduction of 95% in leaning door packages. The solution was then standardized on all the production lines and added to the documented process procedures. The work of this team was completed in four months and the following is a sample of the results achieved:

1. Reduction of repackaging of leaning packages, creating a cost savings of $30,000 per year.

2. Reduction in the amount of scrap doors.

3. Increased order picking efficiency.

4. Increased trailer loading efficiency.

5. Decreased time a tractor trailer has to sit at the loading dock waiting to be loaded.

6. Improved quality of life for distribution center employees.

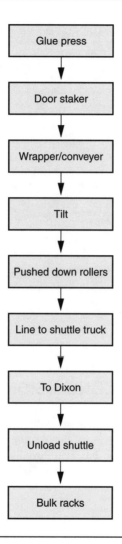

Figure 25.5 Flowchart.

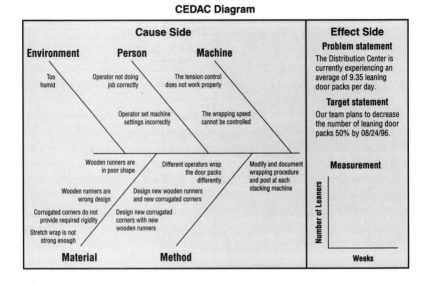

Figure 25.6 CEDAC.

CONCLUSION

EMCO Specialties has been involved with the implementation of the CPI methodology for three years. As of this writing, EMCO has developed nine high-performance teams and has also developed a team of CPI advisors. The goal of the organization is to have 100 percent participation in five years. Currently, EMCO has approximately 30 percent participation within the entire organization.

The application of the systematic process, as discussed earlier, can be applied to any area within an organization. At EMCO, we have had teams from the manufacturing facility, corporate facility, and distribution facility. Teams using the systematic model are equipped with the ability to identify, evaluate, and reduce or eliminate any problem encountered. Some of the highlights of the teams are:

1. Cost savings over the last three years of $750,000.

2. Lower work-in-process (WIP) in various areas of the manufacturing facility.

3. Reduction in the amount of scrap and rework.

4. 50% increase in manufacturing facility attendance.

5. 50% percent reduction in order placement to product delivery cycle time.

6. Decrease in misdirected phone calls.

7. Increase in inventory accuracy.

8. Implementation of a new aluminum lineal cutting center.

9. Improved business relationships among associates.

10. Decrease in leaning door packs.

Recently, an educational program was developed to teach people how to become effective leaders. Nine associates volunteered to go through the 13-week educational process. Upon completion, the leaders were paired together and began facilitating high-performance teams.

At EMCO, CPI is not a program that has a starting and ending date. It is a methodology that is becoming instilled in our daily job activities. Focusing on improving processes within the system is the key to growing our organization.

REFERENCES

Covey, S. R. *Principle-Centered Leadership.* New York: Simon & Schuster, 1991.
Deming, W. E. *Out of the Crisis.* Cambridge, MA: M.I.T., 1986.
Goldratt, E. M., and J. Cox. *The Goal,* 2nd ed. New York: North River Press, 1992.
Ishikawa, K. *Guide to Quality Control,* 2nd ed. Tokyo: JUSE Press, 1986.
Juran, J. M. *Juran's Quality Handbook,* 4th ed. New York: McGraw-Hill, 1988.
Scholtes, P. R. *The Team Handbook.* Madison, WI: Joiner Associates, 1988.

26

Quality Audit: Tool for Continuous Improvement in Disability Claim Operations

Illona Dubaldo and Jeffrey P. Nogas

ABSTRACT

Metropolitan Life Insurance Company (MetLife) was one of the first companies to implement a quality improvement process in a service industry. This paper demonstrates the application of quality audit principles and practices in disability claim operations as a tool for continuous improvement. The Quality Management Department for Met DisAbility Claim Operations conducts quality audits to ensure compliance with contractual obligations, and customer expectations, as well as state and federal regulations.

Quality audit results and subsequent trends and analysis identify operational strengths in addition to opportunities for corrective action. This helps the organization prevent future quality problems as well as focus its resources on the components of the claim adjudication process that require retraining. The end result is ongoing and continuous improvement.

This paper will discuss the following:

- Quality audit commonalities and differences between the manufacturing sector and the insurance industry

- Quality management audit methods

- Use of Pareto analysis in evaluation of audit results

- Statistical reporting of audit results

- Roles of the auditor, auditee, and customer

INTRODUCTION

What is quality? How do we define it? The dictionary defines quality as:

1: the essential character of something; nature 2 a: an inherent or distinguishing characteristic; property b: a personal trait, esp. a character trait 3 a: superiority of kind b: degree or grade of excellence . . .

Synonyms for quality are listed as "property, attribute, trait." The definition may change depending on the context or usage.

Depending on what is being measured, the criteria for quality evaluation will change. In service industries, customer perception of quality influences what is defined as a "quality" product or service delivered.

What does "serve" mean? The dictionary's meaning as a verb is as follows:

3 a: to provide goods and services for (customers) b: to supply (goods or services) to customers 4: to be of service or use; function 5: to meet requirements or needs; satisfy . . .

Manufacturing industries process materials into finished durable and non-durable goods. Juran defines quality as "fitness for use." Service providers, such as an insurance carrier, want their services to be deemed "fit for use" as much as the manufacturing industry does. Service industries have certain characteristics in common: direct contact with the users of the service; benefit provided on demand by being prepared to serve when needed; timeliness of service; intangible benefit as well as a "physical" product.

There are definite quality characteristics, attributes, or traits that apply to a service in order to be deemed "fit for use." Juran lists several: psychological; time-oriented; contractual; ethical; technological. Customer expectations and requirements play a major role in defining the quality characteristics to be evaluated in a service industry such as insurance. Customer *perception* of quality is also critical, which is why "customer satisfaction" is frequently used as a measure of quality service.

Business depends on quality, whether the business is for-profit or non-profit; manufacturing or nonmanufacturing, service or non-service. Most of us are part of the insurance buying public and are, indeed, impacted by the quality of the products and services delivered by an insurance company. Insurance costs are certainly reflected in the premiums we pay and the amount of coverage we have. Don't we all want "the most for our money?" Certainly, marketing thrives on creating this expectation.

However, are definitive quality measurements really important to an industry that produces an intangible product such as insurance? Not sure? Think about that last time you filed an insurance claim for that roof damage, auto accident, dental work, loss of income, or physician expense? Did you care when or if you received a decision on your claim? Did it matter to you if you received a check in a timely manner (one week, two weeks, six weeks, six months) or if the check was for the correct amount according to your insurance plan? Was it important that the check went to the right address or even to the right person?

The focus of this presentation is based on the assumption that we all do indeed want the best quality service we can get. This paper will demonstrate that quality in a service industry, particularly in an insurance company, can be measured, reported, and continuously improved.

BACKGROUND

The current Met DisAbility claim quality management process began in response to a centralization of the claim function into one business unit. While there were, and are, several different claim office locations, each performing essentially the same function, it was also apparent they were essentially operating independently of each other. The current process started as a quest to determine the "best practices" for the newly centralized business unit. The goal was to provide consistency, reliability, timely, and cost-efficient use of resources in order to achieve high customer satisfaction.

The corporate quality vision during this assimilation was always clear: total customer satisfaction by providing a high quality of service to all customers, whether internal or external, corporate or individual. This vision was carried forth throughout the organization.

The current corporate vision also focuses on various elements of a total quality management process: how we provide customer service, delivery of our products and services, information technology, and people as resources to improve quality as well as to achieve quality in personal growth and professional development.

The Quality Management Department of Met DisAbility is an independent, separately organized functional unit in the claim operations area. The unit is composed of a team of auditors in each claim office location, all reporting to the same director (director of development and quality). The quality director reports to a senior management team member and is on peer level with the location operations directors. All report to the vice president of claim. The quality director is also the facilitator for the quality task force for the underwriting and contract issue/administration areas for the business unit. The basic functions of the audit teams include the review, analysis, and reporting of the claim management performance of the location on an individual, unit, and office level. Quarterly reports are prepared summarizing the trends as well as providing a statistical analysis of the data collected. These reports are provided to management of the location, as well as senior management of the organization.

Audit sizes vary from location to location. Depending on the scope of the audit, the overall sample usually exceeds 8,000 claims per year. Cross audits are also performed by auditors of each other's locations.

QUALITY MANAGEMENT PROGRAM

The Quality Management Department for Met DisAbility Claim Operations conducts internal quality audits that can be categorized as either "process quality audits" or "service quality audits." These process quality audits evaluate the claim adjudication process against established instructions, workflow procedures, and standards. These process audits also measure conformance of the processed activity to established and referenced standards as well as measuring the effectiveness of process procedures and instructions. The referenced standards are defined in the disability contract and in published customer time service standards. Established workflow procedures and instructions are defined and located in various claim operations policies and procedures manuals.

The claim operation quality audits are also similar to service quality audits as they are an in-depth examination and evaluation of the quality system as it applies to a particular service, accurate and timely claim adjudication processing. These audits examine all elements of the service and their related quality system elements to evaluate the system against established and referenced standards or procedures for that service.

AUDIT OBJECTIVES

The objectives of the quality management program are as follows:

- to ensure that our customers are receiving quality service that exceeds expectations in regard to decisional and financial accuracy as well as timeliness

- to determine whether established Claim Operations performance goals are met or exceeded

- to identify operational strengths and training issues that include opportunities for improvement and prevention of future quality problems

- to provide quality assessments that are measurable, meaningful, and easily administered

- to ensure compliance with contractual obligations as well as all state and federal regulations

- to assess the effectiveness and impact of the implemented quality system and program

AUDIT ROLES AND RESPONSIBILITIES

Auditor

Quality Audits are conducted by staff from the Quality Management Department that is independent of the areas being audited. These auditors have had substantial experience in the claim adjudication process and possess the appropriate personal attributes that are necessary to be successful in quality management. They are responsible for:

- complying with applicable audit requirements

- communicating and clarifying audit requirements

- evaluating disability claim file documentation based on specified criteria and in conjunction with the applicable contractual provisions

- documenting observations and findings

- reporting audit results

- verifying the effectiveness of corrective actions taken as a result of prior audits

- retaining and safeguarding documents pertaining to the audit as well as maintaining confidentiality in regard to such documents

Auditee

The auditee for quality claim audits is the disability claim case manager, who is responsible for the claim adjudication process and the issuance of disability benefits when appropriate. The case manager discusses the audit results of their claim files with the auditor and uses this feedback as a learning opportunity to assist them in their career development in disability claim management. The audit results are also utilized by the auditee's manager to assess their job performance and career development.

Customer

A question often asked is: who is the customer in regard to claim quality audits? Obviously, the ultimate customer is the policyholder as they are paying the policy premium in order to receive a specified service in an accurate, efficient, and timely manner.

However, in an organization devoted to quality, customers are not only external, but also internal as well. Management for Claims Operations as well as senior management for Met DisAbility are also the customer when conducting audits. These claim audits provide management with critical information as to the effectiveness and performance of Claim Operations and the implemented quality system. As stated earlier in the objectives of the Quality Management Program, audit results indicate whether customer expectations and departmental performance goals are being met or exceeded. Audit results are vital in identifying operational strengths and training issues that indicate opportunities for improvement and prevention of future quality problems. Quality audit truly provides management with a tool for continuous improvement in a disability claims operation.

Other internal customers of the quality audit are fellow employees, peers, colleagues, and departments interacting with other departments as everyone profits from the quality management program.

AUDIT METHODS AND PRACTICES

The quality management audit methods and practices are consistent with those outlined in ANSI/ISO/ASQC Q10011-1-1994 "Guidelines for Auditing Quality Systems." The following paragraphs will discuss these methods and practices.

Audit Scope and Frequency

Claim Operations management makes the decision on audit scope and frequency for the internal quality management program. Management decides whether the entire claim adjudication process is evaluated or just specified components of the process. Generally, each disability case manager is evaluated on the entire adjudication process on a quarterly basis. However, the program is flexible enough to allow for performing specialized *ad hoc* studies or focusing on a particular component of the quality system. Business needs, customer expectations, and prior audit results guide management's decisions on audit scope and frequency.

Audit Preparation

Audit notification is given to the unit manager, and a random sampling of claim files is selected from a system-generated report for each disability case manager in that unit. The applicable disability contracts corresponding to the selected claim files are also obtained. The auditor will evaluate the claim adjudication process for each file against the plan of coverage indicated in the contract in conjunction with established and documented workflow procedures and instructions. The auditor will also identify the appropriate quality review worksheet to be used in the file review. The worksheet is comprised of a checklist that identifies the criteria used in evaluating the claim adjudication process along with areas provided for documenting and reporting audit observations and findings.

Conducting the Audit

The auditor reviews each claim file selected in the random sampling utilizing the criteria identified on the quality review worksheet (see Figure 26.1). This criteria represents the main components of the claim adjudication process and are listed as follows:

- Accepting proper/continued liability
- Correct benefit/benefit calculation
- File documentation
- Timeliness

Date	Claim #	Coverage Type: STD/LTD
Claimant Name		Initial Decision/Continued
Case Manager		Current Claim Status
Reviewer		ICD-9 Code

	Yes	No	
1. Accepting Proper/Continued Liability			
A. Eligible under plan			
B. Disabled while eligible			
C. Timely submission			
D. Definition of total disability			
E. Exclusions			
F. Disability management			
G. Compliance with previous audits			
2. Correct Benefit/Benefit Calculation	Yes	No	
A. Salary			
B. E/P, I/L			
C. Carveouts			
D. Taxes			
E. Calculations			
F. Overpayment			
G. Compliance with previous audits			
3. File Documentation	Yes	No	
A. Occupational information			
B. System documentation			
C. Letters			
D. Decision rationale/future plans			
E. Cost containment referrals			
i. Reviewed for rehab potential			
ii. Reviewed for SS potential			
iii. DNS referral			
iv. Consultant/IME referral			
F. Correct ICD-9 code			
G. Accuracy of system data			
H. Compliance with previous audits			
4. Complete and Accurate File	Yes	No	

Timeliness					
L T D	Initiation of Claim Management	Initial Decision	S T D		
Days			Days		$ File Value
0 to 5			0 to 2		
6 to 8			3 to 4		
9 to 11			5 to 6		$ Financial Error
12 to 14			7 to 8		
> 14			> 8		

Figure 26.1 Quality review worksheet.

Each of these components is divided into subcategories as illustrated on the quality review worksheet. The auditor indicates on the worksheet the conformance of each item of this checklist as well as documenting resultant observations and findings (improvement opportunities). At the conclusion of each file review, the audit results are discussed with the case manager to provide a clear understanding of the results. This discussion also provides a forum for the auditee to present their point of view as well as to challenge specific observations or improvement opportunities that have been identified. The auditee's feedback may clarify or resolve discrepant issues, and the auditor may decide to modify the audit results. If contentious issues still remain, there is a formal rebuttal and arbitration process.

Audit Report, Trends and Analysis

Data is compiled from the quarterly audits on an individual, unit, and office location basis. A cumulative statistical analysis and narrative report are prepared outlining the findings and observations identified on the review worksheets. The data is also presented utilizing Pareto analysis tools (see Figures 26.2 and 26.3). Supporting documentation provides examples and references where claim management deviated from established standards, instructions, and expectations as documented in the contract and claim management guidelines developed for claim operations. Quarterly trends are tracked, and a report is prepared that illustrates office ratings by quarter

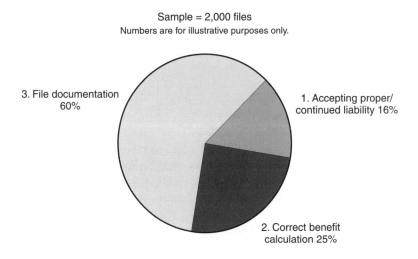

Figure 26.2 Improvement opportunity distribution third quarter.

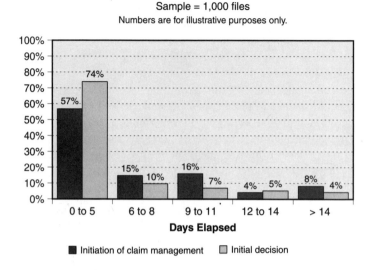

Sample = 1,000 files
Numbers are for illustrative purposes only.

Figure 26.3 LTD time lines—third quarter.

for decisional, financial, and nonfinancial accuracy (see Figure 26.4). A separate report is also prepared for special studies that were completed during the quarter as well as for separate corrective action follow-up audits on improvement opportunities noted in previous audits.

Root causes are then identified that result in improvement opportunities for the staff. This feedback is directly provided to the training unit of each office location. The director of quality is also responsible for office training needs. The quality auditors may engage in providing some corrective action training on an individual and unit basis, serving to promote a team spirit of prevention and yet still maintaining integrity of the audit information.

Upon audit report completion, a copy is provided to the director of quality, vice president for claim operations and each office location director. A meeting is scheduled with the director of each location as the report is discussed with members of the audit team for that location. Following the meeting with the location director, the report is distributed to the unit managers within the location. Meetings are scheduled with the unit teams by the audit team to review the findings and observations presented in the report. A copy of the report is also provided to the location trainer for any necessary training that may be needed, including training to prevent future quality problems noted in the trends analysis.

Sample size = 8,000 (2,000 per quarter)
Numbers are for illustrative purposes only.

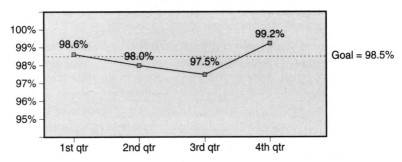

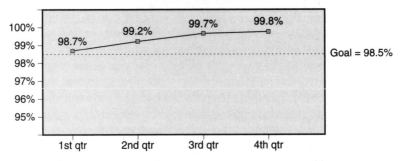

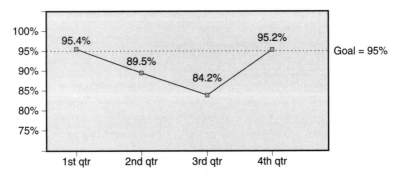

Figure 26.4 Annual quality management trends and accuracy rating.

Once the unit meetings have been completed, the audit cycle is considered completed for the quarter; and the new audit cycle begins.

CORRECTIVE ACTION FOLLOW-UP

Improvement opportunities (corrective action requests) are returned to individual case managers with a copy to the unit manager. Copies of specific financial improvement opportunities are also given to the office director for their follow-up.

The auditees are responsible for initiating and implementing the necessary corrective action on a claim file that is returned for an improvement opportunity. Corrections are expected to be completed within eight days of the return date and notification submitted to the unit manager that corrective action has been completed.

The quality management auditors for the location are not responsible for implementing the corrective action. However, in contrast to the manufacturing audit process, they will identify the references and resources available to assist the case manager in performing the corrective action. In addition, the auditors may assist the office trainer in providing some individual or unit training regarding specific procedures to be followed. This type of "value-added" auditing provides management and the auditee with quality assessments that are both effective and meaningful.

The auditors are required to perform a follow-up audit on improvement opportunities identified in previous quarters. The timing for the follow-up will be determined in part by when corrective action training and resultant procedural changes were completed. This approach allows a period of time for a learning curve.

CONCLUSION

We are all constantly evaluating "quality" in our lives—quality of products we use, quality of services, quality time, quality of life itself. We are all "customers" regardless of type of industry. We must pay attention to customer requirements and expectations. If we fail to meet these requirements and expectations, we will lose customers and, potentially, be out of business.

Quality audits measure conformance to these requirements and expectations. In a service industry, such as insurance, there are specific characteristics and attributes that can be quantitatively measured such as timeliness of claim determinations and correct amount of dollars paid. All of which, when done with a "zero defect" philosophy, will lead to a subjective assessment of good quality by the customer as measured in customer satisfaction surveys.

The future of quality improvement in service industries depends upon forming learning partnerships with our customers to ascertain what matters most to them so that we are quickly responsive to their changing needs. By anticipating these needs, we can provide the appropriate services to meet these needs and *exceed* their expectations. Additionally, the successful learning organization of the future will continuously improve by engaging their employees in the quality process. Quality is not only the responsibility of the Quality Management Department; it is *everyone's responsibility* in an organization, top down and bottom up.

BIBLIOGRAPHY/REFERENCES

American Heritage Dictionary 2nd College Ed. Boston, MA: Houghton Mifflin, 1982.

ANSI/ISO/ASQC Q10011-1-1994. "Guidelines for Auditing Quality Systems." Milwaukee: ASQC, 1994.

Arter, D. R. *Quality Audits for Improved Performance,* 2nd ed. Milwaukee: ASQC Quality Press, 1994.

Ishikawa, K. *Guide to Quality Control,* 2nd revised ed. New York: Quality Resources, 1986.

Juran, J. M., and F. Gryna. *Juran's Quality Control Handbook,* 4th ed. New York: McGraw-Hill, 1988.

Mears, P. *Quality Improvement Tools and Techniques.* New York: McGraw-Hill, 1995.

Senge, P. *The Fifth Discipline.* New York: Currency Doubleday, 1994.

Townsend, P. L., and J. E. Gebhardt. *Quality in Action.* New York: John Wiley & Sons, 1992.

27

Can Benchmarking for Best Practices Work for Government?

Patricia Keehley and Sue A. MacBride

Anyone seeking to improve measures his or her current performance and then looks to other leaders in the same field for comparisons, fresh ideas, and ways to improve. For instance, a runner attempting to run a 5,000-meter race faster may find answers by examining the techniques of the record holder. Perhaps the record holder's starting technique gives her an edge over the competition. To improve her own performance, the runner can adopt the record holder's technique, adjust it to suit her own style, and attain a better performance, possibly shaving seconds off her time.

Like the runner, a public sector agency can use benchmarking to provide better service. First the agency identifies the best in class among those carrying out a particular task. Then, the agency analyzes and adapts the best practices to improve its completion of that task. Benchmarking usually reveals sizable gaps in the organization's performance. For instance, when Lynchburg, Virginia, Fire and Emergency Medical Service conducted a benchmarking study, it found a citizen death rate due to fire that was 150 percent above the national average.[1] Such astonishing results are discovered because benchmarking urges agencies to identify and examine the best performers in their field.

Benchmarking is a method for identifying and importing best practices in order to improve performance. The term "benchmark" has been used in different instances to refer to a turning point, a milestone, a stage, an event, and even a crisis, but it is most commonly known as a standard. In benchmarking for best practices, quality authorities agree that the benchmark means the highest possible performance, referring either to the highest level of performance currently existing or a level of performance yet to be seen but on the horizon. For instance, Joseph M. Juran sees benchmarking as trying to uncover the best performance possible. The method by which that superior performance is achieved is known as a best practice.

Juran once illustrated the concept with a story about German generals who observed an American circus early in the century.[2] Why? Because the circus was expert at moving great quantities of animals, people, food, and gear; assembling and disassembling the shows; and traveling from city to city, sometimes in only a few hours. The generals had the same logistical dilemma: moving masses of people, horses, ammunition, and food quickly and efficiently. These military administrators learned deployment proficiency from the most unlikely of sources, one whose purpose and mission were in no way related to their own. Often, the most significant breakthroughs are made when organizations benchmark not just their competitors, but businesses in other industries also.

THE PUBLIC SECTOR JUMPS ON THE BANDWAGON

The improvements in quality and efficiency obtained by private industry through best practices and benchmarking have been so profound and widespread that public sector agencies—organizations traditionally perceived as slow to plan and implement change—are waking up to the benefits of this powerful analytical tool. The mass adoption of best practices through benchmarking by government institutions at all levels may dispel three myths that have attached themselves to public agencies:

1. There is never any real improvement in service delivery.

2. The only way to improve service delivery is to spend more money.

3. Delivery performance actually deteriorates with increased spending.[3]

Behind the search for best practices lies a new way of thinking about the role of government in American society. Public leaders choosing to adopt best practices understand that government plays a critical part as leader and catalyst in helping communities survive and flourish in a changing world economy, but they also recognize the limits of government as the provider of all things to all people. These leaders are able to deal with the reality in which governments must become better managers of limited fiscal resources by reallocating funds to higher priorities, constraining problems before they progress, and providing a more thorough accounting of return on expenditures.

In light of increasing citizen distrust and the accompanying movement to restrict government revenues, astute public administrators are starting to treat their constituents as paying customers entitled to responsive service, efficient performance, and satisfaction for their tax dollar. Successful managers receive the greatest return on their investment by capitalizing on available tools and methods such as best practices and benchmarking. They are always looking for better ways to do business, cut costs, and work smarter. That is the secret to maintaining performance in the face of uncertainty and constant change, and becoming the leader of the pack.

HOW WAS BENCHMARKING INTRODUCED TO THE PUBLIC SECTOR?

Benchmarking and best practices are not new ideas. Most practitioners are surprised at the length of time over which the concept has developed. Robert Camp traces the origin of the method back to the ageless Japanese concept of *dantotsu,* meaning striving to be the best of the best.[4] Also cited as a benchmarking pioneer is Henry Ford. He adopted the monorail of moving hooks used by meat packers in his auto assembly plant, increasing his output dramatically.

Private sector organizations have been looking outside themselves for improvement ideas for a long time and have been using benchmarking as a key performance improvement tool for at least 15 years. Today's successful companies are labeled as such because they value the successes of others. Motorola's importing of methods from Domino's Pizza and Xerox's study of practices at L.L. Bean are cited by almost every author writing about quality improvement.

Benchmarking for best practices was brought to the forefront in the public sector by Vice President Al Gore's National Performance Review (NPR). NPR recognized that taxpayers were appalled at having to foot the bill for poor service from government agencies. In response to this sentiment, the report recommended a selection of best practices, culled from state and local governments and industry. For instance, the information technology team drafted a plan that called for wider and wiser use of electronic data communications within the federal government based on an existing program in Iowa. The plan included high-speed networks, electronic benefits transfer, geographic information systems, and public access to online data.[5]

In response to the information technology team's plan, nine federal agencies studied Iowa's communications network (a likely best practice in communications), which carries voice, data, and video to state agencies, schools, and libraries through 2,700 miles of fiber-optic cable. The observers found that Iowa's method of service delivery could be applied nationwide. NPR team member Laraine Rogers, director of management information systems for the city of Phoenix, Arizona, said the effort would have failed like other attempts at improving the federal bureaucracy if the team had not sought out best practices and started with a blank slate instead.[6]

Benchmarking and best practices are now the parlance of government reformers. Throughout the years, government has slowly made incremental steps in improvement. With best practices it can operate on a higher plane and change to a new mode more akin to leapfrogging past performance, where the pace of change is faster and the amount of change is greater.

THE PURPOSES OF PUBLIC SECTOR BENCHMARKING

Why do public administrators need to find best practices? Senator John Glenn provided an answer when he remarked on the "profound feeling across the country that government has not been doing its job. Civil servants do not operate in a vacuum, and they are quite aware that citizens, tired of being frustrated, are becoming more vocal about wanting effective and responsive government."[7] Government has been accused of being unresponsive, gridlocked, and too bureaucratic. Voter discussions center on wasted tax dollars, the government's failure to improve the nation's future, and the desire for greater accountability.

In response to this widespread sentiment, Oregon developed a 272-item strategic plan that outlines in great detail where its citizens want to be in the years 2000 and 2010 and how the government plans to get there. The items being benchmarked range from lowering teen-age pregnancy rates to increasing personal income; from boosting the state's manufacturing base to cutting air and water pollution; from increasing Oregonians' knowledge of basic geography to lowering their blood pressure.[8] But, even Oregon—which is recognized to be at the forefront of the benchmarking movement—has been advised that it is not reaching its full potential because it is only looking internally, not externally.

In his presentation to the Oregon Progress Board, John Kirlin of the University of Southern California recommended that Oregon compare its past and current performance with other states and nations, not just itself, to identify the best practices and results. If Oregon were to add comparison data to its tables in the categories of national average, best state in America, best nation, and second best nation, the data would reveal where Oregon stands in relation to others and what services need the most improvement. Comparison data would also help Oregon prioritize its efforts.

According to a survey of benchmarking authorities, there is a wide range of reasons for using benchmarking practices. According to the Public Management Group, the purpose of benchmarking is to identify variability in performance and reduce it by optimizing imported processes. The Oregon Progress Board would add to any benchmarking project the aspiration of assessing "the degree to which a jurisdiction is achieving its strategic goals."[9] Neither of these two purposes includes the concept of surpassing the performance of the organization from which a practice was imported. Any organization can use outcome measures to monitor its internal improvement quarterly, but new horizons can be discovered only through unconventional ideas. This factor is key to benchmarking; without it, breakthrough improvement is impossible.

Besides the general rationales for benchmarking already mentioned, public sector practitioners often cite several other reasons to benchmark:

1. *To determine the criteria that measure performance.* Without criteria, an organization has no basis and no foundation for making comparisons. Comparisons made without criteria will lack validity, as will performance improvement goals based on those comparisons.

2. *To recognize problematic aspects of particular services.* Benchmarking lowest-rated services is only logical. Benchmarking top-rated services will not move the entire agency forward and may leave second-rate services to atrophy even further. Conduct process triage to prioritize which services need action first and which can wait.

3. *To improve service delivery.*[10] Just knowing where an organization stands in comparison to others and why will feel like a significant accomplishment in itself, but do not stop there. Precious money and time will be wasted if the new knowledge and insight are not acted upon and used to bring improvement.

In the public sector, benchmarking should not only change the pace of an organization but should move it forward in time by quantum leaps to allow it to cope with fundamental change, still meet citizen expectations, and avoid disenfranchising any community subgroup. William Gay, in his

August 1993 benchmarking workshop for the International Association of Fire Chiefs, described benchmarking as a "surrogate for the competitive forces that push businesses to achieve higher levels of quality and productivity."[11] Public entities are not vying with each other for the lion's share of the market or even corporate survival, so a driving mechanism is conspicuously absent within government. Through the various awards and honors programs, public programs are now competing with each other for reputation, top billing, and notoriety.

According to Katherine Barrett and Richard Greene, officials in Dallas, Texas, have made a religion out of comparing notes and competing with other municipalities.[12] Dallas leaders are well aware that re-creating the wheel all the time is a waste of resources. Ryan Evans, Dallas director of budget and research, makes a dozen calls a week to other cities. If he finds another city of similar size with a parks and recreation department operating with $10 million less than Dallas, he will investigate and aim to match or beat the benchmark. In the southeast part of the city, the largest of Dallas' six districts, the police have instituted a neighborhood-oriented approach adopted from community policing models in Seattle, Washington, and other cities. As a result, crime statistics in this district have dipped slightly more than in the city as a whole.

Those agencies that do not keep up with the pace of change will pay the consequences, the main one being that citizens will no longer patronize a particular agency or service with a markedly deficient performance level. For instance, had the New York City Transit Authority (NYCTA) not benchmarked its performance in inventory control against similar service providers, continuing poor resource management would have led to high costs and low quality that would have eventually driven NYCTA's patrons to competing transportation providers such as private bus lines, taxis, and automobiles. Because of the lessons NYCTA learned through benchmarking, the agency has probably saved itself from bankruptcy and dissolution. (See the sidebar "NYCTA: A Success Story.")

HOW TO BENCHMARK

Benchmarking has evolved from a nebulous concept into a concrete method used to identify and import best practices. This quality management tool now encompasses a formal, systematic process with its own rules, ethical code, and language. To find a best practice, most practitioners follow some form of these steps:

NYCTA: A SUCCESS STORY

In an effort to provide more service with less resource consumption, the New York City Transit Authority (NYCTA) conducted a detailed study of inventory management. NYCTA's goal was to reach world-class performance levels in inventory and logistics management capabilities. The agency examined practices of leading multimodal transit authorities in Houston, Texas, and Detroit, Michigan; foreign transit authorities in Montreal, Quebec; Stockholm, Sweden; and Tokyo, Japan; and private-sector companies such as Federal Express, UPS, and Delta Airlines.[1] Like the NYCTA, many of these firms were operating under severe budgetary constraints. NYCTA's most significant insights came from analyzing companies and organizations that were not directly comparable to the public transportation industry. To their surprise, NYCTA managers found the following best practices readily applicable to their situation, despite the profound differences of the operating environments of origin:

1. A balanced spreadsheet for transit management that listed inventory and other operating statistics

2. A program tying employee and manager accountability to specific inventory objectives

3. A framework for balancing inventory targets with service goals throughout the organization

Reference

1. K. A. Bruder, Jr. and E. M. Gray, "Public Sector Benchmarking: A Practical Approach," *Public Management* 76 (1994): S9–S22.

---

1. *Determine the purpose and scope of the project.* Before choosing benchmarks or partners, an organization should set limits, boundaries, or parameters, including limits on time, limits on expenditures, number of benchmarks, number of partners, number of internal processes to be reconfigured, number of people on the benchmarking team, and members of the oversight committee. This step includes process triage.

2. *Evaluate the processes.* The organization should analyze its internal processes to gain a thorough understanding of what is really going on. It should dig below the surface of the process to get at the true driving forces behind each action.

3. *Research potential partners.* It is unlikely that the organization will have the time or resources to locate every piece of information on possible partners, but most of the time it will succeed in gathering enough information for the sake of benchmarking.

4. *Choose performance measurements.* The organization should take care in choosing a set of measures that is comprehensive and common for the chosen function. The closer it can approximate apples to apples, the more secure and valid its findings will be.

5. *Collect internal data for performance measurements.*

6. *Collect data from partner organizations.* The organization should do this with as much courtesy and as little time and bother to the partner as possible, without sacrificing reliability.

7. *Conduct gap analysis.* Based on measures and data, the benchmarking team determines the performance gap. It should be prepared for the possible unpleasant nature of results and reactions. The team should present the results to management and share its findings with the partners.

8. *Import practices to close gaps.* The organization should picture this step as a three-part process: borrow–adapt–adopt. It should choose the process or processes, allow for necessary mutations to fit its structure, and implement the processes.

9. *Monitor the results.* Is the organization closing the gaps identified in step seven? If so, how quickly?

10. *Recalibrate the benchmarks based on findings.* By their very nature, benchmarks have an expiration date. Reusing old benchmarks year after year will invalidate results and ultimately may cause a regression in performance.

11. *Return to step one.* In the initial attempt, the organization conducts process triage to determine where best practices should be applied first. Now it should move to the second level of functions that need assistance and conduct the entire exercise again.

This list describes what benchmarking is. Practitioners must also be aware of what benchmarking is not: It is not easy to do, it is not a quick fix, it is not the result of top-down decrees, and it is not simply comparing one organization to another. Keeping these thoughts in mind, project directors will avoid getting sidetracked by coincidental issues and will be able to maintain focus and progress toward the ultimate goal, which is matching or beating world-class performance.

ADVANTAGES AND DISADVANTAGES

In the debate about benchmarking effectiveness, those who oppose emulating the best in the business cite differences in mission between private and public sector organizations, budgetary restrictions, the role of politics, bureaucratic red tape, and the fishbowl environment. Depending on whom you talk to, these arguments may or may not be valid. Several concerns do exist, however, and should be given adequate consideration by practitioners.

First, public sector benchmarking is an inherently political process. To take the politics out of the equation is impossible; administrator or political discretion and subjectivity will always play a small part. Any function a committee or individual administrator chooses to benchmark may still be politically motivated.

Second, agency leaders and managers will be tempted to manipulate the benchmarking results to save their departments and their jobs. "It's easy to talk about what you want to measure, but not so easy to face the music politically when the numbers start coming in," said Max Arinder, program analyst for the Mississippi Legislature.[13] Milwaukee, Wisconsin, administrators experienced such numbers when the city fire department benchmarked its performance against other municipalities. It found an average of three fire deaths per year in benchmarked neighborhoods—a high figure.[14] According to consultant Gay, the Milwaukee Fire Department looked at other departments around the country to find a program that addressed the problem. Milwaukee found a solution in a smoke detector installation program in Portland, Oregon. The Milwaukee Fire Department chose Portland's program as one to which it could aspire and succeeded by following recommended benchmarking procedures:

1. The Milwaukee team began with a literature search for best practices. (It found information about Portland's program in an industry publication.)

2. The Milwaukee officers contacted their Portland counterparts for information.

3. The team conducted a thorough analysis, including geographic location, housing, and victim characteristics.

4. The team adapted the Portland program to its department. After implementing a modified form of the program, Milwaukee's fire deaths in the targeted neighborhoods declined to one in five years.[15]

Third, when choosing performance measures, establishing cause and effect can be very tricky. The benchmarking team must be sensitive to causal relationships and drawing erroneous conclusions. For example, do highway accident rates rise or fall according to the minimum age for purchasing liquor, the speed limit, cracking down on speeders, or a combination of all of the preceding?

Fourth, in some instances, measuring outcomes can be nearly impossible. Some government activities defy gauging and may be of a long-term nature, making data gathering an expensive operation.

Fifth, will benchmarking for best practices really work anywhere? Benchmarking is easy for a community like Sunnyvale, California, which is a small, apolitical, tax-rich community that has "social problems that New Yorkers would kill for."[16] But how effective will the method be for larger, more diverse metropolitan areas? Extremely. It is a highly reliable and valid methodology.

Already, benchmarking has been used to address one of the nation's toughest and most taboo urban issues: AIDS. In regards to AIDS case management, Patricia McInturff, director of the regional division of Seattle-King County Department of Public Health, described the division's partnership with San Francisco, California, as "stealing everything we could."[17] McInturff also noted the advantage of being able to avoid San Francisco's mistakes. San Francisco's glut of AIDS case managers made managing cases confusing and difficult. Seattle first centralized then limited its case managers and stopped the spread of small agencies by forming a coalition. Seattle's "stealing" is actually the best form of benchmarking. By going through the borrowing–adapting–adopting process, Seattle took what was a best practice and created a new best practice. With its fresh approach, Seattle has moved San Francisco's model one step forward, increasing the magnitude of its performance.

Benchmarking is not foolproof, and it is not guaranteed to meet all challenges for public sector administrators, but when used properly, benchmarking can bring significant improvement, multiplying performance tenfold.

Benchmarking can also lead organizations to break the all-too-familiar cycle of putting out fires. In his article "Institutional Renewal in American Cities," Royce Hanson tells that public sector reform responds only to crisis. Hanson claims that public remediation and revitalization projects are market followers, not leaders, because they seem possible only after deterioration has reached a crisis point. Governing institutions change slowly and move behind the wave rather than at its crest. Few agencies have successfully established programs on "anticipatory renewal," are equipped to anticipate change, or are ready to provide transitional leadership.[18]

Finding and importing best practices will encourage public agencies to replace reactionary measures with preventive ones. One of the foremost examples of this is how Philadelphia, Pennsylvania, used public safety best practices from Japan. A *koban* is a Japanese police substation, part of the nation's law enforcement policy of putting officers into the neighborhoods they protect. The premise underlying kobans is that a police presence deters crime before it happens—a preventive, not reactionary, measure. Under the auspices of the Milton S. Eisenhower Foundation, police chiefs from several U.S. cities visited Japan in 1988 to see how kobans work. Philadelphia was one of the first two cities to then employ kobans as part of its community policing efforts. The results were impressive: a 24% drop in crime between 1991 and 1993 in a retail section of Philadelphia using kobans.[19] Through proaction rather than reaction, public entities like the Philadelphia Police Department will be able to shape their own futures.

Other benefits of finding best practices are not as obvious or tangible as performance improvement but are just as important. Best practices encourage agencies to look outside of themselves and may form new bonds between government and business where before there was a wall. Public agencies partaking in best-practice benchmarking searches benefit simply from the communication between localities on the most important social topics of the day, such as crime, homelessness, and revitalization. Best practices are the best means for instigating lasting collaboration and for fulfilling missions and may lead to a new way of doing government business.

THE CHANGING FACE
OF GOVERNMENT

Benchmarks being used as measures of public sector performance are a paradigm shift on a large scale. Benchmarking and best practices force public sector institutions to seek opportunities, solve root problems instead of just delaying symptoms, think entrepreneurially, and overcome long-standing perceptions of poor performance. Like private corporations, public organizations are specifically targeting what they really want to accomplish, and the new degree of concentration seems to be paying off in significant, measurable improvements. Barrett and Greene see benchmarking as the most sensible route for organizations interested in progress; they dedicated their article "Focus on the Best" to helping other municipalities adopt the method.[20] Today, every governing body can look forward to being asked by citizens to do more with less. Productivity and quality improvement are no longer matters of choice for public administrators. Organizational success, competitiveness, and stability will be determined by how well and how fast public agencies improve their business processes. Pioneer organizations have shown that benchmarking for best practices can and will work for a wide range of government functions. Now, it is up to individual agencies to use this knowledge to analyze their own status and tap into the wisdom of their counterparts for fresh ideas and breakthrough improvement.

ENDNOTES

1. W. Gay, *Benchmarking: A Method for Achieving Superior Performance in Fire and Emergency Medical Services* (Herndon, VA: Public Management Group, 1992): 18.
2. B. Ettore, "Juran on Quality," *Management Review* (January 1994):10–12.
3. K. Barrett and R. Greene, "Focus on the Best," *Financial World* (March 2, 1993): 36–51.
4. R. C. Camp, *Benchmarking: The Search for Industry Best Practices That Lead to Superior Performance* (Milwaukee: ASQC Quality Press, 1989).
5. G. H. Anthes, "White House Gets Tech Advice," *Computerworld* 27 (1993): 4.
6. Ibid.
7. R. J. Fischer, "An Overview of Performance Measurement," *Public Management* 76 (1994): S2–S8.
8. Oregon Progress Board, *Oregon Benchmarks: Standards for Measuring Statewide Progress and Institutional Performance,* report to the 1995 Legislature (Salem, OR: Oregon Progress Board, 1994): 2.
9. Ibid.
10. Fischer, S-6.
11. Gay, 1.
12. Barrett and Greene.
13. J. Walters, "The Benchmarking Craze," *Governing* (April 1994): 33–37.
14. Gay, 29.
15. Ibid.
16. Walters, 37.
17. Barrett and Green, 46.
18. R. Hanson, "Institutional Renewal in American Cities," *The Annals of the American Academy of Political and Social Science* (November 1986): 100–119.
19. M. Janofsky, "Japanese-Style Booths Put Police at the Center of the Action," *New York Times* (July 31, 1995): A8.
20. Barrett and Greene.

BIBLIOGRAPHY

Bogan, C. E., and M. J. English. *Benchmarking for Best Practices: Winning through Innovative Adaptation.* Washington, DC: McGraw-Hill, 1994.

Doades, R. "Making the Best of Best Practices." *Public Utilities Fortnightly.* (Aug. 15, 1992): 15–18.

Gore, A. *The Gore Report on Reinventing Government: Creating a Government That Works Better and Costs Less.* Washington, DC: Times Books, 1993.

Hatry, H. *An Assessment of the Oregon Benchmarks: A Report to the Oregon Progress Board.* Washington, DC: The Urban Institute, June 1994.

Smith, G. N. "The Urban Upside." *Financial World* (March 2, 1993): 8.

Weisendanger, B. "Benchmarking Intelligence Fuels Management Moves." *Public Relations Journal* (November 1993): 20–22.

Appendix

Body of Knowledge for ASQ Certified Quality Improvement Associate (CQIA) Certification Examination

(100 Questions, 3-Hour Test)

The topics in this Body of Knowledge (BOK) include subtext explanations and the cognitive level at which the questions will be written. This information will provide useful guidance for both the Exam Development Committee and the candidate preparing to sit for the exam. The subtext is not intended to limit the subject matter or be all-inclusive of that material that will be covered in the exam. It is meant to clarify the type of content that will be included on the exam. The descriptor in parentheses at the end of each entry refers to the maximum cognitive level at which the topic will be tested. A complete description of cognitive levels is provided at the end of this document.

I. Quality Basics (27 Questions)

   A. *Terms, Concepts, and Principles (12 questions)*

      1. *Quality.* Define and know how to use this term correctly. (Application)

For more information about this, and other, ASQ certification examinations, contact the American Society for Quality Certifications Department, 1-800-248-1946

2. *Systems and processes.* Define a system and a process; distinguish between a system and a process; understand the interrelationship between process and system; and know how the components of a system (input/output, process, and feedback) impact the system as a whole. (Analysis)

3. *The importance of employees.* Understand employee involvement and employee empowerment, and understand the benefits of both concepts; distinguish between involvement and empowerment. (Comprehension)

4. *Quality planning.* Define a quality plan; understand its purpose for the organization as a whole and who in the organization contributes to its development. (Comprehension)

5. *Variation.* Understand variation and common and special causes. (Comprehension)

B. *Benefits of Quality (5 questions).* Understand how each stakeholder (e.g., employees, organization, customers, suppliers, community) benefits from quality and how the benefits differ for each type of stakeholder. (Comprehension)

C. *Quality Philosophies (10 questions).* Understand each of these philosophies, know how they differ from one another, and know how to apply each philosophy. (Application)

1. Deming (14 points)

2. Juran (Trilogy)

3. Crosby (Zero defects)

II. Teams (23 Questions)

A. *Types of Teams (4 questions).* Recognize each type of team and how it is structured; know how teams differ and how they are similar; know which type of team to use in a given situation; know the value of using each type of team. (Evaluation)

1. Improvement teams

2. Cross-functional teams

3. Project teams

4. Self-directed teams

B. *Roles and Responsibilities (5 questions).* Identify major team roles and the attributes of good role performance for champions, sponsors, leaders, facilitators, timekeepers, and members. (Comprehension)

C. *Team Formation and Group Dynamics (14 questions)*

1. *Initiating teams.* Know the elements of launching a team and why they are important: clear purpose, goals, commitment, ground rules, schedules, support from management, and team empowerment. (Application)

2. *Selecting team members.* Know how to select team members that have appropriate skills sets (e.g., number of members, expertise, representation). (Application)

3. *Groupthink.* Define and recognize groupthink and understand how to overcome it. (Application)

4. *Team stages.* Describe the classic stages of team evolution (forming, storming, norming, and performing); understand the value of conflict; know how to resolve team conflict. (Application)

III. Continuous Improvement (50 Questions)

A. *Incremental and Breakthrough Improvement (4 questions).* Understand how process improvement can identify waste and non-value-added activities. Understand how both incremental and breakthrough improvement processes achieve results. Know the steps required for both types of improvement. Recognize which type of improvement approach should be used in specific situations. Know the similarities and differences between the two approaches. (Application)

B. *Improvement Cycles (4 questions).* Define various improvement cycle phases (e.g., PDCA, PDSA) and use them appropriately. (Application)

C. *Quality Improvement Tools (30 questions).* Use, interpret, and explain flow charts, histograms, Pareto charts, scatter diagrams, cause-and-effect diagrams, check lists (check sheets), affinity diagrams, cost of quality, benchmarking, brainstorming, and audits as an improvement tool. Understand control chart concepts (e.g., centerlines, control limits, out-of-control conditions), and recognize when control charts should be used. (Comprehension)

D. *Customer–Supplier Relationships (12 questions)*

    1. *Internal and external customers.* Know how customers are defined. Know to work with customers effectively to improve process and services. Know how an organization's internal customers influence organizational processes. Know how to distinguish between different external customer types (consumers and end users). (Comprehension)

    2. *Customer feedback.* Know the different types of customer feedback (e.g., surveys, complaints) and understand the value in using the data to drive continuous improvement activities. (Comprehension)

    3. *Internal and external suppliers.* Understand the value in communicating stated expectations and the consequences of supplier performance. (Comprehension)

    4. *Supplier feedback.* Know the different types of supplier feedback (e.g., surveys, complaints, ratings) and understand the value in using the data to drive continuous improvement activities. (Comprehension)

SIX LEVELS OF COGNITION BASED ON BLOOM'S TAXONOMY (1956)

In addition to *content* specifics, the subtext detail also indicates the intended *complexity level* of the test questions for that topic. These levels are based on "Levels of Cognition" (from Bloom's *Taxonomy*, 1956) and are presented below in rank order, from least complex to most complex.

Knowledge Level

(Also commonly referred to as recognition, recall, or rote knowledge.) Being able to remember or recognize terminology, definitions, facts, ideas, materials, patterns, sequences, methodologies, principles, etc.

Comprehension Level

Being able to read and understand descriptions, communications, reports, tables, diagrams, directions, regulations, etc.

Application Level

Being able to apply ideas, procedures, methods, formulas, principles, theories, etc., in job-related situations

Analysis

Being able to break down information into its constituent parts and recognize the parts' relationship to one another and how they are organized; identify sublevel factors or salient data from a complex scenario

Synthesis

Being able to put parts or elements together in such a way as to show a pattern or structure not clearly there before; identify which data or information from a complex set is appropriate to examine further or from which supported conclusions can be drawn

Evaluation

Able to make judgments regarding the value of proposed ideas, solutions, methodologies, etc., by using appropriate criteria or standards to estimate accuracy, effectiveness, economic benefits, etc.

Index